MILK SPILLS
& ONE-LOG LOADS

FRANK WHITE

with an introduction by
HOWARD WHITE

MILK SPILLS
& ONE-LOG LOADS

Memories of a **PIONEER TRUCK DRIVER**

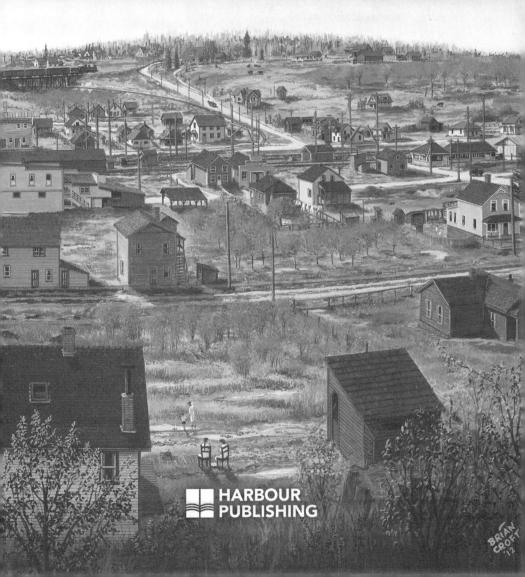

HARBOUR PUBLISHING

Harbour Publishing Co. Ltd.
P.O. Box 219, Madeira Park, BC, V0N 2H0
www.harbourpublishing.com

Edited by Howard White
Text design by Mary White
Front cover—truck logging, Gordon Labredt illustration
Title page—Abbotsford, 1922, Brian Croft painting
Printed and bound in Canada

Canada Council   Conseil des arts
for the Arts   du Canada

BRITISH COLUMBIA
ARTS COUNCIL
An agency of the Province of British Columbia

Harbour Publishing acknowledges the support of the Canada Council for the Arts, which last year
invested $157 million to bring the arts to Canadians throughout the country. We also gratefully
acknowledge financial support from the Government of Canada through the Canada Book Fund
and from the Province of British Columbia through the BC Arts Council and the Book Publishing
Tax Credit.

Library and Archives Canada Cataloguing in Publication

White, Frank, 1914-, author
    Milk spills and one-log loads : memories of a pioneer truck driver / Frank White.

Includes index.
ISBN 978-1-55017-622-3 (bound)
ISBN 978-1-55017-734-3 (paperback)

    1. White, Frank, 1914-. 2. Truck drivers--British Columbia-- Biography. 3. Working class--
British Columbia--Biography. 4. Trucking--British Columbia--History--20th century--Anecdotes.
5. British Columbia--Description and travel--Anecdotes. 6. British Columbia--Biography. I. Title.

HD8039.M7952C3 2013   388.3'24092   C2013-904491-4

Contents

Introduction

Howard White

This book was dictated to me by my father, the 99-year-old former truck driver, logger, excavating contractor, gas station operator and all-round *mensch* Frank White, and is organized (or disorganized) along the lines of a casual conversation. As such it is a bit different to read than a conventional book and I feel the need to repeat a caution I have used to preface other books written in the vernacular style. At first it's a bit like dropping in on a heated conversation between two old campaigners who have already been carrying on all night. The air is thick with unfamiliar names and obscure work issues you can't at first make whole sense of. But you don't need to know exactly how a pig is butchered to get the point Dad makes about it, which is that it was damn ticklish business for a twelve-year-old kid and his school chum working on their own. All you really need know about turn-of-the-century butchering, driving early milk trucks and hauling giant logs on creaky old three-ton gas pots with mechanical brakes—not to mention hunting basking sharks and holding your own in a brawl—you will know by the end of the story. Dad doesn't always begin by giving you all the background of the 1930s dairy wars or potato smuggling, but he gets around to it once he's got your interest aroused and you're ready to listen. He's a bit post-modern that way and if you just relax and listen in, I think you will soon find yourself fully engaged.

Milk Spills and One-Log Loads is a kind of book that doesn't usually get written and not just because its author is in his 100th year. Dad is not the sort of guy who would normally consider his life worth writing about. I don't think he ever would have got the notion into his head if not for a trick I played on him back in 1972.

I was trying to write an article about the rise of BC coast truck logging for my historical magazine *Raincoast Chronicles*, and turned to Dad for help. Like most young people I didn't give my father much credit for knowing anything truly important but I had sat through enough of his tales about banging around in trucks to know he had been in the game early on and might at least be able to give me the names of some truly important figures that I might go talk to. Dad wasn't offended by this assumption of his own historical insignificance—he had never thought of himself as anything but a bit player in the forest industry and it didn't occur to him he had anything quotable to offer either. He felt badly that he wasn't able to come up big names who were still living, or even any who weren't.

"Jeez, How, there's a lot of jaws been broken over the question of where and when trucks first got into the woods—hell, they can't even settle on where the first logging railroad was, and trucks are a lot harder to keep track of than trains," he mused in his typical way. "I'd hafta say though, if I had to give you one name it would be old Bill Schnare…"

At first this didn't seem helpful. I had heard Dad talk about Bill Schnare (which he pronounced *snar*) many times and regarded old Bill as just another one of those foot soldiers he had worked alongside in his own modest career. But the more I searched libraries and archives, the more I came to appreciate just how little had been documented about recent logging history in BC circa 1972 and the more I began to think maybe Dad's eyewitness recollections might be the best I could do.

I got a crazy idea. What if we printed Dad's take on logging history just the way he said it, in his own sidehill lingo? It doesn't seem at all daring now, but that's how much literary technique changes in forty years. Barry Broadfoot had not then written *Ten Lost Years, 1929–1939: Memories of Canadians Who Survived the Depression,* making ordinary people speaking in their own words a popular and acceptable way of evoking the past. *The*

Foxfire Book was yet to be published. *Working: People Talk About What They Do All Day and How They Feel About What They Do,* the bestselling classic by Chicago author Studs Terkel that put oral history on the map, would not be published until 1974, two years later. Oral history was not then an established phrase. The idea of letting a regular guy whose only qualification to talk about an industry was having worked in it for thirty years, and especially letting him speak in the words he would use on the job talking to his fellow workers, was untrod ground as far as I knew. My

Frank White was still monkeywrenching trucks in 1972 when he unknowingly authored the groundbreaking article "How It Was With Trucks" about the early days of truck logging. CLAYTON BAILEY PHOTO

heart was in my mouth as I copied down my dad's man-in-the-street views on how the truck logging revolution had come about, and prepared to send it to the printer illustrated with snapshots of his impossibly huge logs on sagging little trucks no bigger than modern delivery vans. I gave it the title, "How It Was With Trucks," a phrase Dad often used.

When the logging issue of *Raincoast Chronicles* hit the streets in 1973 the first reaction came from the one local resident who had shown interest in our coastal BC history project, the Gibsons writer and teacher Lester Peterson. I'd come to realize each BC region had its local history maven and Peterson was the recognized oracle for the Sunshine Coast. He had graciously agreed to sit on our inoperative "editorial board" and had even contributed a couple of articles, written in the fusty old local history style we were trying to break away from. Peterson was outraged by my dad's "incoherent ramblings" and served notice he was resigning his honorary post. He was particularly upset by Dad's use of the term "cakzickers." He opined that although he had personally witnessed some use of foul language in his many years observing the coastal forest industry, "it had never helped get a single log in the water."

I was pretty sure he was wrong about that.

Apart from Les, the general reception of the logging issue was pretty good. The first printing of 5,000 sold out in mere weeks and we went back to press for a second 5,000—a little too many as it turned out, but its popularity still amazed Vancouver booksellers. We got a lot of attention, and every review singled out Dad's verbatim reminiscences for special praise. "How It Was With Trucks" was widely reprinted and ultimately seen by tens of thousands of people. Dad and I were invited to go to Vancouver where Mayor Art Phillips presented us with that year's BC Media Club Prize for Best Magazine Feature. (The original article is incorporated into Chapters 14–17 of this book.)

Through all this notoriety, Dad was somewhat bemused. It was the first time in his life he'd seen his name on public view and like most people of his pre-social media generation, he found it a shock. It didn't help that the article made him sound like, well, a truck driver. A bit of a damn rube, in his view. Dad is no snob but he is very well read and on the rare occasion when he sits down to write a letter, he does so with a graceful formality.

He considered that his true writing style and would have appreciated it if I had given him the chance to clean the article up a bit so it sounded more like himself. I argued that even when Churchill was speaking off the cuff he sounded a bit like an old truck driver, or at least an old cavalryman, and a person's natural manner of speaking was more himself than an artificial writing style learned in composition class.

Dad was not convinced. This was a man, after all, who didn't leave skin mags in the washroom of his gas station, but copies of *Hansard*. He was also a modest man who would never have set himself up as an authority on such a solemn topic as truck logging if it were left to him and he was worried that the truly major players of his era would think he was stepping out of line. It helped when the BC Truckloggers Association invited him to address their 40th anniversary convention and treated him to a lengthy standing ovation. The fact was, the major players of his day had long since shipped out to that big bunkhouse in the sky without leaving any record at all, and Dad's version of events was the best thing modern truckloggers had ever heard about the shaky beginnings of their industry. His thesis that his old crony Bill Schnare was the Henry Ford of BC truck logging became widely accepted and the many writings that began to appear on forest history invariably quoted Dad as an authority on the subject.

Of course many of the reviewers and readers of "How It Was With Trucks" suggested we keep on and write up more of Dad's memories, and at first he flatly refused to consider it, but after awhile I realized he was quietly working away on his own, doing just that. He never fully admitted he was writing a book, only "buggering around with some of the old yarns." Once in awhile he would show me a sample, and sure enough it was composed in his formal letter-writing style reminiscent of the brittle pioneer memoirs I was familiar with from my work as an editor. The originality, colour and energy of his natural speaking style was largely missing and he seemed stuck on trying to reconstruct shadowy memories of early family and childhood history while ignoring his own well-remembered experiences as an adult as if they were too recent and commonplace to be of interest. But I encouraged him and he kept pecking away, using a series of computers he had built himself from plans in *Popular Electronics*, which in his typical way he spent more time monkeywrenching than writing on.

This went on for decades. He didn't retire from his last job as a municipal waterworks operator until 1990 when he was seventy-six but even that didn't make much difference to his progress. My mother had died in 1978 and in 1982 he partnered up with a former New York journalist named Edith Iglauer, who introduced him to a new life of society and travel. I despaired of him ever getting on with his life story and urged him to start a list of topics that he could add to randomly as he thought of them. This suggestion he took to heart and while the finished parts of his saga remained mired in the early 1920s, he eventually compiled a minutely detailed list of the people, places and events that encompassed the whole span of his life. The list was almost the length of a book itself and is such an impressive document that when he showed it to an anthropologist who came to interview him about BC resource communities, she asked his permission to attach it to her PhD thesis. She described it as "a kind of poem" and I don't know if that's what it is but it is indeed a remarkable document. Once I started reading it I realized that this was essentially a complete draft of his book and all that remained was to expand his shorthand notation into full sentences. A sample:

Memories of life on County Line Rd. 1916–18 Neighbor sawing wood at fence, We kids enjoy the noise and the sawdust. Hazel (Dolly) is out with Beryl and I. My first girl friend, Rose. I insist Gladys be named Rose. Walking from Rose place with Beryl and ?? a hired girl or an aunt. Cooking the small potatoes for the pigs, Breaking the windows. in the old house his father built. The baker, Albert Lee. Dr. Swift. Doctor Swift Calls. Mr Lee Calls. Dad comes home in his Model "T". We kids recognized each one coming down the road by the sound of his car...

About the time Dad turned ninety and was starting to slow down a little, I decided I better get involved or his great literary labours might come to naught. Using his master-list of topics as a blueprint, I began asking him to explain his notes and taping what he said. Then I went home and transcribed the tapes. This worked well. His notes to himself triggered his memories precisely and by the time we'd worked our way to the end of the list we had a manuscript of 180,000 words. I printed it off on 1,000 pages of typescript and presented it to him.

"What the hell is this?" he said, staring at the tall stack of paper. He had read it in pieces but hadn't seen it all connected up before.

"This is the book you've been writing for the last forty years," I said.

"Ha! I wasn't writing any book. I was just trying to put down a few of the old stories…"

"Well, take a read of it and see what you think. Mark down anything you want to change."

I left it with him for a week. Complete silence.

I went over to check in and asked him if he'd read over the manuscript. I could see he wasn't overflowing with joy.

"Yeah, I went through it," he said.

"So, how does it strike you now that it's all in one place?"

"I can't believe a man's life can be made so small."

"What do you mean?"

"This barely scrapes the surface of what really went on. There is so much more I could have said about it."

"Holy cow, it's already longer than *War and Peace.*"

"All I can think of is what's not there."

I gave him a lecture about how no autobiography tells the whole story of a life and the important thing is what it does place on the record, not what it leaves out.

"Most of what you've written here is the only place these events and people will ever be mentioned. You're all that stands between them and complete oblivion," I said.

I could see he wasn't going to take my word for it so I asked his wife Edith and their Filipina caregiver to serve as an impartial jury while I read the manuscript aloud to them with him listening in. It took us about six weekends and they were laughing and crying the whole way through. Dad was, too. The jury congratulated him and said they'd had no idea he'd had such an amazing life and from now on they were going to look at him with new eyes. After that, he allowed maybe it hadn't been a total waste of time after all.

In the end the book was just too bulky and unleashed just a bit too much raconteuring at one go, so we split it into two volumes. This is the first and takes him from his birth in 1914 up to the end of the Second World War. It is a bit of a cross between Dad's verbal and written styles. The anecdote of the boys playing with dynamite in Chapter 3 was one that he wrote out rather than dictating and is an example of his more studied composition. By far the bulk of the material was spoken, but his conversation sometimes betrays an awareness it is being written down and sometimes doesn't, so there is occasional variation in tone. The editors worried about this but decided to forgive it on the basis that it isn't uncommon for the tone of a conversation to vary depending on subject and mood.

I'm too close to the material to judge its ultimate merit. It is, as I said at the outset, the kind of everyman story that doesn't often get written and I think that gives it a certain novelty. It was Dad's idea to frame it as a story about transportation and how trucking in particular developed in the first half of the twentieth century and it certainly provides insight into that process. There is an undeniable fascination in listening to a man talk about anything from the perspective of having observed it over the course of a whole century, be it the evolution of trucking, ladies fashions, sexual mores, or a hundred other things he touches upon in these pages. But I suspect the main exhibit here is Frank White himself, an unassuming man who in his plain-spoken way reminds us that the most ordinary-seeming life, on close inspection, can be found to be full of unexpected riches.

Frank White with great-granddaughter Katy Plant, 2011. WHITE FAMILY

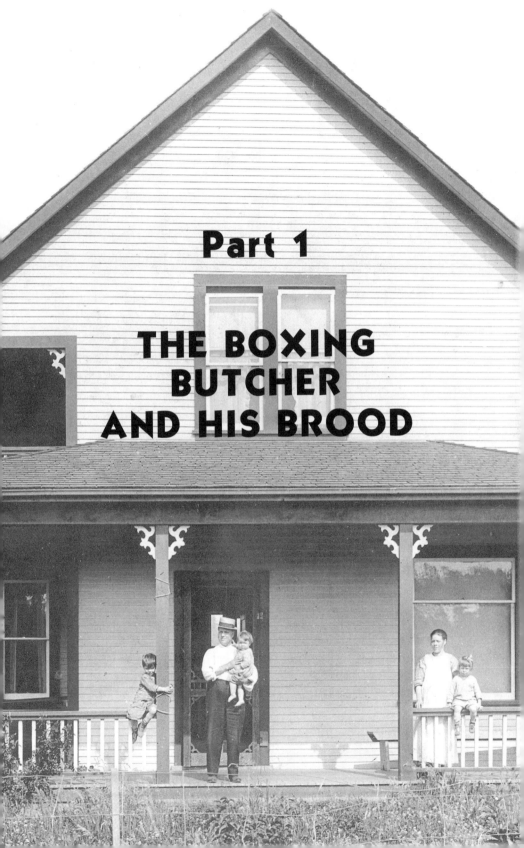

Part 1

THE BOXING
BUTCHER
AND HIS BROOD

I Get Born in
the Wrong Country

sometimes think the real story of my time is the story of transportation—how it developed and changed the way we live, and how my own life has been tangled up in that process. People today have become so blasé about flying around the world and being able to go wherever they want whenever they want, they never stop to think that there was a time not so long ago when just going to the next town down the road was something you had to plan for days ahead, and only did once or twice a year. One of my earliest memories is of going on a ride with Uncle Tom, my mother's younger brother, from my father's farm in Aldergrove, BC, to my grandparents' place in Bradner, an easy fifteen-minute drive today but then a long, dusty crawl in his old horse-and-buggy. He drove in the middle of the road and let the team find its own way, like a pioneer version of cruise control. The road ran die-straight for miles so he decided to catch a snooze and tucked his chin down on his chest. "Wake me up if a car comes," he said. That was how you got around in those days. It took a little longer, but there was no road rage.

Many more buggies and wagons than cars passed our house back then, and we came to recognize the few cars there were—Doctor Swift's and Albert Lee, the baker's—by the differing sounds they made, announcing their approach long before we could see them. When Dad went to work for Canadian Immigration he acquired a Ford to commute to White Rock and I remember my sister Beryl and I running to see Dad drive up the lane when we heard his distinct *putta putta putta* coming down the road. Incidentally, these Fords were all Model Ts but we just called them Fords. There was no need to say what model it was when only one model existed. If we wanted to call them something besides a Ford we said Tin Lizzie or Flivver. It wasn't until 1927 when the Model A came out and there were two common models of Ford that the term Model T came into popular use. Up to that time the Model T pretty much owned the road. If you passed ten cars, nine of them would be Model Ts. There have been models since that sold more copies but never one that dominated its market so completely. That's why they say it was the most successful car ever made.

Long distance travel was by train, but that meant going where the railroad went, and when it chose to do so. The train that went past our farm was the Great Northern, and when I was about to be born our family physician, Dr. Swift, arranged for Mother to take the train north to New Westminster, but when Mother's time came it happened that the Great Northern was going south towards Sumas, Washington, and so she arrived in the hospital there and I was born in the USA.

My parents always carefully declared any groceries or other goods they might be bringing from back from visits across the border but they failed to declare me. The only record of my birth remained the hospital registry in the State of Washington. This would create a very interesting foul-up later in my life. I would spend the next sixty-five years developing quite a grudge against Americans over one thing and another only to have the Canada Pension office tell me that in the Canadian government's view I was myself an American and had been one since I first drew breath in that Sumas hospital. If you think that was easy to straighten out, you've got another think coming.

It would have been alright if I was able to prove either of my parents was Canadian, but my mother was born at home in Kenora, now part of Ontario but then called Rat Portage and part of Manitoba. There was no record of my father's birth in Ottawa, Upper Canada as it was then, since neither Canada nor Ontario had been created yet. To try and get some proof my father was Canadian I went to interview another old relative who was something of an authority on family history. This gruff old gal was the daughter of my Aunt Mattie, my father's sister (or half-sister?) who had married into one of the prominent families of New Westminster, the Gilleys. Gilley Avenue is a big important street in New Westminster. She insisted that I had it all wrong and my father wasn't born in Ottawa in 1865 but at sea in 1862 and quite possibly out of wedlock as my grandparents had eloped to the New World. This was a revelation to me but I couldn't dismiss it out of hand because it triggered a distant memory.

The future wrangler of trucks and scourge of BC forests at about one year. They say I was a sickly baby with bad jaundice but I look to be ready for action by the time this picture was taken. WHITE FAMILY

I had barged in upon my father in the middle of a bull session with one of his cronies back when I was a boy in Abbotsford, when he'd been talking about some fellow who had been working on a farm in Ireland and had run off with the boss's daughter. There was something about the hushed tones and the way he clammed up that caused me to make special note of it, and it would now appear that he was talking about his own parents. According to this old Gilley woman they had landed in the US and lived in Duluth, Minnesota, for a time, which only made my immigration problem worse, so I decided to ignore everything she said. I was on quite good terms with our Member of Parliament, Ray Skelly, so he went to bat for me and took my case to the highest levels of Ottawa officialdom but still couldn't get anywhere. At one point one of the bureaucrats told me I should go to the US government and apply to get my old age pension from them. I didn't know what to do.

One day when I was driving through Whalley I noticed a small office with a big flag in front and an immigration department sign in the window. On a whim I went in and found a solitary young woman in charge, obviously very junior to the mandarins who had been bouncing my application all around Ottawa and telling me I should go peddle my papers to America. She listened to my story and said, "My goodness, if you are not a Canadian, I don't know who is. We'll settle this right now." Bang! She stamped everything and told me I was now officially a Canadian. I couldn't quite believe it and confessed to her I had already been turned down at the highest levels in Ottawa. "I'm sorry to hear that," she said. "Anyway, you shouldn't have any more trouble now. If you do, come back and see me." I was a little dubious at first, but she was as good as her word. Before long I started getting my pension, I got a Canadian passport and I never heard another word about not being a proper Canadian. Sometimes you don't have to take on the whole system, you just have to find one person with a bit of sense.

I was born the year the First World War started. By the time it was over I was four. My father was born during the American Civil War. So if you shake my hand, you're shaking the hand of a man whose father was around when there was still slavery in the States. That is how much history just two lifetimes can cover.

What I remember about the First World War is my dad holding me in his arms out on the porch of our house in Aldergrove. It was cold and there was a hell of a racket going on: *bang bang bang.*

"Hear that?" he was saying to me. "That's the Germans coming."

I wasn't sure what Germans were. I had them confused with germs and had a vague impression both were bad. What was going on, I've figured out since, is this was the Great Ice Storm of 1918. In the first week of January freezing rain fell on all the trees around the Lower Mainland and instantly froze until so much ice built up it would break off the limbs and that's what was making this racket, frozen tree limbs snapping under the weight of ice. To him it sounded like an infantry barrage, although of course I didn't get the joke because I had no idea what an infantry barrage was. I'm told modern parenting experts warn against this kind of kidding and say you should explain everything clearly. Father would have laughed and said giving kids puzzles to solve never hurt them, although he would have been disappointed it took me damn near a hundred years to solve that one.

I've often asked myself what it is about those early memories that makes them stay with you when so much else is forgotten. Another scenario comes to mind: we, that is my sister Beryl and myself, watching Dad cook a bunch of potatoes for the pigs. He had built a fire under a huge iron pot hanging on a framework and was boiling the small potatoes left over from the digging. I seem to recall a large garden and field of potatoes out near the barn. This was the land my father and grandfather had homesteaded around 1900 on County Line Road, just south of where Sixteenth Avenue crosses now. They had at first built a smaller house where they all lived together: my father, his father, his sister Mattie and his two stepbrothers, Nelson and Albert.

Now that I set that down I have a lot of questions I never thought to ask anybody who knew. What was this extended family doing out in the wilds of BC, all jammed together in a small farm house? Why had they left Ottawa, where they had been established for forty years, and left

The home my father built near Aldergrove, where we were living when I was born and where he took me out on the porch to hear all the trees cracking during the Great Ice Storm. That's me hugging the post, Dad holding my sister Hazel and my mother with sister Beryl c. 1918. WHITE FAMILY

one daughter, who married a local fireman named Thompson? All that background is lost. The days of our lives, it's all so damned important to us it drowns out wars and famines while it's happening, then a few years later all trace is gone. This is what makes it the west, I guess. I'm sure out east or back in the old country where families stay in the same brick house for 600 years they can all trace themselves back to William the Conqueror, but out here where we move around so much and build our houses out of flimsy stuff that rots after twenty years we barely know who our grandparents were. Anyway it gives a guy an excuse to try to jot down even a little of what happened on his own watch.

Soon after the bunch arrived in BC they started a butcher shop over in Cloverdale, which was the nearest town of any size, and that went quite well. They built a big white house on the hill above town, which was still there in 2013, but in 1911 when my father and mother were married he got out of the Cloverdale operation and built a third house back on the County Line farm where my grandfather was still living.

I gather I was a sickly baby with a bad case of jaundice that kept me very weak through my infancy. My mother had lost her first baby to meningitis just a year before I was born, which had left her emotionally shattered and possibly not in the best shape to be having another child. But we both survived. We lived at the County Line Road place until I was five, but I have only scattered memories and one of the clearer ones is of those small potatoes I started out to tell about a few paragraphs back. I can't be sure of the date but it must have been at least 1917 or '18 because my second sister, Hazel, was walking by this time and Beryl and I had to look after her. I can remember some fussing with my mother about our babysitting duties, and constant crying from Hazel. Anyway Dad fished out some of these baby spuds, stuck them on splints of wood and handed them to us. I've forgotten the births of my sisters and most of the major events of my early life but I still vividly remember how good those little potatoes were.

Another early childhood memory that endures is of the time I broke the windows. What is it about little boys and windows? I can still see this small, empty, dark one-storey house that had belonged to my grandfather, George White, and stood empty after he died in 1912. I never knew my

My sister Beryl and me about 1917. We were good buddies from the start. WHITE FAMILY

grandfather, but I heard the story of his death many times. It was a few days before Christmas and a hell of a storm blew up during the night. They had a big old barn out behind the house and the wind blew one of the doors loose so it was banging back and forth with each gust. The old man got on his boots and slicker, lit a hurricane lantern and headed out into the driving rain to fasten this door before it beat itself to pieces. He pushed the barn door shut and to hold it shut he started driving a wooden stake into the ground with a sledgehammer. They heard him strike one blow then there was a flash of light and all went silent. When they went out he was lying dead from a heart attack. He'd been holding the lantern when the attack hit him and he must have thrown his arm up, which caused the flash they'd seen. I never knew when this happened until a few days ago, but thanks to Google I can tell you it was on December 18, 1912, and he was seventy-four years old. All my life I've thought of him as old beyond counting, and it is a bit of a shock to think that if I ran into him now, he would strike me as a young fella. I was still working at a full-time job when I was seventy-four.

My dad never talked about his father much but he must have been quite a man. Later in life I belonged to the Elks Club for a time and once at an Elks meeting in Aldergrove (only about seventy years ago) I met a Mr. Andy Jackman. He was a well-known Fraser Valley pioneer and friend of both the Whites and my mother's people, the Carmichaels. He had homesteaded on the road that became Jackman Road (272nd Street) near Langley. Andy wanted me to know that my grandfather was a good man and very highly thought of in the community. In those days there were no veterinarians and George White was known throughout the area as the man to get for a sick horse or any ailing animal. He was also a good blacksmith. Jackman told me that they came to get him to fix a plough or a wagon or shoe a horse. He was a very capable man in many fields. But by the time I came along all that remained was his old house, which we were not supposed to play in. Somehow I got the idea its windows needed to be broken, and I suppose there was a licking involved but those details my memory has conveniently deleted.

There was a bachelor who had the place next to us on the north side and Beryl and I used to go through the fence to watch him saw firewood. I remember the long shavings his crosscut saw made—he must have been a good filer. We gathered the shavings to play in. He was sawing a large log, splitting and hauling it to the house on a stone boat. He built huge conical piles at his house, which seemed a very long way from our house.

Our neighbours to the south of our place had a cute little girl named Rose and I was madly in love with her. The place must have been a mile from our house and I remember walking with Mother's hired girl and Beryl to visit Rose one hot, sunny day. I can still see a bridge and a hill with a turn in the road at their house. The fact that there was a hired girl probably meant that my third sister, Gladys, was either just born or about to be born. When Gladys was born I insisted that she be named Rose. A compromise was reached and she became Gladys Rosella White.

That's about all I remember from that place where we lived from the time I was born to age five. Funny, eh? You'd think I'd have better memories of that farm but when I took my son down to show it to him awhile ago, I couldn't exactly place where it had been.

There's other memories from the same period, but they didn't take place on the farm. I guess my father was having a tough go—he wasn't really a farmer—so he took a job with Canadian Immigration. He became an immigration officer. I have faint memories of riding to the immigration office at Pacific Highway about 1917. The station at Pacific Highway had some kind of a traffic separator extending north and I was fascinated by the flashing red lights—it seemed like Christmas. Father was in charge of the Patricia (Aldergrove), Pacific Highway and Douglas (Blaine) crossings. I do not remember an office on the road at Douglas and his own office was in the Great Northern station in White Rock. I believe we moved to White Rock and lived there for a short time, but now couldn't say just which year this was.

Dad often took me with him to work. I remember going out to meet the train at the US border at Blaine. The tracks ran along the edge of Boundary Bay and there was a little shack on the shore where we waited for the train. In those days Canada armed its immigration officers and Dad carried a Colt automatic pistol. To kill time while we waited he would take this gun out, lean out the window of this little shack, and shoot at ducks swimming in the bay. He had me pull the trigger while he held the pistol.

He laughed and had a great time but I hated the noise. I didn't know what was going on but remember seeing the splash where the bullets hit the water. I don't think we ever hit any ducks—we couldn't have picked them up anyway. When a train arrived, Dad would board it and I would follow him down the aisle as he checked the passengers' destinations and passports.

Mostly we would spend our time at his office in the White Rock station, and being a major border crossing they had a small lockup with bars on the doors and windows. Occasionally he would have to rush off to attend to some matter where a little boy couldn't follow, and to keep me out of trouble until he got back he would shoo me into the jail and lock me in. I was quite happy in this oversized playpen chasing cockroaches and admiring the interesting artwork on the walls, but one day I was interrupted by a commotion in the station and my father appeared at the door with a great big black fellow in handcuffs. He unlocked the door and hollered at me to clear out, whereupon he shoved this hulking character past me and slammed the door. I remember feeling slightly miffed at having to give up my private playhouse to this stranger and wondered what he'd done to deserve it.

It's hard to imagine the Canadian Border Service allowing one of its officers to drag a small boy on his rounds today, and they might not have

The border crossing at Blaine, Washington, was one of the ports of entry my father, Silas White, had to watch over during his stint as an immigration officer. THE REACH P3867

When Dad was working as an immigration officer from around 1916 to 1919 his main office was in this railway station at White Rock. He used to take me with him and keep me out of trouble by locking me in the station's little jail. WHITE FAMILY

been that keen about it even then if they'd known. Dad was never one to go by the book, either in dealing with bureaucracy or raising children. Maybe the bureaucrats did object, because right around that time he left the immigration job, voluntarily or not I never knew. Anyway, around 1918 or 1919 he found himself needing something else to do so he threw in with my uncle Fred Carmichael and bought a butcher shop in Abbotsford.

The Pugilist and the Bloomer Girl

hy Abbotsford I don't know except that there was a man there named Charlie Sumner who had a butcher shop he was willing to sell for a price my father and uncle could handle. On the surface it didn't look like a gold mine. Abbotsford had four butcher shops serving a population of probably well under 1,000 people. Raoul Des Mazes had all the Catholic trade. Albert King had the English trade. Coppings and Dad went at it hammer and tongs for the rest. All told the sales of the four of them wouldn't keep one decent business going now, but of course things were different then. Diets were simpler and meat was a bigger part of it. Canada Food Rules hadn't been invented yet. Meat and potatoes, those were your basic food groups. We had vegetables, mostly root vegetables like carrots and turnips, but not the variety there is today. Meat was the main item. And since there was no effective refrigeration, people depended on butchers to get meat from local farmers or slaughter-houses and bring it fresh to market.

Des Mazes had his butcher shop at the back of a grocery store, the Pioneer Market, but generally stores didn't carry meat—you could only get it at a butcher shop. There was a lot more work to butchering then and the butcher played a much more prominent role in feeding the town. Dad spent a lot of time out buying live animals, which he would move to his own pasture for conditioning before slaughtering them in his own slaughterhouse. His shop wasn't the biggest or best and it was down at the

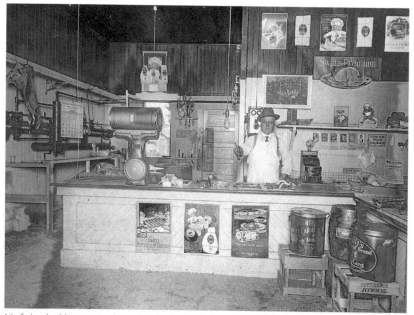

My father had been trained as a butcher by his father and took up the family trade again in 1919 when he bought this butcher shop on the main street of Abbotsford. This picture was taken after 1922 because it shows the cooling pipes of his revolutionary new refrigeration plant along the left hand wall. WHITE FAMILY

bottom of the hill on the wrong side of the tracks that cut the town in half. As the town grew, it grew away from him. Uncle Fred left the partnership after a short while to go into meat wholesaling.

Dad rented a house on Hazel Street down near the railroad tracks for the first year we were in Abbotsford, then moved us into a house he bought up Old Yale Road just as it came down the big hill into town. It was a beat-up old thing he got off some farmer for $2,500. Three rooms upstairs and four downstairs. It had a queer design, it was like two narrow houses pushed together, so that if you looked at it from the end, there were two gables. Why they built it like that I don't know—maybe they had actually pushed two smaller buildings together.

It was cramped and uncomfortable, but it served our growing family until the middle years of the Great Depression, when my mother lost it. It was on a good-sized lot, an acre or so with a small barn and a chicken coop where we kept chickens. There was no running water and no water on the property until my father dug a well. Then we'd go pump a bucket of water and bring it inside. The stove had a big copper boiler attached to it for hot water, and we'd keep that full. The house had no insulation and on winter mornings we'd all come pouring down the stairs shivering in our pajamas and dress around the tin heater, which Father would have started before setting off to work earlier. Once I bent over to put on my socks and backed into the red-hot heater, which woke me up quick. I had a scar on my butt for a long time. Maybe I still do, it's been awhile since I was able to see back there.

My father was a jolly, outgoing guy. He had a big round face that was un-blemished despite the fact he'd spent years in the ring, first as an amateur boxer, then as a touring prizefighter. People liked to be around Si White. He liked a drink and he was good company. He practised what was known in those days as "elocution." He'd fling out his arm, throw back his head, and let fly with some fancy piece of speechification. One of his favourites was, "Say not the struggle naught availeth / The labour and the wounds are vain / The enemy faints not, nor faileth / And as things have been, they remain…" He was also big on *The Rubaiyat of Omar Khayyam*: "Oh fill the cup that clears / Today of past regrets and future fears…" I don't know where he'd picked this talent up, he just had a high school education. I guess it was more common then.

He'd had quite a life. I always thought he was born on the family homestead in Ottawa in 1865, which is what he always wrote down, but his niece's story about him being born on the immigrant ship coming over from Ireland in 1862 puts that in doubt now. I don't know anything about my paternal grandmother, the Irish estate manager's daughter who supposedly eloped with my grandfather. I don't even know her name. She died very soon after they arrived and the old man got married a second time to a woman who had two sons of her own, Nelson and Albert. There were two daughters, Mattie (Martha) and Eva. Mattie was five years younger than father and I always understood she was a full sister but I couldn't swear to that now. The timing would seem to indicate the second wife was her mother.

So Dad grew up in Ottawa. But he wandered far in the course of his life. He toured with carnivals, fighting small-town tough guys for a few bucks. He would sometimes tie one hand behind his back, but he always won. He wasn't a big man, he stood five foot nine and weighed 165 pounds in fighting trim, but he was skilled. When he was an old man he had this trick, he'd place his handkerchief on the floor and put one foot on it. Then you'd have to try to hit him and he'd bob and weave without moving the foot off the handkerchief. You couldn't lay a hand on him. I saw guys go at him like a windmill, get all sweated up cursing and grunting. Sometimes he'd reach out and give them a little tap when they were off balance and sit them on their ass, not to hurt them, just to make the point that boxing was about skill, not strength.

He'd been all over the continent, New York, Chicago, New Orleans. He used to tell me stories of this wonderful new bridge called the Brooklyn Bridge, he said he walked across it when it was just recently opened. He told me about a cog railway that went up a mountain—a technological wonder of the day that is still operating in Bretton Woods, New Hampshire, only now it's considered a historical artifact. A funny-looking little old steam train. I went to see it myself a few years ago and tried to imagine my father as a young man, riding on it when it was considered a futuristic development. He spent time in Duluth, where there was a huge open-pit mine said to be the world's largest man-made hole up to that time. He was well acquainted in the boxing world and often spoke of making the rounds with John L. Sullivan, the great American heavyweight.

During the 1890s there was quite a mining boom, with mining camps springing up all through the Dakotas, Wyoming, Montana and Idaho, and Dad worked his way west in towns like Deadwood, following this boom until he ended up in the BC boom town of Sandon. A man named Pat Burns had set himself up supplying meat to the mines and railroads—this was the founder of the Burns meat-packing empire—and my father got a job managing the Burns outlet in Sandon. Burns was just on his way to becoming one of the richest men in Canada and Dad didn't have a lot of use for him. He said he was one of the crudest bastards he ever met. He had a story, one time Burns was at some big do in Ottawa with black ties and tails and visiting royalty and he took on a heavy load of booze and needed to take a leak. He's up at the head table and there's some potted plants off to one side so he just goes over to these plants and takes a leak right there in the foliage. He was so goddamned stewed he thought he was out in the bush somewhere.

Sandon was a wide-open town with gambling dens running round the clock, shootouts in the street, rampant prostitution, et cetera, and Dad would tell us stories about it, without saying anything about the prostitution, of course. He was a man of the world but observed the proprieties of the Victorian age when in mixed company. I sometimes wondered if he had any women friends or long-term relationships during his long years as a bachelor, but he was very closed-mouth about his private life. At the same time I heard him jawing with his cronies often enough to know that he enjoyed the company of women, so I can only assume there is a lot of his life I never did find out about.

Sandon seemed to be a high point of his wanderings and I don't know why he left it when he did but I have read that the town was levelled by fire in 1900 and that could be the reason, because right around that time he teamed up with his father's family and helped them get established in

Dad enjoyed about 20 years sowing wild oats around various parts of North America and spent the 1890s prize fighting and hustling cattle in mining boom towns across the west. By 1900 he was managing the Burns meat market in Sandon, BC (above). CITY OF VANCOUVER ARCHIVES CVA 2-33, RICHARD HENRY TRUEBLOOD PHOTO

BC. Again, I never knew why he decided to look homeward after all his years of wandering, or why his father decided to leave Ontario after forty years in business as a butcher and blacksmith. All I know is that sometime around 1900 they were travelling around BC looking for a suitable piece of land where they could pursue the family trade of raising and selling meat. They almost bought an acreage on Hornby Island, but chose the farm in Aldergrove as having superior soil and being closer to markets. They must have spent some time casting about doing one thing and another to survive because I remember talk of taking a contract to clear part of Moody Park in New Westminster. An incident they always spoke of concerned a blast that got away—they must have overloaded a stump and hit some nearby houses with flying roots, something I've done myself.

The family's meat business in Cloverdale was quite successful and I have vague memories of my mother being unhappy that the big house on the hill went to her sister-in-law Mattie instead of her. I don't know if there was friction between the stepbrothers or if it had been Father's plan all along to butt out after he helped them get established. That would have been in character for him. I remember talk about Mattie's husband, Ben Whitely, being a bit of a stumblebum and it may be he wanted Mattie to have the Cloverdale house because he could see Ben would never be able to get her into a decent place on his own. Dad remained close to Mattie until she died in 1923 or '4, the result of complications in childbirth. He always maintained her death was unnecessary. After that we never had much to do with Ben or Dad's two stepbrothers, Nels and Albert. I have completely lost touch with that branch of the family.

My father was nearly fifty when he married my mother in 1911 and middle-aged already by the time I was old enough to hang around with him—although as I say that I realize he was fifty years younger than I am today. He'd been a bachelor so long he never got completely domesticated. He was a good provider as long as his health lasted and he took good care of my mother, but he spent a lot of time out. Just where, we were never sure. My mother wouldn't discuss it. She was very religious and refused to have alcohol in the house, while he never turned down a drink. He was no drunkard, but he liked drinking and talking and playing cards, and I guess that was what he was doing most of the time when he wasn't at home or working. He was quite a sportsman too, and he was always organizing local boxing clubs and training the young fellows how to box.

He was a master of the butchering trade. He didn't just stand behind the counter handing out packages brought in from some big centralized packing house the way they do today. He made sausages, he made headcheese, he made pickles and sauerkraut, he smoked bacon, he corned beef, he made mincemeat, he did a thousand things that used to be part of the butcher's craft. He also husbanded animals. Buying animals on the hoof was a big part of the meat business and he was always dashing off to look at a cow some farmer had for sale, often bringing it home to tether in the pasture beside our slaughterhouse until he was ready to slaughter it. He had to have an eye for livestock; he had to be able to look at an animal and make an accurate estimate of what it weighed and how it would "cut out"—how much of its weight would be saleable meat as opposed to waste—because it varies greatly from one animal to the next and if you guess wrong, you end up working for nothing. Often he would buy a cow cheap because it was poorly and losing flesh and the farmer was afraid of losing it, and Dad would figure out what was wrong with it and bring it round, fatten it up. Then he'd maybe trade it to a different farmer for a couple of hogs, sell it back to the same farmer for double what he paid or do whatever he could to get a few bucks ahead. A butcher in those days had to be part veterinarian, and father had a real touch, which he had picked up from his father. Often farmers would get him to look at an animal if they couldn't get the vet, and most times Dad could help them out. He was an easygoing guy who didn't mind doing a favour for a friend and likely all he'd take would be a drink or something from the farmer's garden.

He was a master at his trade but not really that great as a businessman. He was too good-hearted and people knew they could put the touch on him. He knew it too, and he didn't mind as long as he figured you were playing straight with him. But you didn't want to cross him. I remember one time this great big bull of a guy from over in Clayburn, Buster Mutch, came into the shop and tried to throw his weight around. He owed Dad some money on some deal and was refusing to pay on some pretext. I remember Dad standing behind the counter and saying to him, "Buster, you know that's not right." And Buster, he was saying back to Dad, "What

Butchers had a more important role to play when the meat and potatoes diet reigned supreme. Here meat cutters plough through sides of beef at the big Burns packing plant in Vancouver. CITY OF VANCOUVER ARCHIVES CVA 1184-1788, JACK LINDSAY PHOTO

you goina do about it, Si?" This got my attention, because I knew and everybody in town knew, you didn't talk that way to Si White. Buster knew it too, but he was a great big ox of a guy well over six feet with a reputation for brawling and he thought he could get away with it. The old man wasn't that big, with chronic asthma, a generous belly and in his sixties. Also, there was a meat counter between them. To get out, the old man had to go eight feet down to the end and come up around the outside, but he did it a hundred times a day and he was out there in the blink of an eye. I saw the old man's arm shoot out, heard the "smack!" and saw Buster hit the floor. The way the arm flicked out, you wouldn't have thought there was that much power in it, but it did the trick. It was taking quite a chance because if the punch didn't land this big goon could have broken the old man in two. As it was, Buster was finished for that day. And that wasn't the only time. More than once I saw Dad take men out with a single punch, usually somebody who really needed it. He had been the Canadian welterweight champion when he was eighteen. I guess it was amateur, but the line between amateur and professional wasn't as clearly drawn in those days. He had a beautiful belt with a big silver medallion on the front. Mother sold it to a junk dealer after he died. She didn't get anything for it. The fact was, she was glad to get it out of the house. She always considered his boxing connections an embarrassment.

I admired my father tremendously. He was quite a man around town, more because of his manner and his personality than anything else, but he was respected by all sides. All sides, that is, but the Catholics. Catholics weren't acceptable to my father. He was an Orangeman. He was prejudiced. In many other ways he was very open-minded. He was liberal for the times, you'd have to say. But he would be the least liberal person you could find now. He voted Conservative all his life. But Conservative then meant tied to England. It meant honouring traditional ideas of good citizenship and gentlemanly conduct. He wouldn't have gone for all this heartless, let-the-buggers-starve attitude you see with modern conservatives of the Margaret Thatcher–Stephen Harper stripe. He was very compassionate. All the poor people in town came into our shop, and he'd always have something set aside he could give them for a few cents or whatever they had. He had no use for big corporations. He absolutely despised them. "They'll poison you!" he'd say. Somewhere he'd got this thing that corporations were a menace without heart or conscience. Perhaps he picked it up working for Pat Burns, I don't know.

Dad with my sister Beryl about the time our family moved to Abbotsford in 1919. If you look closely you can see the tip of his nose is slightly off-kilter, but otherwise his face betrayed little evidence of his years as a prize fighter. WHITE FAMILY

He was a good father. He had his own name for each one of us kids. My oldest sister Beryl was Teetee. I was Bud, Hazel was Dolly, Gladys was Happy and Wesley, the youngest, became Wes. These were our names at home always, although mother did give me Franklin at times, mostly in a reproachful attitude. Sometimes Father would take us for a ride, go on picnics. He'd burst in the door with a big whoop and announce we were going on an outing. Mother would get a bunch of stuff together, we'd all pile in the car and off we'd go, to some place like Starr's Ridge on Whatcom Road, which my mother named "the pretty place." My mother and father didn't mix up much socially with the local people. When we had company or went out, it was to see Mother's brothers and sisters, the Carmichael clan, visiting them if there was any visiting to be done.

Father had all the tools to be quite successful, but he was not financially ambitious. He disdained men who would make fools of themselves over a dollar. He was by far the best butcher in Abbotsford, maybe in the Fraser Valley, and with his winning personality he could have owned the meat business if he'd been inclined that way, but he wasn't. He was content just to provide good service to Abbotsford's Protestant meat customers and live according to his own code of good conduct. As long as he was healthy, there was never any shortage of money. But he never really got ahead. He never saved any or used one dollar to make another dollar. Our old shop needed a coat of paint when we got it and it still needed it when we sold it. Technology was changing, but he didn't keep up. He did put in one of the first refrigeration units, but in that case he was actually a bit ahead of his time and got stuck with a primitive system that cost too much and didn't work very well. It was a huge, heavy thing with pipes running all over the place, it had a big motor with a long slapping belt driving a compressor unit that stood ten feet high, a noisy bloody thing right in the shop. It worked with ammonia and the ammonia leaked, which made the whole place smell like piss. It was more of a drawback than anything, and he paid way too much for it. It wasn't long before they came out with a much more compact deal, which came as a self-contained unit and worked a lot better. Des Mazes got one of the new small ones that both cooled and froze, and the old man was left behind. Then he got sick and couldn't keep up, and suddenly we were poor.

My mother and father were not well matched. She was a Carmichael, from a family of hardbitten Scots Presbyterians who'd settled in the valley in the 1800s and hadn't been out since. She was devout and parochial and private. He was worldly and good-natured and outgoing. He'd been everywhere, seen everything and done everything, including having once operated a physical fitness emporium in Duluth under the name of

"Professor White." Maybe that was what she liked about him. He was so different from the men she knew. There was a difference in laughter too. He laughed. The Carmichael men snickered. I never learned any details of how they met. Mother had gotten tired of being cooped up on the family farm in Bradner and took a job as a telephone operator in Vancouver. At twenty-seven she was getting to be an old maid by the standard of those days, but she was still twenty years younger than Father. Somehow they met, married in 1911 and by 1920 produced six kids, counting the one she lost. Whatever initial attraction was there, the differences in their personalities brought them into conflict before long. I was aware of friction between them. She'd do a lot of scolding. He would never answer back, he'd just get out of the house.

Early on she'd gone through a period of being what they called a "Bloomer Girl" and went around wearing these big baggy pants like something out of a Persian harem as an act of rebellion against Victorian strictures on women. This was considered very wicked. Bloomers were only supposed to be worn by women athletes as part of their uniform, or as the lower part of a bathing suit. Other than that, women had to wear dresses down to the ground, even hoeing the garden or making munitions. A woman's reputation could be ruined by exposing her leg. The only official erogenous zones were the ankle and the waist, which was cinched up with whalebone and laces to make it appear unnaturally small. I grew up with a very confused idea of female anatomy. Pornography, which came in the form of what they called "French postcards," didn't help much. It mainly showed plump ladies stripped down to their underwear, which in those days covered everything from the neck to the knees in billowing fabric, though we managed to get just as steamed up looking at those pictures as young fellows do now looking at *Hustler*.

My mother wasn't what they called "fast," far from it, but early on she had a touch of this suffragette radical stuff. This was right in the thick of the battle for the women's vote, which most men in a place like Abbotsford thought was utter foolishness. Women were supposed to stay at home and have babies according to the old way of looking at it, and I fully subscribed to this for most of my life myself. I didn't know any better— how could I? Every man I knew thought that way and so did most of the women. I know now that there were liberated thinkers over in Europe preaching equality of the sexes back in the 1900s, and right here on the BC coast Finnish immigrants had a colony based on equality of the sexes up at Sointula, but we had no way of knowing any of that. People in small towns like Abbotsford were very sheltered.

Communications—there's another thing that has changed so completely—we didn't even have telephones. There were a few around, but it would take years before they caught on to the point every home

My mother, Jean (Carmichael) White with her fourth child, my sister Hazel, born 1916. Mother had apparently kicked over the traces a bit when she was younger but was all church and respectability by the time I came along. WHITE FAMILY

had one. For one thing, there was no dominant phone company, just a bunch of local gyppos who didn't necessarily hook up to each other. I think there were three different phone companies in the Fraser Valley alone. It's hard for someone today to understand just how isolated a small country place like Abbotsford was in those days. It had many of the same features a small town today has, but it was magnified. We were more myopic. Each town was its own little world. People in different towns had a different sound to their voices and were thought of as foreign. People from a town of 10,000 laughed at the people from a town of 5,000, imitated the way they talked. Regarded them as rubes. The outside world was just a kind of a shadowy myth. Our only contact with the outside world was the occasional stranger who would come through with some news, a travelling salesman or occasionally a lecturer. Somebody from the Women's Christian Temperance Union would come through and speak to a small group of women in a church basement. The women's rights ideas that were acceptable focused on men drinking in taverns and were closely tied to the church. With her strict Presbyterian background, this went over big with my mother, and hardened the tension between her and my father.

She had a hard time of it, though it wasn't until years later I began to feel any real sympathy for her.

Early on my mother had ambitions to be a writer and took lessons by correspondence, but all that got put aside when she got married and started having babies. It was a lot to handle and she wasn't equipped for it. My father was a different kind of man from anything she'd known. Mother's family thought she had married beneath her, they had a very high idea of themselves for a bunch of poor dirt farmers from Bradner. Grandmother Carmichael referred to Father as a "pugilist," which was not meant as a compliment. She made much of her descent from old New Brunswick United Empire Loyalists named Wetmore and Belyea (aka Bullier), one of whom was supposed to be a heavyweight in the Bank of Nova Scotia. She had a lot of heirloom furniture and household belongings with her when they first moved to the valley, but they didn't allow for tide when they tied up their barge at Barnston Island and it heeled over, dumping all grandmother's prized possessions into the muddy Fraser. That left them without anything, jammed together with a bunch of kids in a log shack in Bradner, although they did carve out a decent farm in time. In my grandmother's mind they were always a cut above everyone else in the neighbourhood. Religion was a big part of this. They were Presbyterian through and through. The living room of their house had a pedestal right in the middle with a great big bible on it and my grandfather would often stop on his way by and begin preaching out of it. In the old Presbyterian way of thinking, religion was a personal responsibility. The father was the minister to his own family and each person was the guardian of his own conscience. They were very big on original sin and individual guilt and had a strong sense of superiority to anyone who didn't go around carrying as big a load of guilt as they did. After I retired I spent some time tramping around New Brunswick looking up Grandmother's ancestors in various small-town churchyards and couldn't help but notice what a hidebound, uptight, churchy society that was, even heading into the twenty-first century, so some of the narrow-mindedness I always blamed on the old Scotch Calvinist thing might actually have an East Coast twist to it.

Once when I was a little older I went out to help my uncle Bob move into a new place he'd bought on Sumas Prairie. It was a boiling hot summer day and something was haywire, either the stuff we were supposed to move was late arriving or Bob hadn't got ready for us, and we ended up standing around all morning in this baking sun. There was no explanation, no apology, no water to drink, no lunch, no nothing. I was old enough to be smoking then, so to help pass the time I took out my makings and lit up a cigarette. I was aware smoking was considered sinful by the Carmichaels but I was pissed off and didn't care. "Wham!" My whole body lit up with pain and I went flying forward onto the ground. Uncle Bob had come up behind me and kicked me as hard as he could right on the tailbone. "No smoking on this property," he thundered. I was paralyzed. It was days before I could walk straight. I had nerve trouble in my leg for the rest of my life; I have pain in my heel right now I trace back to that righteous Presbyterian kick. But he felt perfectly justified, because I was a lowly sinner, spawn of an ungodly pugilist. That was the Carmichaels all over.

3

Biting Dynamite and Derailing Trains

Father was not an ideal husband. He provided well as long as his health held up, but he didn't help much around the home. Not that Mother encouraged that. Home was where she reigned supreme. She managed to create a very confining atmosphere. There was no place for fun or relaxation in our home. She was just a slave to the church, and her father's brand of strict Presbyterianism. She would put up a fight about things like going fishing on Sundays. She was constantly fretting about one thing or another, and the fact she often had good reason made it no easier to take. My father dealt with it by being absent as much as possible, and as soon as I was big enough I began to follow his example. The shop made for an easy getaway.

Working alongside my father brought us close together. Once I became his helper at the shop, he became very devoted to my education, both as a butcher and a man. He delighted in getting me to do things, like handling big knives, that shocked people coming into the shop, and I soon became quite addicted to showing off my precocious talents in front of surprised and alarmed customers. Despite the fifty years between us, Father and I became real buddies and my admiration of him verged on worship.

I sometimes stop at the corner of Hazel (now George Ferguson Way) and Railway streets and try to see Abbotsford as it was when we moved there in 1919. It was a little mill town built up around the large mill and logging show owned by Sam and Joe Trethewey out at Mill Lake. The mill on occasion cut 100,000 board feet a day, which was very impressive for that time, although it wouldn't amount to much today. It was a railroad show and they had probably 300 men in the woods, the mill and the railroad. They had a great barn for their horse teams, which were used for local deliveries and laying track. The Tretheweys were Abbotsford's aristocrats. Joe, who was boss during my time, had made his money in Cobalt, Ontario, where he had operated then sold the rich Coniagas Mine in 1906. Then he returned to BC and got into the family lumbering business, which his descendants kept up until recent years, although the Abbotsford operation shut down decades ago.

There was a small downtown built up along the Fraser Valley's main road, the Old Yale Road, soon to be renamed Essendene Avenue where it passed through town. Essendene ran down a long hill to where it crossed the CPR tracks at the bottom of the valley, then reverted back to its Old Yale name and begin winding up a smaller hill east of downtown. The shop my father bought was in the oldest part of town, the first block east of the tracks. Across the street were a number of other old commercial buildings built of wood, including a small hotel, which was owned by the Haddrells. There was a station house beside the railway and a barbed-wire

Downtown Abbotsford c. 1922. My father's butcher shop is the one with the lower cornice and white awning just to the left of the parked car. The large white building two doors over is the Pioneer Market, owned by Raoul Des Mazes. THE REACH P12983

fence guarding the yards. A long wooden trestle emerged from a ravine now filled and covered by a shopping mall, crossed Montrose Street and ended at Railroad Street. It carried the tracks used by the Tretheweys' mill to ship their products to the far corners of the world. They were known as the "dinky" tracks and the two small locomotives that ran on them were the "dinkys."

It was quite a change moving from a farm in the countryside to even as small a town as Abbotsford was then, and one of the first changes was that I now had to start school, a year earlier than usual probably because of my brother Wesley's imminent birth, which according to Google took place on July 27, 1920. I can't swear that I can remember the first day that I attended school. It does seem to me that I walked alone to the old Orange Hall on what is now Montrose Street. I have no recollection of either of my parents ever coming to the school. The Orange Hall was being used as a schoolroom for first- and second-year pupils while the new Superior School was being built on Hazel Street. The next term we went to the basement of the United Church and Beryl reminded me that we went to the Masonic Hall for a short while, I think because of some unforeseen delay in opening the new school. I do remember our first day in the new school and being scolded by old Mr. McPhee, one of the trustees, for running on the stairs.

Beryl and I were somewhat careful, each a little jealous of the other, but as I see it now she gave me more respect than I deserved. We played together inseparably until I was five and started school. During one of our too-rare sessions of reminiscing before she died, Beryl reminded me that I was supposed to take her to school on her first day, but left her halfway there and went off to play with some other kids. It was hard to go past the Great Northern bridge without stopping to mess with the sand and stuff under the tracks. I do remember the incident and that she was scared, and I thought she was a pain for crying and shouting at me—I was just not waiting for her enough. I think she must have been six years old and as a mature scholar of seven I resented having to look after her. It was about a mile from our house to the Orange Hall. I recall the long walk up Montrose Street with Beryl behind me crying, lost and scared. She also remembered and told me what she thought of me that day, eighty years

When the Superior School was opened in 1923 we thought Abbotsford had really arrived. THE REACH P5606

later. They say time heals all wounds and I guess it does but what they don't tell you is scars last forever.

In 1923 we were able to attend the great new school. Eight rooms—imagine! Two rooms were empty, to be filled with high school kids in a few years. The design was what we knew as a Superior School and it was a design that was replicated all over BC. It was an L-shaped, two-storey affair with clapboard siding and a trademark round vent at the apex of the gable. During the 1920s and '30s they popped them out like pancakes. I've seen identical examples all over BC. There are two good specimens still being used in Sechelt and Gibsons, where one has been given heritage status and nicely restored by the local school board, of which my grandson Silas White II is currently chairman. I should ask him if he knows the story behind that particular schoolhouse design and how BC's ministry of education came to be so stuck on it in the early days. In Abbotsford, we thought our Superior School was a modern wonder that showed Abbotsford had finally arrived. I lived long enough to see it become outdated and demolished—a good many years ago, because I bought the windows from it and incorporated them into the two shop buildings that now house my sons' businesses.

My earliest memory of school concerns my first teacher, Mrs. MacDowell. To a scared and timid five-and-a-half-year-old she was a most ferocious old ogre. Some distant officials in the education department had prescribed a system of penmanship that required each letter to be formed in a round, flowing style using only the muscles of the upper arm without moving the fingers. This ill-advised system, called the MacLean Method, has long since been abandoned, but it was used to torture generations of students across Canada.

Mrs. MacDowell was a true believer and scolded the classes, second-year students and beginners alike, to produce nothing less than the ideal script using this impossible method. Her great pleasure came from stalking up the aisle waiting to catch some slight movement in someone's fingers, whereupon there would be a whack as her pointer cracked across a small set of knuckles, often my own.

I don't know how many penmen she turned out but I do know that her spectre hangs over my shoulder any time I pick up a pen, and try as I will the pen wavers and the old fear returns. I have never been able to write legibly in my life, and if I can't blame her entirely I can say she sure didn't help.

At recess we used to go to the stream that ran beside the hall to torture frogs and get as wet as possible. One day I was so terrified of returning to that old monster and her pointer that I stayed out in the woods and hid 'til noon. No one bothered to look for a missing pupil but when I made the mistake of trying to sneak in during the afternoon I was found out and soundly strapped. I wish that I could remember the name of the teacher that replaced Mrs. MacDowell. She was as kind as MacDowell was mean and used to take us out in the woods between the hall and the tracks looking for morels. If only teachers realized what lasting effects they have on people's lives, I can't help but think they would tread a bit more carefully.

I was lucky to have some great teachers before I was done. There was a man came to Abbotsford who was a bit of a weird duck, Mr. West. He was a bachelor and kept to himself, but he was a true scholar and had a university degree, which was rare then. I think he'd been an engineer, but he'd gone overseas in the war, and for some reason got into teaching. He was up on all the latest scientific theories and it was him who freed me from all the biblical nonsense I'd got from my mother and Sunday school, and opened my thinking to Darwinism and atomic theory and all the modern ways of understanding the world. He was outspoken. He said the bible was all b.s. I was surprised, but I was ready to hear this.

Suddenly everything began to make sense and it's no exaggeration at all to say that teacher changed my life. Mr. West taught that there are no mysteries and magic, there are just things we don't understand yet. He gave me the approach I carried through my life—if you find yourself facing something that stumps you, don't wring your hands in despair, just put on your thinking cap and figure out how it works, whether it's a car, a computer or a natural wonder. I was soon reading every scientific book I could get my hands on—I still get *Popular Science* and *Scientific American* to this day—and I would go home and try to get my mother to see the error of her thinking. "Don't you see? Don't you see?" I remember myself saying, in desperation. But of course she didn't see. That was another lesson I was learning: just because you give people the tools to make sense of the world doesn't mean they will use them. Often as not they will fight them and denounce them as the work of the devil.

Things change, but they're not what you think. All the hardware, the horseless carriage and the aeroplane, they are just the outward trappings. When I was a boy in school, it was common for a desk to be empty where one of your chums had been sitting the day before. They would say, Oh, Bobby's not well. Eventually they would take the desk away and you would figure out that Bobby had died. Classmates would just disappear like this and nobody would make too big a deal about it. There were so many childhood diseases. Diphtheria killed tens of thousands. George McGowan next door got something that crippled his arm, something I'm sure they would knock out with a pill or a shot today. There was no health care and what medical help existed was limited. They didn't have antibiotics or any drugs worth mentioning and they didn't know what they were doing most of the time. If a child came down with something serious, it just died. My mother lost her first child to meningitis, and she was lucky, only losing one. Her mother lost two and for many families the toll was higher. Today if a child has a medical problem, they spare no expense doing everything modern science can do to bring it through. If a child dies unnecessarily, they have an investigation. So that's been a big change, the availability of truly effective medicine and the value that has allowed us to place on life. And yet, we got along. There was nobody to tell us how bad off we were, so we didn't let it bother us, and it seems there were about as many good days then as there are now. I am going to keep thinking about what has really changed and will let you know as soon as I think of something.

I adapted without too much trouble to living in town, at least at first. Kids that young take what comes. Abbotsford still had lots of wide-open spaces in those days for a kid to get into mischief, only now I had playmates to aid and abet the process.

We moved up the hill to the house Dad bought after the first year but the Hazel Street flats behind our first house remained a favourite playground. The area until recently occupied by the Clayburn Industries brick plant was covered then by a heavy growth of broom and wild hazel bushes. I suppose that the area had been cleared and levelled for some kind of camp and shop during the building of the BC Electric and the CPR spur that had been put in a few years earlier. Scattered through the brush were relics of these former activities and among them was a water tank off

Blasting stumps, a time-honoured Fraser Valley tradition. Instead of spending weeks hacking and burning, you could make stumps disappear fast by digging a hole between the roots and loading it with several dozen sticks of stumping powder—on a long fuse. It made great entertainment for small boys. THE REACH P12385

some ancient locomotive. This tank was huge and had served as a home for various homeless characters from time to time.

Jack Copping owned the next field, containing the old powder plant. He had decided to clear the stumps from the field and we boys became a very interested audience. In those simple days, at the end of a working day it was enough to put the box of powder under a piece of blasted stump out of the rain, and then do what thirsty blasters have always done after work. I do wish that I could remember who all was there, but there were four or five of us, all aged about ten or twelve. We had by this time become quite knowledgeable in the ways to make a real blast and at the first chance helped ourselves to a representative sample of blasting supplies: caps, fuse, and eight or ten sticks of twenty-percent blasting powder.

In the fastness of the bushy jungle we felt safe to pursue our research into various causes and effects, now focused on noise. After a few tentative shots, someone proposed dropping a small shot in the tank to see what would happen. A quarter stick was prepared with cap and fuse—and I might add, as we had watched the blaster do, we likewise carefully crimped the highly explosive cap onto the fuse with our teeth.

The fuse was lit and the charge dropped down the manhole. Now eighty-five years later I can still feel the excitement as we scurried for cover, having no idea what was going to happen. It seemed forever before we were rewarded with the most gratifying boom we had ever heard. The old tank acted like an enormous drum, and as a bonus we watched in awe as a great smoke ring rose in the air, higher and higher.

The smoke ring became our centre of interest. With such success to our credit it was only natural to pursue the research with vigour and naturally, next a half stick, and of course, soon a full stick.

In our single-minded pursuit of science it had not occurred that others might also have an interest in our research.

It happened that the police station was only what would now be a couple of blocks away and that the magistrate, George Pratt, was holding court that afternoon. He became curious as to the source of the interruptions to His Majesty's proceedings. At last he dispatched an officer to investigate.

Cars were much noisier in those days and we heard him approaching long before we saw him. Of course the officer had no idea of what he was looking for and we watched from our jungle as he searched around the open area; we left very shortly, not wanting to bother him in his duties.

I have often wondered what his conclusions were and what he reported to the court.

Another caper didn't turn out so well. I think this would be earlier, when I was maybe seven or eight. Somehow we got the idea in our heads of putting a tie across the dinky tracks. I guess we must have heard somebody talking about it, or else we just came up with the idea ourselves of putting something in the little choo-choo's way to see what would happen. We certainly had no concept of what would really happen or we would never have had the nerve. Somehow we dragged an old cast-off tie up onto the tracks, and this is what made it worse, we dragged it along to the high part of the trestle and placed it crossways on the rails. Then we hid in the bushes and watched the dinky come down from the mill up at Mill Lake, loaded with three cars of fresh-cut lumber for shipment on the CPR.

The little engine was pushing the string of cars and the hogger (engineer) back in the locie didn't see the obstruction before the train

The main employer in town was the Trethewey brothers' Abbotsford Lumber Company, which operated its own narrow-gauge railroad locals referred to as the "dinky." THE REACH P998

slammed right into it. There was a brakeman riding in the forward car and he was supposed to be watching the track but he must have been lighting a smoke or something. It must have been a boring job, going back and forth on this short piece of track where nothing ever changed—except on this day it did. I don't know what we were expecting. Maybe a bang and wood splinters or something. We often put smaller things on the tracks, rocks and coins and sticks, and came back to find them satisfyingly mashed. But we were totally unprepared for the effect of our latest effort. The first car bumped up onto the tie and jumped the track, lurched and plunged down off the trestle onto the ground below, pulling the next two cars with it. The drop was fifteen or twenty feet. Thankfully the locie broke away and didn't get toppled as well, but the brakeman went over and got busted up pretty bad. It's a miracle he wasn't killed. We kids of course were horrified and beat it out of there as fast as we could. We were never caught, although there couldn't have been much doubt about who the culprits were, there was a small bunch of us playing around the tracks all the time and I'm sure my father had to do some fancy talking to old Sam Trethewey, the mill owner, who happened to be his best meat customer. I got a lecture out of it but he left it at that—he could see I had learned my lesson well enough, he didn't need to drive it in. He was right about that. I have been having nightmares about that caper for the ninety years that have passed since and the thought of it still makes me cringe.

Boy Butcher

never had the old man's easy manner and slick way with words; I was awkward around kids of my own age, especially girls, and was always self-conscious about the way I looked. My hair was wiry and stood straight up on my head, and I was a bit pop-eyed as a kid—I thought I looked like a clown. I was no good at sports, either. Somehow I could never kick a soccer ball with any authority, and I just couldn't make a bat connect with a baseball. If I was forced into participating in sports day, I came last in every event. The only thing I was halfway good at was schoolyard brawling, but that didn't get you any ribbons.

My escape was the butcher shop. Dad was down there all hours and was always glad to have company, and gladder yet to have a helping hand. I soon learned that if I did a few chores I had an ironclad excuse for being away from home as much as I wanted. It also gave me a place where I wasn't just an awkward kid, I was somebody special, waiting on my classmates' mothers and wowing them with my grown-up skills.

I'd always had a dog—when I was young it was a mutt named Leo that I used to pull a wagon and had a lot of fun with, and when I was nine or ten I got my own horse. I bought it myself with money I'd earned selling papers and magazines. *Mechanix Illustrated* and *Liberty* used to be sold door-to-door in those days and I had a route. One day I was walking by the auction just as it was winding up and this oldtimer came staggering away with an old horse he'd been unable to get anybody to bid on. I offered him two dollars but he wouldn't take that so I threw in some books, a pocket knife and some other stuff up to a total of about five dollars and I became the proud owner of a very old horse named Fanny. I knew my mother would be irate but I counted on Father to back me and he did. It suited his idea of adventurous kid-raising and he helped me keep her fed by scrounging the odd sack of oats or bale of hay. Fanny was well known around Sumas Prairie where this old farmer had used her to ride and pull a wagon, and people would often come up to look her over and caution me about looking after her properly and not working her too hard. I had no saddle—I just rode bareback, and I had to shimmy up on a stump to get on her.

She was very patient but like every horse she had a mind of her own. The first day I had her I took Beryl for a ride and the horse promptly lined up with a low-hanging cherry tree and scraped us off onto the ground. But she proved to be a great old horse and I had some wonderful, carefree times wandering over roads and trails far beyond my normal haunts. Once when I was wandering through some bush on the outskirts of town I came across a heap of trash left by someone who was cleaning out a house. Among the effects was a collection of medical books, which I carefully collected and took home. These were serious medical textbooks that must have been owned by a doctor and they were a revelation to me. I was already familiar with basic mammal anatomy from helping my father in the slaughterhouse and had often wondered what all those glistening organs with all their strange shapes and colours were for. Now I was able to find out and I studied the books with a passion. I was soon giving my father lectures on the names and functions of cow parts he had been handling but taking for granted all his life, which greatly impressed him. Like any parent who predicts his kid will become a rocket scientist because he can add two plus two, he took my medical bent for a sure sign I would grow up to be a doctor and began encouraging me. That suited me fine and that became my main ambition throughout my years at school.

I had a few friends my own age. My main sidekick early on was a kid from next door named Rendall McKinnon, whose father was a millwright for Trethewey's sawmill. He liked to hang around the shop with me, and Father undertook to teach him about the butchering trade as he taught me. On Thursday afternoon the shop was closed so we would beat it down there and be turning the grindstone for my dad sharpening knives, cleaning up, changing the sawdust on the floor. We did it for fun. My father had a knack that way. It was fun working for him. He had a way of treating kids as equals and letting them do grown-up work and it felt damn good. He'd had an insight that kids could handle a lot more responsibility than they were usually given and relished the chance to show what they could do. At the same time, a well-trained kid could be a great help to a guy like him. He always had some young fellow hanging around trading work for training.

Sometimes I'd skip school and go out and get a cow in—I brought cows in for miles. Get them on the road driving them, leading them. You could do it then. Once my father bought a cow out on Matsqui Prairie, four, five miles out. There was no way to get it home, so would I go bring it in? So Rendall and I went out, started to drive this cow home. It's all low land in Matsqui there, with deep black muck and deep, water-filled ditches to drain it. Well, this goddamn thing took off and tried to jump the ditch, hit the fence and bounced back into the ditch. It was lying there in this soft mud, we had to hold its head up, the water was building up, had a hell of a time. Finally some guy come along and he helped us and we got the cow out of there. Touch and go, oh boy, we felt like we'd been to the wars and back by the time we finally handed that muddy cow over to my father. He just shook his head and laughed.

By the time I was twelve I was going out to kill pigs on my own. That was quite a piece of work for a kid. You had a big table you'd put up in parts. Then you had a cut-open gas drum of water with a fire under it and you'd set up a hoist and kill the pig. When the water was just right you'd hoist the pig up and dunk it into the water and out, into the water and out, and eventually you got it so you could scrape the hair off with a scraper. If you got it right the hair would just roll out, but it was tricky. You didn't want to give it too much or you'd cook the hide and spoil the meat. A hundred and fifty-five degrees. You didn't have a thermometer, you'd test it with your finger—if three quick dips just about made you scream, it was just right. But the pig cooled the water so you'd have to keep the heat coming and make sure you didn't splash water on your fire, or yourself. It would be pretty easy to scald yourself or your helper if you got careless and jolted the barrel or dropped the carcass too fast. I would have Rendall with me. When you got the hind end done you'd switch ends and dunk the other half. You did the front end first and put a gambrel on the back end so when you were finished scraping you could go right ahead with splitting it open and pulling the guts out. It was a lot to ask of a twelve-year-old, but my father had been bringing me along since I was eight and had confidence in me.

It must have been 1927 or '8 when I was fourteen and Rendall McKinnon fifteen or sixteen when we found ourselves commandeered by my father on a summer day to help him kill a cow that he had

Killing and butchering a pig is normally considered a job for an experienced man with a helper or two. My dad started sending me out on my own when I was 12. THE REACH P12431

bought from an old friend, Howard Boley. At that time Howard farmed what was known as the Old York Place, a large dairy farm beside the Sumas River in what is now Abbotsford municipality.

It would almost surely have been a Thursday afternoon, since the town closed down every Thursday afternoon, especially during summer holidays. I remember the bright fields, mown, and the river, even then looking sullen and hopeless from the indignities forty years of farming had imposed on it.

We arrived at the farm as usual, with block and tackle, knives, buckets, a hammer and all the paraphernalia needed to turn an unsuspecting animal into beef. A site was chosen in the barn and the gambrel and tackle were hung from a convenient rafter, then the cow was led out and promptly dispatched. My father had a very undramatic way of killing a cow. A lot of guys would get all hopped up and start yanking the cow around and yelling and before they knew it the cow would get all jumpy and fighting the rope and they'd be jumping around hammering away on its head making a bloody mess and spoiling the meat, but Dad would calmly lead it over to the place he wanted it to drop and place a handful of hay on the ground. When the cow put its head down to get the hay, *pop*, he'd bang it on the head with the hammer. It doesn't take much of a blow to conk out a cow if you hit the right spot. You only want to stun it, not kill it. It would flop down and Dad would open the throat and let its still-beating heart empty the carcass of blood. The cow would pass away peacefully without getting stressed. If you stress it, it fills with adrenalin, the heart rate goes up, all kinds of chemical changes go through its body and it taints the meat. This is something they don't bother with today. In those big production-line slaughterhouses every cow dies terrified and bawling.

As the job progressed we became aware of some younger kids furtively peeking through the cracks in the barn wall, giggling and shushing each other. They turned out to be a girl about twelve, tall and slim, a younger sister and a young boy about eight or nine. We tried to talk to them but they were too shy and intimidated by us busy craftsmen. The tall girl, whose name was Kathleen, had a striking beauty that blazed out of her like a flame, even though she was about two years our junior and much too young for us big boys to admit an interest in.

While Dad was finishing up, Rendall and I as usual cut out the bladder and blew it up with a straw to make a very serviceable football. We then proceeded to show off with it, pretending to ignore the pretty girl as she pretended to ignore us. She and her sister and brother were too shy to enter into the game but stood off watching us kick the ball around. It wasn't until we left they ventured out to inspect the rather grubby item and try kicking it around themselves. They had a great time with it and kept at it until their mother pronounced it the work of evil city boys good children like them should have nothing to do with. This proved to be about as effective as most parental advice. Twelve years later that tall, beautiful girl became my wife. But that is getting ahead of our story.

Rendall and I hung around together for quite a few years. I remember once Dad says, "Time to go home"—he's counting the money. He didn't usually count the pennies and gave us this big pile of pennies to count.

Then we're going home and getting in the car—*tinkle, tinkle. Tinkle-tinkle.* Pennies dropping on the floor. McKinnon had filled his pockets with them. The old man never said a word, he just laughs. "That's Rendall." This was his way. It told me something. You could have somebody who was your best friend who would still steal anything he thought he could get away with, and you could just laugh and go on being his friend, while taking note of the way he was. Things aren't cut and dried in the real world the way they made you think in school, and unlike most adults who try to communicate a black-and-white version of morality to kids, my dad was all live and let live. But keep your guard up. Any time he encountered one of these funny contradictions he'd just laugh. He had a wonderful, wise laugh that I learned to pay attention to. We weren't entirely surprised a few years later when Rendall took all the knowledge Father had drilled into him and went up to Coppings, our main opposition, and gave all our trade secrets to him. By that time he was a first-rate butcher's helper. That was the end of our close friendship. I saw him around after that and we had the odd drink together as young men but we never palled around again. I'm not even sure what became of him. He went to work at the mill with his father for awhile, then the mill shut down and I'm not sure what he did. Those childhood friendships seldom do survive into adulthood in my experience.

Another kid I knew from the earliest days was Bud Haddrell. His father's hotel was across Essendene opposite Dad's meat market. Bud was an entirely different kind of a guy. He was a brash character, a motormouth who was into every kind of a racket you could imagine. One of the first I remember was marbles. I don't see them playing marbles anymore. In those days you'd see them start up in the spring. As soon as it dries up and you can play in the sand. Everybody had marbles. I forget just what the rules were. You'd make a ring and put one of your marbles in there and everybody shoots to knock it out. Hit this one, bounce over, hit another one, you got two. If you called your shot you got credit. The object was to accumulate the most marbles as the season wore on. The good players' bags would get bigger and bigger, the bad players' smaller and smaller. But Bud wasn't content to win the slow way. He invented his own game. He brought in a little box with a hole in it. I forget just how it worked. He'd have a bunch of good-looking marbles on top of the box and if you hit the hole you won all the marbles on top of the box, but if you missed he got your marble. Damn few ever hit the hole. Before long Bud had most of the marbles in the school. He needed a gunny sack to drag them around.

After school he'd go to work in his old man's hotel. It wasn't a big hotel, a frame structure—I couldn't guess how many rooms. A dozen maybe. It had a café. If a car stopped out front, *swish*, little Bud comes out wearing an apron, "How ya do, Missus—," find out their name, bring them in, "We got nice washrooms, c'mon in…" On the way out he would try to sell them ice cream cones. He was the goddamnedest guy you ever saw. If you were on the inside track you could walk into Bud's—"Gimme a root beer!" So he'd put up one of those stone crocks they used for root beer, but in it would be real beer. Cops would walk in, you'd talk to them without letting on, you'd feel you'd arrived. He did some bootlegging, always. He had an older guy, Nosey Campbell, who bought for him. He catered to every whim. You wanted anything, why, talk to Bud, he'd try, he'd break his goddamn neck to get you what you want. If it was a woman you wanted, no problem. They were a pretty rough bunch.

By the time Bud was in high school he had his own motel. Up the hill behind just as you went out of Abbotsford. He had a row of twelve, fifteen

The Abbotsford Hotel, directly across Essendene Avenue from my father's butcher shop, was owned by Charles and Annae Haddrell. Their son Bud became a lifelong friend, despite being the most eccentric individual you could ever want to meet. THE REACH P1216

cabins there. The old man set him up I guess. He was barely a teenager. We were still playing with goddamn marbles when he was running the motel. Well, during the day when he was at school, the motel would fill up with Americans who drove up from across the line to get a bit of booze and have a good time. Prohibition had been repealed in Canada but not in the States. Scotty Coutts was a few years older than us and he used to run this motel 'til Bud got out of school. Scotty would put these people up, rent out rooms, rent gramophones, but he wasn't allowed to open up the liquor cabinet. Bud had to be on deck before any booze could come out. So all these Americans had to wait 'til school was out before they could start drinking. Bud never had trouble with the police that I know. Everybody knew he was a bootlegger. Cops might have been paid off but I can't see anybody stooping that low, to take money from a kid, even though this was no normal kid.

There was this girl, Georgia. We're getting on now, maybe Bud was fifteen. She was older than him, maybe sixteen. From a respectable family. All of a sudden—great big explosion. You know how it is in schools. Bud has been doping girls. Bud did this and Bud did that. It turned out he'd been feeding Georgia dope. Her mother raised hell. Then, a big investigation. Second day of the investigation they got Bud up on the carpet, hashed it out. Anyhow, Bud said, I just gave 'er some Aspirin tablets and she just came right across like nothing.

End of the big doping case.

The whole town is chilled off when this goes through, believing the worst of Bud all the way. Bud came off clean as hell. The girl—she survived.

Bud never worked a day in his life. His old man's hotel burnt down and they rebuilt it. I don't know if Bud built it but Bud got it anyhow. He never left the place. He started on his own some time in the twenties. He made everybody come to him, sitting there. People went to him for money, you see. A big part of his business was loaning money to farmers and that. But that was the extent of it. When he was younger you'd hear people predicting he'd become a big tycoon and end up owning half the country, but he was limited in his ambition. I guess he had a few million tucked away when he died, but he never went big.

Bud was a funny guy. Funny situation. He had a special place. You couldn't call him a great friend or anything. He was his own friend. He had a woman around for awhile but he never married. I guess if he had a real friend it was his father. They say he used to ride his bike out to his father Charlie's grave at Hazelwood Cemetery and read him the stock market listings. I kept up with him over the years and used to go visit him in his little house on the hill above his old hotel. He had the place full of cuckoo clocks, all telling different time and making an unholy din, cuckooing at random. He claimed some of the clocks were antiques he'd paid a lot for, including the first cuckoo clock ever made, but of course Bud was a world-class bullshitter. He also had about, I think he said, 700 pairs of shoes. Fancy shoes, ordinary shoes, shoes of every colour and kind—spilling out of every drawer and closet. Plaques with corny sayings all over the place. "I may be the miller's daughter but that doesn't mean I've been through the mill," one said. He must have dreamed them up himself. He rattled away mile a minute about anything that came into his mind, just like always. He was a baseball nut and personally attended every World Series for sixty years or some such thing. I took my son to see him once and he thought Bud was cuckoo, but if so he'd been that way a long time. His two brothers, Ace and Glen, were normal. Later he moved to the Bevan Lodge seniors' home and I visited him there, too, but the last time I went he was dead. He only made it to ninety-four.

When we Googled his name to get his dates we came across a story by a woman who had been living in Abbotsford after Bud died on May 15, 2004. He'd been born on April 5, 1911, in Spy Hill, Saskatchewan. This woman had been living higher up on the hill and noticed a yard light on in front of an abandoned house and went down one day to check. It was Bud's place and it had been ransacked by vandals and taken over by squatters. She found papers strewn all over the yard including his father's last will and testament and pages from Bud's diary. These were disturbing. Apparently in his last years Bud had been terrorized by some local no-goods he referred to as the "Dummies" who made raids on his house and carried away his possessions while he cowered in the bathroom praying. He had never mentioned anything of this when I visited him in Bevan Lodge, but by then his grip on reality was getting pretty slack. While this woman was at Bud's a couple of guys came in with crowbars and started pulling up floorboards. They told her they were from Kelowna and had heard there was a house in Abbotsford where an old man had died leaving vast amounts of money hidden. They had actually found hundreds of dollars tucked in old stoves and behind mirrors etc., and were convinced the motherlode was still lurking somewhere. This was quite believable to me. Money was Bud's lifeblood and he had cash coming in from little loans and deals in all directions. His pockets were always stuffed with it and it would be like him to squirrel it away in hiding spots and forget where he'd put it. One of the most telling details in this lady's story was of finding an old penny wrapped in lined paper with the note saying it was the first penny Bud ever earned, from sweeping off his father's hotel roof. He devoted every minute of his life to pinching that penny and adding to it but what good did it do him in the end?

I don't remember how I first got started fighting. I guess it was my old man's fault. He said, "You'll never be a fighter." He always had other guys he was sparring with and training. Boxing was a popular sport then, every town had a club or two where the young fellows would go to learn the gentlemanly art of self-defence. But when it came to me he said, "No, no, you can't do it." That burned my ass so I did what any kid would do, I set out to prove him wrong. It takes a special person to be a boxer—light and fast. He said I had too much Carmichael in me. He was right, no question. But that didn't make it any easier to take. One of the articles of faith between us was that the Carmichaels were a step behind the Whites, and I had assumed I was with him on the White side of the fence. I felt betrayed. I didn't understand it. I still don't. He could have indulged his own son and given me the tools to defend myself, but he didn't think that way. Boxing to him was an art, and if you couldn't do it right he wanted no part of you. It was his whole approach to life. Whatever you were doing, whether it was boxing or killing a pig or conducting yourself like a gentleman, there was one right way; you learned that and stuck to it with no regard to whether it was to your immediate advantage, and that was that. End of argument. He was gruff about it. I guess my mother was a part of it, she would have been all against getting me involved in "pugilism." I think he also felt that if he gave me the tools to fight, I would only get myself into a lot of trouble.

Well, he wasn't as good a psychologist as he could have been. Being the son of the town's famous fighter makes you a target to start with, and all the more if guys think you're not very good. This guaranteed I had more than my share of schoolyard scraps from the start, and it also gave me something to fight for. I soon found out that I could fight pretty damn effectively, as long as I got in the firstest with the mostest and didn't worry about getting scuffed up a bit. The fact is, most boys don't fight very hard. It's all bluff and bear-cub wrestling. If one kid goes in there with a bit of blood in his eye, he can pretty much clean up. It was a great relief to me to find I wasn't born with some kind of handicap after all, and I didn't pass up many opportunities to prove it. I soon worked my way through my own weight class and found myself up against the bigger boys, but I tackled them the same way I did the little ones and I found it worked just as well. Better, because they soon realized tackling me was a no-win proposition in which they had nothing to win and a lot to lose, like tangling with a

Boxing clubs were all the rage in the 1920s and my father, as former Canadian welterweight champion, was in great demand as a trainer. He refused to train me, thinking it would only get me into trouble, but I found ways of my own. VANCOUVER PUBLIC LIBRARY 18380, HAROLD SMITH PHOTO

rabid chihuahua. They were unlikely to get out of it without a black eye or a torn shirt, no matter what, and they knew I wouldn't stop as long as I was conscious. I guess I hoped if I beat up enough of his protegés, my old man would hear about it and have second thoughts about my promise as a fighter, but no such luck. He only had disdain for street brawlers and had quite a vocabulary of put-downs for that kind of fighting. He had fought hundreds of brawlers during his prizefighting days and knew all the dirty tricks himself.

His lack of approval disappointed me, but it didn't stop me. Being able to take care of myself became one of the things I was known for, and it made life a little easier. I was always the last one picked for a game of scrub baseball, but if there was any rough stuff going down everybody wanted me on their side. It set me on a path that got me into more than my share of trouble in time to come, just as my father had feared. As I got older, I found men were the same as boys, no matter how tough they might talk, ninety-five percent of them will pull in their horns if they see you're actually prepared to mix it up. And of the ones who don't back off, ninety-five percent of them have no idea how to handle a guy who knows what he's doing. It's that last quarter percent you have to watch out for. The damn trouble is, once you get known as a brawler, all you ever seem to run into is other brawlers. My own nose has been broken more times than I can count. I had to have it re-bored one time so I could breathe. This is just the fate my old man hoped to save me from by refusing to teach me how to box scientifically. Talk about unintended consequences.

When my father and Uncle Fred bought the butcher shop in 1919 they also bought a 1919 Model T Ford one-ton truck, with cattle racks on the back. I remember Father decided to spend an extra $100 and buy a self-starter so he wouldn't have to crank it. It was $900 with, and $800 without. There were very few trucks in Abbotsford at that time and he bought it primarily for hauling his own goods, but people were constantly coming to him for hauling of one kind or another. When there was a breakdown at the mill, Sam or Joe Trethewey would call him up to hire the truck for an emergency parts run into Vancouver, at the very least a

A Model T pickup truck similar to the one my father taught me to drive on. This fine specimen was owned by Edgar Boley (standing) who later became my uncle-in-law. THE REACH P4852

two-day trip in those days. Dad would get one of the young helpers he always had around to do the driving.

Father did it as an obligation because he sold meat to the logging camps, but he wasn't too happy, partly because he couldn't get over worrying about what the driver was doing on those nights in Vancouver. There were no trucking services for hire in those days and if he'd only stopped to think about it, he would have realized here was an opportunity to get in on a business that had a lot more future and a lot less competition than the one he was in, but he wasn't thinking that way and it wasn't until the Tretheweys took their business to other truck lines that sprang up that my father started to see what a chance he'd missed. It would be my fate to try to follow up on this missed chance, but by the time I got my turn the opportunity to get in on the ground floor had passed.

The thing was, the old man was never comfortable at the wheel of a motor vehicle. He grew up driving horse teams and when he wanted to stop he would yard back on the steering wheel and push down with his feet and holler, "Whoa, damn you, whoa!" As long as he was driving a Model T he got away with it because it was operated by three floor pedals—one for forward, one for reverse and one for brake, and if he stomped at least two out of the three, the vehicle would buck to a halt. In 1926 he bought a new Chevrolet with a modern stick shift and clutch, brake and gas pedals on the floor. It was the only new car ever in our family—to this day. It was black or dark blue and had a chrome-plated rad and completely enclosed all-metal body with seating for five and looked very modern to our eyes. But coordinating the foot-operated clutch with the lever-operated gearshift was beyond my father and when he resorted to his instinctive stomp-and-holler technique to avoid a slow-moving buggy, he'd hit the clutch and gas and the car would start freewheeling forward with the engine racing. The very first day he had it, he was taking a load of us kids to school. We were late, and he was angry, and getting started in a rush he broke the gearshift handle off. There was an old blacksmith named Bill Schnare setting up a primitive service station across town and Father got him to weld up the gearshift but he'd had it with the Chev and its newfangled controls, and just let it sit in the yard and went back to driving the Model T.

I was twelve then, and had been sitting in father's lap steering cars for years. I was as fascinated by modern machinery as Father was stymied by it and I started fiddling around with the Chev, got it going, drove it around the yard, back and forth. And around and around. Took it out on the road the next day. Went up and down the street shifting gears until I could double clutch without grinding. I'd been going for several days when Beryl told on me. I figured I was in for it, but instead of getting mad, my father said, "Let's see you drive!" That was just what he wanted. When he saw that I had got the hang of it, he ordered me to drive him out to the mill boarding house to pick up a meat order, and from that time forward I was the family's designated driver.

As luck would have it, my father was riding with me one day when we passed Mr. Greenwood, the resident member of the BC Provincial Police. We had just gotten back to the meat market when Greenwood showed up and in a grim voice said, "Si, that kid of yours has got to get a licence, I've seen him driving all over the place." Didn't say how old is he or anything else. That was the tipoff for the old man. Ok, ok. Backroom now. He marched me up to the police station after rehearsing me on my new birthdate: 1912 instead of 1914, and Mr. Greenwood happily issued me a licence. It was many years before I got nerve up to straighten my age out with the Motor Vehicle Branch. My dad was happy because I had solved an embarrassing problem with the Chev and turned what was beginning to look like a costly white elephant into an asset. He still had the Model T truck for meat deliveries and now I could drive that as well and spent a lot of time delivering meat to the mill boarding house and the various logging camps, one of which was just north of where the Matsqui Municipal Hall is now. I was on top of the world. I loved driving and couldn't get enough of it. How were either of us to know the degree to which this turn of events would shape my life?

The 1926 Chevrolet touring car that my father bought then abandoned because he couldn't figure out how to work the newfangled stick shift. This was taken a few years later on an outing with my pal Chip Parberry and his girl. WHITE FAMILY

5

My World Turns Upside Down

Dad always had asthma. He would get attacks of coughing. Things wore down toward 1928. He was sick and coughing all the time. He was losing weight. He wasn't making a very good picture in the shop. He'd get these big coughing attacks that knocked him right down, right flat. I spent more time helping him as he got sicker. It got to where Dad couldn't work at all. He sold what was left of the business back to Fred Carmichael in 1928 and I went to work for Fred.

Far from being the good-natured uncle, Fred turned out to be an unforgiving slave master. "Things are going to be different around here now," he lectured me. He never missed a chance to make the point my father hadn't run things very well and he was the guy to straighten everything out. This was hard for me to take, admiring my father as I did and knowing that when he was healthy he'd been twice the man Fred was, and would be again when he got well. One episode I recall that did not help our relationship occurred the very first day I worked for him. The water tap in the shop had a slight drip and Fred made a big production about it. "Haywire just like everything else around here. Well, that might be your father's way but it's not my way. When I see something that needs fixing, I stop and fix it!" He sent me outside to turn the water off. This I did. After studying the situation I worried that it was not fully off and gave the valve another turn. All hell seemed to erupt inside and I hurried in to see what was wrong. It seems Fred had removed the tap handle and had been looking down the open valve and I had given him a blast of cold water full in the face. When I got there he was trying to hold the water back with both hands, soaked through. I had never seen such an enraged man in my life. I think our relationship never really recovered, although I was to work for him another four years.

The situation with Father worried us but he was always going to get better. Just be alright in a little while. And he might well have if he'd had any kind of medical care worth the name. It's hard for a modern Canadian to understand just how primitive things were as recently as 1929. They had stopped drawing blood but that's about all you could say for them. They had no antibiotics. They had no X-rays. They had no ECG. They had no heart surgery. There was no hospital, all we had was a house up on the hill. Just a regular house. Mother would look up at it and say, "The lights are on. Somebody's in trouble." That was small-town medicine. Women had their babies at home. Everything depended on one overworked guy, Dr. Swift. He was honest and tried his best but he didn't have the drugs they have today, or the knowledge. He worked himself to death in 1927 and was replaced by a new doctor whose name I can't recall. This new man was trying to treat Father with some kind of staff, like an electric wand. Electricity was new then and people thought it had healing properties. This wasn't voodoo, this was mainstream medicine. We laugh now but I wonder how many of our modern treatments are going to seem just as foolish in eighty years' time.

I have read things now that make me realize they understood about cancer and biopsies and a lot more than we ever saw in Abbotsford, but that involved travel to Vancouver and specialists, and who was going to pay? This was the thing. In those days before medicare the average family couldn't afford anything beyond the most basic care, so there was little incentive for small-town doctors to improve their service. I went with Father to see the doctor in his office sometime early in 1929 and he said, "Your bill is pretty big now, Si. You owe me $300. I don't know, Si, maybe you should try some dry air." The doctor well knew that the charges were for a broken arm for me, tonsils and other childhood maladies of us kids, amounts that father could easily have paid a short while earlier. He wasn't a bad doctor, he was a good guy, but he could see Father's finances were shot

Tom Swift, Abbotsford's resident doctor, loved fishing but seldom had time to do it. The lone doctor in a vast area, he eventually worked himself to death. THE REACH P1274

and if he sent him into Vancouver to find out what was really wrong with him, there were just going to be a lot of specialists demanding money and not getting it. So he took the easy way out and recommended Father go live with his relatives in the dry climate of the Okanagan for a spell. Dad had a cousin in Oliver, Bill White.

Plans went right ahead from there on. We still had the 1926 Chev and it was decided that I would leave school early and drive Dad to the Okanagan to visit Uncle Bill (as he was known to me) for the summer. All preparations were made, the car greased and tires blown up, cooking and sleeping equipment stowed, spare clothes and everything my mother could think we might need was loaded and we were off. I remember leaving the bunch that morning, Mother's tears, Dad's fond farewell to the girls, Wesley begging to go and my excitement.

From a distance of eighty years it is hard to imagine the state of road travel then. Blacktop was unknown. Outside of the city a few miles were paved with concrete but gravel was the rule. Sumas Lake had been drained five years earlier by virtue of the soldiers resettlement plan and the route led out on Vye Road to the old substation at Vedder Mountain then straight north across the dry lake bottom to the bridge over Sumas River near the pumping station and on to Chilliwack. It's just a few minutes' drive now on the freeway but at that time it was a long, lonely trip on washboard gravel. The government had persuaded some farmers to grow peas, tobacco, hops and other crops to develop some humus in the unfertile sand of the old lake bottom but there were huge open areas and very few people were living there yet. When the wind got up there were dust storms just like on the Prairies. The returned soldiers weren't terribly impressed with this gift of land and a lot of it ended up going to Mennonite immigrants who created the town of Yarrow near the northeast end of the old lake bed. They were willing to put up with the hard work and long hours of scratch farming needed to build up the soil and eventually turned it into good farmland. I remember those Mennonites. They dressed like Russian peasants and couldn't speak English worth a damn, but they would work for a half what a Canadian would and once they got on a job they'd immediately begin lobbying to bring in more Mennonites. "I like to bring my cousin Helmut. Him strong like ox, work all day, no stop." They took up most of the casual labouring jobs that way—ditching, fencing, picking, milking. The employers loved them but working stiffs like me hated them. That didn't bother them. They stuck together, worked their butts off, supported each other and eventually they took over most of the central valley.

After leaving Hope there was a feeling of adventure as we passed Hills Bar and entered the storied goldfields of the Fraser. We looked for the old landing places at Yale, the head of navigation in the early years, and felt some kinship with the old miners of the 1860s. The CPR had obliterated the first Fraser Canyon wagon road when it was blasting its roadbed from Lytton to Yale some forty-five years earlier and the road had been rebuilt in 1924 with a toll gate at Spuzzum and a new bridge at Alexandra, so the road was only five years old in 1929 when my father and I tackled it in the old Chev. It was narrow, rough and steep; much of it was built on timber trestles around cliffs, later to be blasted into the modern highway we see today.

Travelling from Yale to Lytton the roadbed was often too narrow to pass without slowing down and scraping by and the many steep grades really tested the little Chev. Not many remember the long haul up Nine Mile Creek just north of Boston Bar or the horrible climb up Jackass Mountain. Any story of the Canyon Highway of those years must mention the Charles Hotel at Boston Bar, operated by a very colourful character

The Fraser Canyon section of the old Cariboo Highway was a severe test for the kind of cars we had in 1929. CITY OF VANCOUVER ARCHIVES OUT P544

named Cog Harrington. One old story tells of the Alberta-bound couple who arrived at the hotel so traumatized by what they'd seen of the canyon road they abandoned their car and finished the trip on the train. It would be interesting to look up the history of Boston Bar. It was surely a stop on the old Cariboo Wagon Road, but what was happening there from the time the CPR knocked out the old wagon road 'til the canyon highway was put through some forty years later?

Anyway, in 1929 about all there was to Boston Bar was the old two-storey green hotel and the CNR station and buildings. We pushed on up the Nine Mile Creek, back on the other side and over the hill and made camp on the side of the road beside a small stream a few miles short of Lytton. I have spent many nights there since and as trucking developed many other truckers made a point of stopping there after a hard day's drive from Vancouver. It always brings back memories of that first trip—the sense of adventure at going to a strange part of the country, the excitement of long-haul driving, the enjoyment of my father's company and the vague concern about his condition hanging over us like a dark cloud. We passed Spences Bridge and on down to Princeton, then Keremeos, where we explored an old mine that had shut down not too long before. I could never find that spot again. We got in a bunkhouse there. The Spences Bridge–Merritt road was just rebuilt from an old trail.

From Keremeos we jostled and jerked over to a town on top of a mountain with a big hotel left from the gold rush days, I can't come up with the name. That road was an old stagecoach run. Finally we pulled into Oliver where we stayed with Uncle Bill. He had moved there from Peachland in 1927 and was just getting started with a new meat market. I never quite understood his relationship to my father. It was another one of those silent zones the older men kept to themselves. I heard my father say something one time about double first cousins, two brothers who married two sisters. My father and Bill looked like identical twins. When he visited us in Abbotsford he would put on my father's big white apron and everyone who came in would think it was Father. Once one of Father's regular customers came in while Bill was at the counter and Bill told her an off-colour joke. The old biddy was shocked and so was Father when he heard, but Bill thought it was the greatest laugh ever. They made quite a pair.

Oliver was a new town. The fruit farmers were just getting started and shipping tomatoes, cantaloupes and tobacco while they waited for the fruit trees to grow as the South Okanagan reclamation scheme got underway. There was another cousin, George White, who was an old hand in the fruit-packing plant and got me on as an apprentice box-maker. Box-making was one of the coveted jobs in the packing plant world. You were paid by the piece and a good box-maker could make decent money. George was one of the best. He could make fifteen dollars a day and knock off at noon. He showed me how to do it. You had different templates, or shooks, for the different sizes of box—apple box, cherry box, apricot. You were paid different rates for different boxes. The shook for apple boxes was bigger and had cleats on it. You'd get your end pieces in one pile, your side and bottom pieces in other piles, stick as many tacks as you could fit in your mouth, and go at it. *Bangbangbang*. George could sink his tacks with one stroke. There was a trick to it I never quite mastered, though I got pretty quick and got to where I was making seven or eight dollars a day, damn good money in 1929.

We rented a cabin down the road from Bill's. Dad cooked the meals, looked after the house and made friends with many of the neighbours while I worked. It was a special time. Bill was great company and Dad and I helped him with his meat business when we could. I remember this one time Bill bought six cows to slaughter. As butchers will, we fell to speculating how they would cut out—how much weight in saleable meat they would produce once they were bled, gutted, skinned and quartered. We each wrote our guesses of live weight and finished weight before we started, then checked when we were done. As I've said before, this is quite a tricky calculation and draws upon all the experience a wily old butcher can muster. Well by God, if I didn't guess closest on five of the six cows! Bill was amazed, because you can't be lucky five times out of six, not with a thing like that. It was a sign of just how much I'd learned by hanging around the old man all those years.

Oliver was full of young people working in the orchards and the packing plant and we'd all go down to the lake at night and make a bonfire

During the summer of 1929 Dad and I went up to Oliver to see if the dry climate would help his asthma. The fruit harvest was in full swing and I got a job making boxes at the packing plant.
ROYAL BC MUSEUM, BC ARCHIVES 06876

and sing and swim and flirt. Here was a hell of a lot of young people, fruit pickers and guys with ukuleles, cigar-box banjos with one string—and Jesus Christ, that was living. A lot of people just picked fruit for the kick. It was mean work and low pay, so they didn't go just for the money. It was an adventure, young people testing their wings. I don't know if they still do that or not. Some of the really nicest times I ever remember in my life were down there on the shore of the lake. Just warm nights and a bunch of young people. More good-looking, friendly girls than I'd ever dreamed of and I was crazy about one after another. It was the kind of magical summer you think is going to go on forever, but really only happens a few times in a long life.

Sometime in September Father told me we had to go home, he was no better and he wanted to see Mother before it was too late. When he tried to tell me he was dying I would not accept it.

"But you're getting better," I said. As a matter of fact he was losing a lot of weight. The dry air probably helped his coughing; at least I made myself believe it was. But he knew better.

"I'm not going to make it, we got to go home now," he said. "I don't want to die up here." I couldn't believe what I was hearing. He had never talked about dying before. It was always, "when I get feeling a little better." Another time he said, "I want you to tell your mother how I loved her." I couldn't bear to hear that. I just knew it couldn't happen. I had grown up that summer with him, I learned so much from him. We were pals. A great bond had developed between us.

"Aw Bud, if you were only a little bit older," he said. I didn't know what he meant. I thought I was doing pretty good for a fourteen-year-old, but he knew more than he was saying. He was afraid he couldn't make it home in time.

We went home through the States where the better roads made the trip easier on him. When we got to Abbotsford he went straight to bed. His health worsened steadily until November 10 when he had a horrible coughing attack in the middle of the night and we called the doctor. He came to Dad's bedside, took a look and got out a needle. "We'll have you right in a minute, Si," he said. He slid this big needle into Father's arm and pushed the plunger and Dad jerked and went, "Yarp!" He was dead before the doctor could get the needle out. I was standing there watching. I don't know to this day what was in that needle. People have said it was probably adrenalin. I never put it down to a doctor's mistake, though I might now.

"Quick, have you got any whiskey?" the doctor said. If there was ever a time my mother regretted her hard Presbyterian rule against liquor in the house, this might have been it, but anytime the doctor starts calling for whiskey you can be pretty sure he's out of ideas. I took off at lightning speed to McKinnon's house, where I knew there was plenty of whiskey, but by the time I got back they had pulled the sheet up over him.

God knows what he had. I guess you can die of asthma, but it doesn't come on suddenly like that. It was probably a heart attack at the end, and it may have been heart failure all along. I've often wondered if it was lung cancer. Country doctors didn't always know what to call cancer then. It could have been a number of things, many of them quite curable today. If Father had lived in my time frame he might have lasted to ninety-nine too.

6

On Our Own

They had a funeral. Mother got one of her bible-thumping preachers up there who gave one of these left-handed eulogies about even sinners being welcome into heaven—I never forgave her for that. We buried him in Aberdeen, just the other side of Aldergrove, in one of the graves he'd bought when my grandfather died in 1911. I went over to check a few years ago and there's still one waiting—for me, I guess, but I don't think I'll accept the invitation. If it was possible I'd like to go overboard out here in the chuck and go back to where I belong. I don't believe in this being burned and going into the atmosphere. Go right back into the food chain again where you belong as directly as possible.

Try as I will, I cannot remember Christmas or the New Year's following our father's death. I was the most lost person you ever saw in your life. I could not bring myself to realize that he was gone. It was the end of the world for me. I still believed a year after he died I'd go back into his shop and see him standing there behind the counter, singing out some funny greeting with that big welcoming grin on his face. He was like a big brother to me. My whole life was shaped around him. The other kids weren't as close. I was his right hand. I was... Bud. There is something so incomprehensible about death when it hits you like that, it doesn't make any sense. Nothing in life prepares you for it.

I was lost. I couldn't talk to my mother. It was many years later I told her how Father had entrusted me to tell her how much he'd loved her. That broke her all up. "Why didn't you tell me before?" she said. I said I thought he told her himself, he had lots of opportunity after we got back. But I guess he didn't. I never understood their private life.

We were broke. The whole country was broke. Father died just a month after Black Tuesday of 1929, which marked the beginning of the Great Depression. By some stroke of unlikely good fortune the government took it into its head to bring in a widow's pension just around that time, so Mother had that. I think it amounted to a dollar a day. Her only other money came from a social column she kept up in the town paper, but that was peanuts. With that and what I earned she had somehow to manage to feed five children, the oldest of whom was fifteen. She never complained, that we heard, but I was often aware of her crying to herself in the night.

Beryl worked. I worked. When we got back from the Okanagan we found out Uncle Fred had sold Dad's old meat business to Safeway. Safeway started twenty-five stores in western Canada in 1929 and Abbotsford was among the lucky towns that got a franchise. Fred closed the old man's shop and took over Safeway's meat department. It was a smart move business-wise, because supermarkets were the wave of the future and the days when you could have an independent meat market on every corner were numbered. They talk about Walmarts putting local operators out of business today as if this was something new, but I'm talking here about

By 1929 a Safeway store had come to Abbotsford and my uncle Fred Carmichael moved Dad's old meat business into it. I went along with the business and worked there for four years. THE REACH P13252

1929, and the process was already well underway in the grocery business. Of course these weren't Walmarts, they weren't even supermarkets by today's standards, but they were bigger stores than we'd seen up to that time, and they had multiple departments all under one roof—meat, groceries, produce, bakery goods, some dry goods—which was a change from the previous single-product style of shop. It was the last thing my father would have wanted, given his dislike of big companies, but it didn't bother Fred. He was a born clerk.

As soon as I got back he promptly fired the man he had hired and put me to work. He never let me forget what a big favour he was doing by giving me a job when there were so many others better qualified and made it clear it was only out of concern for my mother that he did it, not because I deserved it. He seemed to feel he had to make up for his generosity by making me do things he wouldn't have asked anybody else. He made me go down an hour before school and kept me until the last minute so I had to run five blocks to make class by nine o'clock. Then I had to come and tend the shop at lunchtime and as soon as school got out I had to come straight down and stay 'til closing time. If I wasn't there right on the dot I had to explain what happened. He left at six but I had to stay for an hour cleaning up. I did all the glass, all the floors, put everything away. Friday I worked late making sausage. There was a sausage special on Friday that generally sold 200 pounds. Gotta pickle the pork. Saturday nights I worked until eleven or twelve.

I was making twelve dollars a week at the best but they kept cutting down, cutting down as the Depression deepened. When I swept up at the end of the day I'd often find a dime or a quarter under the counter, where somebody had dropped it and hadn't bothered to look for it. Sometimes there would be a buck or a buck and a half's worth of change down there. It was a nice little perk and made a difference at home. Anytime there was a few cents left over Mother would run out and buy two rolls of toilet paper. They were seven cents each. That was luxury. We would use only little bits to make it last longer. Long after the Depression was over, I would catch myself still using tiny bits of paper to wipe my ass. What the hell, I would think, the Depression is over, and pull out a longer stretch. But I felt guilty doing it. That was how the Depression left its mark.

I kept my little treasure hunt for dropped coins to myself as long as I could but eventually Fred found out and demanded I share half of what I scavenged with him. But by that time I was finding less money. It kept going down until by 1933, instead of a buck, you were lucky to scrape up ten or fifteen cents. That told you all you needed to know about the state of the economy.

I remember the day the crash happened. A bunch of the local businessmen had a kind of stock-buying club and every morning they would get together in the office of the Safeway store manger, Harry Schafer. They would all be joking and bragging about their big wins and slapping each other on the back. The stock market was booming and it seemed everybody who could borrow a dime was playing the market. One of the members of Harry's club was Mike Shore, the CPR station manager. He had free access to the railway's telegraph and could get early reports on the market, which he would bring over to the meetings each morning, usually with a lot of fanfare and teasing, "You'll wish you hung onto those pork bellies when you see this" kind of thing. This morning his face was like a death mask and he was waving a telegram and saying "She's all over, boys. The whole bloody thing is down the drain." It was weeks before the full story came out and people began to realize what this meant to them personally. My wages went down I think to about nine dollars a week.

Another sign of the times was the influx of dustbowl refugees. Abbotsford was a big, long, dusty street between two hills. In 1932 you could look down the street and all you would see would be these old jalopies with stuff piled all over them. There might be fifteen or twenty of them. This was a constant stream. Started in '31, '32, '33, I guess '34 was the worst. I didn't know then. People just talked about those bums coming from the Prairies and what the dirty bastards were doing. They were blamed for everything from stealing chickens to causing impetigo. Now I know how beat they were. I seen a guy cry one time. His wife was pregnant, he'd lost everything, he'd come to the coast where it was supposed to be better, and nobody would look him in the eye, let alone give him work. "What can I do?" he said. What can you do when you're married to a woman and you can't afford kids but the kids keep coming? There was nowhere to go and nothing to do.

I worked at Safeway through grade twelve. I did pretty well on the exams considering I had no time to study and missed a lot of days. There were two or three always ahead of me in English but I usually beat them in science. Sylvia Harrop was the top student in my year. Her dad was the Imperial Oil agent in town. Camille Trethewey, whose father owned the mill, was another one I was always competing with. One time I remember, the department of education made us write a provincial test, kind of a general-knowledge thing, and I got the highest mark in the Fraser Valley. But in grade twelve there was a course called English 40 that required a lot of reading I had no time for and I failed it by one or two percentage points. I was supposed to go back and rewrite it in the summer but I was working and never did make it up.

I had always assumed I would carry on to university and take medicine and some of my teachers were still pushing me to do it, but with Father's death and the struggle to survive, university had pretty much gone out the window. The district inspector came around and talked to Mother about it. It really didn't take that much money then and he had some scheme in mind for getting what was needed, but with no income and five children living at home Mother didn't want to hear about it. As for myself, I would have dearly loved to pursue the educational dream but I was spending time on the trucks and was ready to drop the whole idea and go work. Sometimes as the years went by I would think of that lost dream of education that once burned so bright in me and try to imagine how my life would have unfolded if a couple things had come up differently, if my father had got the right kind of help and lived a few more years, or if my mother had been a little more far-sighted and pushed the college bit. One is tempted to imagine a great career with a lab coat and test tubes making great discoveries, but of course most people who graduated from medical school in those days went on to hard careers working long hours and didn't even make a very good living. I'm not sure working all night on broken-down people would have been that much better than working all night on broken-down machinery. It's impossible to say how things would have worked out, except my life would have been completely different and I would be writing a completely different book—and not necessarily a more interesting one. Once you've had kids you can't really wish your life was different because if one small thing was changed, then those kids would not exist and you can't wish that, especially when those kids—and their kids—are your main reason for believing your life did serve a purpose in the end.

Apart from Fred, I liked working at Safeway. I stayed there almost four years. I loved going in in the morning and putting on that apron. I had been doing the work for years by that time and I was about as good at it as you can get. A clerk like that is master of his little world. You have a big jump on your customers because you're there every day, you think about nothing else, you know what they're going to ask for before they know themselves. You have even cut out the piece you're going to sell them the day before, knowing just what you have to say to make them take it.

The carriage trade would come in around eleven in the morning. They were where the money was and you'd have your good cuts ready for them, figuring to persuade them to spend a bit more than they planned by playing up the quality: "Now before I cut those chops, I want to show you something I've been saving just for you, Mrs. Trethewey..." And she'd go out of the store having spent twice what she'd intended but thinking

These sausage choppers are from a later time in Abbotsford but they could just as easily be Fred Carmichael and me. I loved going in mornings and putting that white apron on. You got to be master of your own little world and I was happy there—until I got a taste of truck driving. THE REACH P1089

you were the greatest guy in the world. The poor people would come in just before closing time looking for a bargain. We hated them because they took so much time trying to get the most mileage out of the few cents they had left after the old man spent his paycheque at the pub, and they often made you late closing up. But you'd be ready for them too, with a big bunch of hamburger you'd stretched with fat then mixed with blood to redden it up. You'd put it on a few cents below normal and they'd load up on it. You played the whole town like a little ringmaster, knowing people's habits and figuring how to take best advantage of them and get this week's sales total up a couple percentage points over last week's.

The people kept it interesting. Some were godawful cranks who were always bringing back half-eaten cuts saying they were too boney or too fatty or slightly off, even though they bought them on sale for just that reason. We groaned when we saw them come through the door. Others were always smiling and ready with a quip, and we loved to see them come in. Peggy Fishlock was a lively little thing who always had some line ready like, "Do you boys keep dripping?"

"Just for you," I'd shoot back. Dripping, of course, was the term for strained fat, a cheap substitute for lard. Sometimes when we had nothing better to do we would "keep dripping" by melting down the fat trimmings; sometimes we didn't bother.

Peggy Fishlock was one of those people who seemed to make a career out of making people laugh. You could follow her progress through the store by the shrieking and commotion that accompanied her. I sometimes wonder what became of her, if she went to her grave cracking wise and breaking people up. There ought to be a special medal for people like her who make it their business to go around lightening things up. There are not enough of them.

We had another stunt, we'd pretend to be adjusting the fan and accidentally stick a finger in it, only it wouldn't be your real finger, it would be a pork sausage. Meat would fly all over, you'd scream and hold up a bloody hand with one finger bent back—the customers would just about faint. Anything to lighten it up and make a bit of fun. Being behind the counter in a store is like being on stage playing the same role over and over. You'd get all your moves down pat and nobody could catch you out. You got to thinking you were pretty smart. But only as long as you were behind that counter, hiding behind your big white apron. Once you undid the ties and hung it up and went back out on the street, it was like Superman changing back to street clothes, you were back to being a nobody.

Those were lonely times for me. I had few friends and was painfully shy, although I did manage to get in on the odd bit of fun with a few of the guys. We were always after the girls in the next town. During summers Hatzic used to be the hot spot when the berry pickers were there. Hatzic Island was a big, low-lying island in the middle of Hatzic Lake across the Fraser River from Abbotsford and it was solid berries. I don't think there's a single berry grown on Hatzic Island today but then there were dozens and dozens of farms. Millions of berries. I don't believe there was anything else. I don't know why Hatzic should have been that hot for berries but it was and by July there would be thousands of pickers, mostly teenage girls from Vancouver, but a smattering from every part of the country. Each farm had quarters packed with these young lovelies looking for a bit of excitement and we were eager to give it to them—if only we could figure out how. Mostly it just amounted to tearing up and down the road in old

The high point of the year for young Abbotsford guys was the berry harvest, when hundreds of young maidens would pour in from all parts of the country to pick the crop—and, if we were lucky, consent to the odd jalopy ride. THE REACH P12742

Model Ts—it would be worth a laugh to see it now. I was always able to borrow a jalopy and get a couple of guys willing to go over and terrorize these pickers. It seems a lifetime ago. It's just begun to seem that way the last little while. For a long time when people said, oh that was a long time ago, I never was able to feel it, to me it was just yesterday, but lately it's begun to seem like it was a long, long time ago. At a certain point age hits you, a long time after it has been obvious to everyone else.

> *Lo! some we loved, the loveliest and best*
> *That Time and Fate of all their Vintage prest,*
> *Have drunk their Cup a Round or two before,*
> *And one by one crept silently to Rest.*

Part 2

TRUCKING MILK

7

Milk Politics

As my hours shrunk down at Safeway I began looking for something else to fill in and I started to get a bit of work driving. People had seen me driving the old man's truck all around town and knew I could do it, and I spent my spare time hanging around Bill Schnare's garage where the town's few cars and trucks were coming and going. I can see now I was ripe for a career in trucking. I was nuts about trucks. There was this fellow named Jimmy Ross who was driving a truck into Vancouver and I would spend hours shining his truck all up, polishing the engine, and sometimes he'd flip me a dollar. It wasn't like today when people look down on truck drivers. When I think of those very first truckers who were in on the start of the rural truck lines, they were larger than life. Guys like Herb Wareing, Bob Groat, Eric Fox, Jimmy Vanderspek.

Herb Wareing was hauling freight to my dad in 1926, '27, '28. It always made our day when Herb showed up. Towards the end, I remember particularly the old man was sick and failing and had no money to pay for his COD shipments, but Herb would give him the goods anyway and trust him to come up with the money later. Of course then the old man would bust his gut to get it back to him. Herb always brought news from down the line and had a story to tell. I remember one day he said he was going through Green Timbers in Surrey and two truck wheels came rolling along past him. "Now, that's damn funny," he thought. "Whose wheels could those be?" Just then the rear end starts bouncing and scraping gravel and

The early freight lines in the valley had to depend on slow, clumsy old trucks that were a real challenge to operate. The men who drove them were a special breed. VANCOUVER PUBLIC LIBRARY 611

he realizes they're his own wheels that came loose and took off down the hill past him. Another time just as he was approaching the bridge across the Nicomekl River, a car came flying along and crowded him into the railing. It was a metal railing and it broke loose and came through the windshield and ripped his guts out. So here's Herb, walking down the road holding his intestines in his arms. We don't see him for a few months, but one day, there he is, back on the haul, staggering in with quarters of beef. I liked Herb and I liked the trucking business. I looked up to truckers. They were the only people who saw the country in those days. They were respected. People sought them out, wanted their opinions. They were men of special experience.

There's a lot I don't know about the earliest days of rural BC truck lines. Long before I got involved Chapman Motor Transport was hauling milk from the Pacific Milk condensery at Delair outside Abbotsford. They got a contract as soon as Pacific Milk started up in 1920, hauling that case milk into Vancouver using old hard-wheeled trucks. I think it was Federals mostly. Slow, low-geared, hard-riding old brutes, my god, a guy'd be damn near dead by the time you pounded all the way in over those potholes with those hard tires. The thing you have to understand is that this was still the dark ages in terms of truck technology. The modern truck with powerful engines, pneumatic tires, good suspension and good brakes capable of keeping up to traffic on the highway had not been built yet. Just the same there were some pretty fair trucks on the road by 1930. All makes you never hear of anymore—Federal, Fageol, Reo, Gotfredson, Day-Elder, Hayes-Anderson, Leyland, Thornycroft, Diamond T, Packard. There were so many makes it was rare to pass two the same or even know of two exactly the same at first. A lot were built in machine shops on special order, and there was no standard rating.

Those early trucks were made out of pretty standard parts and any well-equipped machine shop could bang one together. Just brace up two pieces of eight-inch channel for a frame, Timken axle, Eaton transmission, Hercules motor. Any blacksmith could make the springs and driveshaft out of stock, and the radiator just hung in a cast-iron frame. The radiator frame and the cab were about the only places they had any chance to use their imagination, and a lot of them just bolted an open seat across the frame.

Actually they were good trucks. You could throw a hell of a load on one of those old crocs. Just make sure you're on good ground. A touch of downhill helped too. Too much and they'd be scraping you up though. The goddamn brakes on those things weren't meant to be taken seriously.

You did have the emergency brake. Great big squeeze-handle emergency brake on the side of the cab. That was the true measure of the truck, the emergency brake. The bigger the truck, the bigger the handle. Some came right up to your chin. I remember when the Detroit trucks first came out, they had a little handbrake inside with the button on top and the guys'd be peering in the cab and saying what kind of chickenshit truck is this? Those old emergency brakes would work alright, but one good stop was about all they had in them, and you damn well saved it for an emergency.

Some had the gearshift on your left too, but mostly it was where it is now, on the right. All the selector part of the gearbox was open—big sliding cast bars always full of mud and sticks. It'd take a twenty-pound pull to shift. Took just about the full reach of your arm. With sixty-five horsepower to work with, you did a lot of reaching.

But those old Hercs, they had damn near a six-inch stroke and you could lug them down to where you could count the revs like cows going over the mountain. You'd wait 'til one wasn't going to make it, then pull 'er out and stomp the gas down for an eternity to get the revs up to where you could get into the next gear.

The only way they could even those old four-bangers out was to hang huge cast-iron flywheels on them, absolute top they could stand would be maybe two thousand revs. Any more than that the flywheel would come right through the floorboards at you. More than one man was killed that way—going down a hill with too big a load, the flywheel exploded.

The steering wheels were great big wooden things about three feet across and flat. Had to be, because they didn't have much reduction and you were hanging on for all you were worth all day long. That was the main battle, to keep the front wheels going where you wanted to go and not where they wanted. You studied the road a long ways ahead. Under normal conditions you had the edge in brute force, but a rock or a rut could tie you in a knot. The spokes would blur just like an airplane propeller. Jesus, if any appendage was in the way, you could write it off for about three months. Next time you see an oldtimer driving, take a look how he holds his thumbs. Outside the wheel. It'll take three generations to wipe out that habit. Once the flying saucers cleared out of your head, chances are you had a broken front wheel to deal with too—wooden spokes couldn't stand the least amount of sideways pressure. They were a real headache, wooden spoke wheels. In dry weather the spokes would get loose in the felloe and clatter. If you didn't fix them quick the wheel would collapse like an old wooden chair. They had special little half-round wedges and you'd see guys stopped on the side of the road banging them in.

Driving truck in the very early days was one of the real bull work jobs, besides all the problems of being something new. Those first truckers, the men who brought trucking in, were a special breed. Half Edison and half Sasquatch.

The Fraser Valley Milk Producers' Association (FVMPA) had a big cheese plant in Sardis, and they had trucks hauling in and out of that, too. Chapman became Rapid Transit, which was BC Electric. BC Electric was hauling freight, Great Northern was hauling freight and of course CPR was hauling freight. They had a truck division even then, running heavy old A-model Internationals with the bulldog nose. Those first trucks were limited because they were so slow, clumsy and expensive. Yet you could see it was the coming thing and was going to open up the country in a way railroads never could. Then Detroit began mass-producing trucks and they became easier to get. That's where I come in at, when trucks started to become more common and small operators started to get involved.

It wasn't long before somebody put out the word they were looking for a kid to do a bit of driving and my name came up. This was how I got working for Milton Nelles, an Abbotsford farmer who ran a creamery in town and was trying to get a bit of a freight business going as well. He had a half-ton delivery van and I got on that. I worked my guts out and did a good job, so Nelles got more business and increased my hours until I was pretty much full time. So I quit Safeway and went driving for Nelles. There wasn't much money in it but I was through school and tired of Fred and ready for something different.

Now, Nelles was one of these restless types who never did particularly well at any one thing, like running his farm, but was always branching out

Hauling milk in the bad old days before the arrival of the modern trucks with pneumatic tires. Your arms would be stretched double by the time you loaded all those cans on the roof, and my kidneys ache just thinking about pounding over the potholes on those hard-rubber tires. ROYAL BC MUSEUM, BC ARCHIVES C-02426

into some new venture. I'm not sure but I think he'd been a teacher back east. However he came by it, he figured he was smarter than the average bear. There was a whiff of scandal around him always. He'd got hold of the Old York Place after Howard Boley lost it and people accused him of burning down his barn and burning all his cattle—for the insurance. He also had a reputation for coveting his neighbours' wives. He thought he was a little too good to be true.

One of the ventures he got involved in early on was hauling milk. He had this little creamery and had a need to transport milk in from the farms that supplied him and then to haul the butter and other products to the market in Vancouver. So Nelles got a three-ton truck and started hauling in and out of his own plant but it wasn't long before some farmers started hiring him to haul bulk milk to dairies in Vancouver. Now, Nelles's daughter Florence had married a young fellow named Les McGarva whose family was from the wrong side of the tracks if anybody could be said to be from the wrong side of the tracks in a little pissant town like Abbotsford was in those days, and Nelles put Les to work driving this milk truck. Les already had a reputation as a drinker and hellraiser, which most people figured was just what you'd expect from a McGarva, but Les wasn't stupid. He saw an opportunity to really go after the business of trucking milk in a big way, much more aggressively than Nelles was doing it, so he went out and bought a truck of his own and devoted it exclusively to hauling milk from dairy farms around Abbotsford in to dairies in Vancouver.

Apart from being surprised such a no-count had managed to talk some unlucky dealer into trusting him with an expensive truck, the wise heads around town didn't put much faith in this new enterprise because in those days milk was not hauled by truck, it was hauled by rail. The BC Electric ran a special string of cars out through the valley to Chilliwack every morning as part of its interurban service. All the dairy farmers for miles around loaded their daily output of full milk cans onto wagons and trundled them down to the nearest interurban stop, where they wrestled them onto the milk train and sent them off to Fraser Valley Milk Producers' Association (FVMPA) dairies in Vancouver.

BC Electric ran a good service and nobody at that time saw any reason to do anything different. This young upstart McGarva was just trying to complicate things by offering a service there was no need for and he was going to go broke in short order, is how the local businessmen probably viewed it. The wise heads at the BC Electric and the FVMPA had freight costs tied into the milk payments and they would see to it that McGarva didn't get a chance to cut into their business. But Les saw that things were changing in the milk business and trucks had something to offer that farmers would have a hard time resisting. It was a hell of a lot of trouble to harness up every morning and wrestle those 125-pound cans onto the wagon and haul them down to the railroad. For some of the outlying farms it was several hours round trip and it was a damn nuisance. With a truck, you could go right to the farmer's barn and save him all this trouble.

This still wouldn't have got anywhere if you couldn't break in on the FVMPA monopoly, but here again, Les saw something that others had missed. The FVMPA had originally been brought in by the farmers themselves to protect them from being exploited by privately owned dairies in Vancouver. The private dairies had been notorious for playing games with milk prices, often paying below cost of production or refusing

Up until the early 1930s most Fraser Valley dairy farmers got their milk into Vancouver via the BC Electric milk train, which ran on the company's interurban line. VANCOUVER PUBLIC LIBRARY 20586

An old hard-tired truck making a delivery to a milk train platform. Farmers started using trucks to move milk cans short distances in the 1920s but a rig like this was too slow and hard-riding to compete on the long haul into Vancouver. It wasn't until Detroit started coming out with 3-ton trucks that milk hauling by road took off. THE REACH P8118

to buy at all during the spring flush when cows started producing milk all at the same time. So the farmers organized themselves and bought the dairies out and replaced them with their own cooperatively run super-dairy that guaranteed every farmer could sell all his milk at a fair price— the FVMPA. The FVMPA developed a large retail market for its fluid milk and also a large industrial market that could absorb the surplus milk for making cheese, cottage cheese, ice cream, sour cream, condensed milk, powdered milk and so on. The FVMPA was the saviour of the farmers, it was a great success and everybody assumed it would go on controlling the milk business in the Fraser Valley forever. The FVMPA was God, and the BC Electric was its designated hauler. This was the situation in 1930 when Les McGarva entered the scene.

What Les had figured out that only a few others had was that the private dairies were starting up again. Hoy, who originally coined the Dairyland name, sold out to the FVMPA then started up again. Louie Powell started National Dairy and Crystal Dairy started up. Nelson was back. It was haywire for the FVMPA. You'd have thought they would have made the dairies sign covenants preventing that, but maybe they had run out or something. Hoy started up under his son's name, Doug Hoy. So the independent dairies jumped in and they started going to a guy with a nice herd and giving him about twice as much as he's getting from the association, from the FVMPA. Old Acton Kilby over in Harrison Mills and old Basil Gardom (whose son Garde later became Lieutenant-Governor) got together and created an Independent Milk Producers' Association and they built up quite a big dairy called Jersey Farms that supposedly sold a higher quality of milk. They put on a nice show and developed their own retail market in Vancouver with their own door-to-door service. There was another group called Guernsey Breeders. Old Jeremiah Crowley started Avalon Dairy on Wales Street in Vancouver in 1906 and epitomized the independent approach. He was a story in himself. He was the last guy in BC delivering milk in a derby hat and a horse wagon. That was the ancient trademark of the horse-and-buggy milkman, the derby hat. And his family kept right at it, right up to the present time, running what is now the oldest dairy in BC. The other independent dairies went after the big commercial contracts like the General Hospital and the big restaurants, bidding down all the high-volume stuff. The General Hospital contract bounced back and forth like a football for years. The FVMPA was really hurting from losing all this business to independent dairies it was supposed to have replaced, but it stumbled along paying even lower prices to its remaining shippers. It was in really tough shape during the thirties. And the poor old farmer, all he can do when he's faced with low prices is ship more milk until it reaches the point he's getting less than it's costing him to ship, then he's dumping it and feeding it to the pigs.

How Les got hooked up with these independent dairies in Vancouver I don't exactly know, he was just an illiterate hayseed with big ideas and no money, but it was one of his traits that he was able to make important contacts, mostly by getting drunk with the right people. He made deals with several of these private dairies, most notably the National Dairy, which was owned by a Greek named Louie Powell. So now he had all the pieces of the puzzle. He'd go right in the farmer's yard and haul his milk out for half the price the BC Electric charged. On top of that he was often able to get the farmer a better price for the milk at one of his independent dairies. The FVMPA was like any other union, the good and the bad were all treated equal. This was great for the poor farmers with scrub herds and inadequate feed who produced milk with low butterfat content, but the good farmers who took the trouble to build up their herds, manage their feed and control their milk flow were penalized because they got no more for their trouble.

The private dairies weren't bound by any such one-for-all, all-for-one pricing and could pay more to the farmer who took the trouble to produce clean, rich milk and regulate it so it wasn't coming on stream at the same time as everybody else's. A lot of the guys who had the best milk were already chafing under the yoke of the FVMPA and were goddamn glad to have a choice. These became McGarva's first customers. But many farmers felt a strong solidarity with the FVMPA and could vividly remember the bad old days before it stabilized the dairy industry. Milk politics was serious stuff in the Fraser Valley and there was a lot of hard feeling between the association farmers and the independents. The FVMPA made it difficult for members to leave and successfully lobbied for legislative protection. The independents challenged the legislation in court and kept gradually gaining until by 1939 they controlled eighty percent of the fluid milk

During the 1930s the FVMPA monopoly was challenged by a new generation of independent dairies, of which Jersey Farms was one of the more successful. ROYAL BC MUSEUM, BC ARCHIVES F-03038

market. I can see now we were on the wrong side of the battle, pulling every dirty trick to tear down something that existed for the farmers' own protection, but it gives me comfort to know there was a handful of true believers who stayed true to the co-operative ideal, and they pulled the FVMPA through the Depression and later built it back into a dominant force, a position it maintained for another fifty years. Its Dairyland brand is still dominant in the Lower Mainland, though the FVMPA itself merged with a national co-op then sold out to the Montreal cheese giant Saputo in 2001. I guess it outlived its time, but the FVMPA had a great run and has to be counted as one of the big successes of the co-op movement, I would think.

By 1932 Les needed an extra truck during the spring flush when all the farms were producing at top volume so Nelles said, "I've got a good young driver for you." I hadn't met Les before but I knew his sister—I went to school with his younger sister, Rita. I thought she was pretty hot stuff. The business was picking up all the time, so Les bought a second truck and put me on it.

I remember well some of the trucks I drove on the 150-mile-a-day route between Abbotsford and Vancouver, mostly loaded both ways: a 1929 Chev one-ton; a 1931 Ford I drove briefly until I tried to escape the oil fumes by plugging the filler pipe with a rag and promptly blew all the oil out the crankcase and had to be towed home; a 1932 Chev, a real nice truck; a 1934 Chev, wonder of wonders with five speeds. We mostly used the trucks up in a year, though some of them made it to 70,000 miles, which would be around two years. In 1936 Dodge came out with a truck approaching modern standards: a three-ton model with a six-cylinder "T120" motor that was around for many years. The first truck I drove for Les was the old '31 Ford. Then he got the two Chevs and I got one. They still had cable brakes on them. I think the '36 Dodge was the first model with hydraulic brakes. Oh, beautiful. The earlier ones had puny little four-cylinder motors and we couldn't put a full load on them.

The money was better than it had been at Safeway. It still wasn't great, but it was the only money to be had. People were standing around out of work. The guys who'd been hauling the milk on the railroad were losing their house and their cars. Us kids were hauling their milk. We were driving right in the yard.

We'd start picking up the milk around six or seven in the morning, seven days a week. Our area was mainly around Sumas Prairie. You'd hit fifteen, maybe twenty farms and then you'd beat it into Abbotsford. We'd have anywhere from 100 cans to 140, depending on the time of year.

Having 140 cans is a big load, even for a six-cylinder truck. Those old ten-gallon milk cans weighed 125 pounds full so that's over eight tons you'd have to lift by hand onto the truck deck, then lift again to make a second deck of cans—we'd double-deck them inside the box of the truck. Then we would move them all a second time when we put the trucks together to switch cans, we'd rearrange the loads because we delivered to several different dairies spread out across Vancouver, from East Hastings to the University of BC, and you didn't want both trucks chasing each other from dairy to dairy. You'd want all the National Dairy cans on one truck and all the Crystal Dairy cans on the other truck. But the way we picked them up, the other truck had some of your cans and you had some of his. So before we set out for the city the loads had to be pulled right apart. Everything had to be rearranged so that when you pulled into a dairy those cans that were going were ready to come out the door, there was nothing loaded in front of them.

We'd be coming in to Abbotsford at about ten o'clock and pull into Slim Webb's service station parking lot and line the two trucks up side by side. They were built with side doors halfway along the box on both sides and we generally loaded and unloaded them through the side. You never loaded through the rear as a rule, because that meant dropping the tailgate and swinging cans across the tailgate, which was a lot of extra work. When you were moving a hundred 125-pound cans, you didn't want to move them six inches further than you had to. Generally you'd have all the cans in the back half of the load just one row high with a cleat on the floor holding them back, then an aisle in the middle running across the truck deck two cans wide, and the front half you'd pile two cans high. In spring flush you'd have to go two cans high in the back half as well, but that would be a pretty heavy load. Sometimes you'd even hang the tailgate on its chains so it was like a three-foot extension of the truck deck, and you'd

When Detroit began mass-producing 3-ton trucks at the end of the 1920s, heavy trucks became affordable and small operators began adapting them to all sorts of new uses. In Abbotsford Irving Parberry and Lester McGarva began hauling farmers' milk into Vancouver in competition with the milk train. WHITE FAMILY

load that with a double row. You'd didn't want to because it increased the risk of a spill, but sometimes you had no choice.

You didn't carry the cans any further than you had to, you rolled them. Not on their sides, the lids were just held in by friction so you were always worrying about a lid popping out and losing a bunch of the farmer's milk. So you'd cock them up on the bottom rim and give them a spin and they'd roll along pretty good tilted at an angle. You know, the lid just slips around in your hand. You just flip them. You get pretty good at it, it's just like they had wheels. They're slopping out, some of them, the ones with poor lids. Some of the farmers tied the lids on but mostly they just stuck in there. When they were tied you couldn't spin them because the rope would catch on your hand and you had to carry them, so you hated that. Of course it was always the same slack-ass farmers who had poor milk, got it out late and made you lift it out of their tanks who had the bent-up old cans that needed to be tied. You'd be so goddamn mad you'd be ready to kill that farmer, although you couldn't say anything because to McGarva every customer was precious.

Picking up full cans from a farmer's milk stand. Note how the driver is tilting the can so it rolls along on the bottom rim. You never lifted full 125 pound cans any more than you had to, but even at that you might have hand-bombed 20 tons of milk before the day was done. VANCOUVER PUBLIC LIBRARY 81072A

Losing milk cans was the biggest thing. A lot of farmers owned their own cans. At that time they were worth five or six bucks. A farmer would have to have two sets, so if he was shipping ten cans, he had a lot of money tied up in cans. People were always claiming we beat them on their cans. We did, too. If we saw a loose can, we grabbed it. We tried to keep extra cans around in case we picked up a new shipper and they needed cans to put their milk in. Some dairies supplied the cans but some didn't. We were always stealing cans one way or another. There was a lot of fucking around.

In the course of a morning you'd have gotten to know those cans pretty good. You'd have pulled them out of the farmer's cooling tank, rolled them out, lifted them up to the deck of the truck, which was about a four-foot lift, then you had to jump up on the truck and roll them back and set them up on the double deck. You'd have personally lifted twenty tons I guess, by the time it was all said and done. Just right out of this world by today's standards. Only a young guy would do it. You had to be young to be able to do it and you had to be young to be dumb enough to put up with it. But then again, what else *were* you going to do? I could have hung on at Safeway but I didn't like Safeway, or at least I stopped liking it once I got a taste of truck driving. I went back to put in a few hours on occasion but I couldn't bear to be cooped up there after tasting the freedom of the road.

8

The City

Being in constant contact with the city gave you a special status in the small-town world. We knew all the stories about town, all the bad things in town, all the hot spots in town—it really got you over with the girls as far as that goes. There'd often be guys wanting a ride to town so you had a bit of help if you needed it to load some freight or something. You didn't want them handling the milk cans, they just got in your way there. One day I counted twenty-two people that got on and off the truck. They'd ride from here to there. One of the local RCMP officers, Doug Wesley, used to take the trip just to see what was going on. He was a good guy and we became friends. The RCMP were a cut above the provincials, they were pretty good all-round men in those days. We were on a schedule so it was almost like a bus line. You'd maybe get two-bits or four-bits if they were going into town. It sounds like small change now, but it all helped. Of course we had a special rate for pretty girls. There were quite a few of them trying to slip away to see the city and get a little excitement into their lives. It took me awhile to figure out what the drill was.

One day when Les was still driving I was following him all the way in, over the bridge, down Kingsway, then I lost him. I got to the first stop where we were supposed to meet to switch some cans and he wasn't there. I didn't know what the hell had happened. I didn't know where he'd got to. I was worried maybe he'd had a breakdown and I somehow missed seeing him on the side of the road, though I didn't see how that could be. The guys at the dairy swore he hadn't come by. Then after about half an hour he rolls in and I asked him what the hell happened, how he got behind me. He grinned and said, "Well I had Mrs. Laird along and she couldn't wait so we hadda make an unscheduled stop." The bugger, he'd pulled off into the brush at Cedar Cottage to screw this woman he'd been giving a ride to, the wife of one of our shippers. The brush was so heavy then, right around Kingsway and Victoria, you could pull off the road one block and be all on your own.

Les didn't miss many tricks. I remember there was this other old gal, she had a chicken ranch just outside of Abbotsford, a pretty hard case, but one time Les got her in the truck and went a round with her.

"What was that like?" I asked.

"Barnacles right to the knees," he says.

There were no paved roads in the valley to speak of except the Pacific Highway and we'd come rolling down that. There wasn't a single traffic light on it then. There were hardly even any traffic signs. You could go all the way down and not meet a car 'til you reached New Westminster, on a Sunday morning. Green Timbers was just a raw logging slash. When I first went over that route with my father in the twenties it was the most beautiful stand of first-growth Douglas fir you ever saw, tall and straight—even then

Green Timbers was the name given to a magnificent stand of old-growth Douglas fir along the Pacific Highway just outside Whalley. Even as early as the 1920s people understood such stands were disappearing and fought to save it but it was clear-cut around 1930. To appease public outrage the government made a show of replanting the area. HARBOUR PUBLISHING

people realized this was something special, the last of the old-growth forest that had originally covered all the Lower Mainland, and they would come from all over to see it. Now here's something you might not know: there was quite a campaign to preserve that forest, and it developed into a real tug-of-war between the nature lovers and the loggers as long ago as that, in the 1920s. The very same arguments, the very same words even, as you hear today between the Greenpeacers and the forest industry. That's how long that battle has been going on in BC.

Around 1930 they clear-cut the whole thing and then promptly made a big show of reforesting it. It must have been the first large-scale reforestation project in the province, but it was more of a hoax than anything, an attempt to make up for the fact they'd allowed this popular attraction to be destroyed. Eventually they made it into a park—an urban forest I believe they call it, but it's only a small fragment of the forest that was there originally. You hear the forestry guys saying there's nothing wrong with second growth, it's a pretty good forest, all greened up with trunks three feet through and lots of underbrush, and they're right—people who never saw old growth can look at it and not know the difference. But oh boy, if they'd ever seen what real old-growth Douglas fir looks like, they'd know this is just a baby forest. Those great old trees, they made you just kind of gasp. There was something about them that just filled you with awe, like a great cathedral, no matter how many times you saw them. You can get a small taste of it at Cathedral Grove on the road to Port Alberni, but keep in mind that is a very small patch and not by any means the best of the timber there was.

When I first started driving, the slash at Green Timbers came up all to brambles. The goddamnedest blackberries you ever saw, and people from Westminster would come out and pick them—kids, families—pick wild berries and sell them alongside the road. Nickel a pound or something. Jesus they were lovely. There were stands all along. They just got pennies, but people would do anything to earn a few cents in the dirty thirties. Then the reforestation started in. They set up a relief camp and put unemployed men to work clearing away the brush and planting trees and that was the end of the berries. God they were nice berries.

When you got down to the Fraser River, you'd have cross on the old railway bridge at New Westminster. It was the only bridge from the valley and it'd just take one line of trucks at a time. You'd drive up a ramp to get on, then straddle the tracks. You had to wait 'til the light went green, then you'd jump out and throw the hand signal and that threw the light at the other end. Sometimes you'd see a truck a way ahead of you and take a chance you could catch up and bluff your way through instead of waiting another turn. But you had to be careful. There were times somebody had to back up half a mile or so, you really didn't want to be the one doing that.

When the Pattullo Bridge opened up in 1937 we couldn't understand what the hell it was for. What would they ever do with all those lanes? It seemed like the height of extravagance. It's hard to get used to all this talk now about how it has long outlived its usefulness and needs to be replaced with something bigger. This is another sign you've been around too long, when bridges you remember being built start getting torn down because they're too old.

The old bridge would deliver you right into Westminster and you'd plough down through Columbia Street and grind your way up Twelfth Street hill. Columbia was a miserable street. Slow. People wandering around. On Friday they had a farmers' market—all the farmers came in, jammed the place up and wandered around. They had streetcars going right up the middle—there were overhead steel posts. I just don't recall now when they took them out. They may have been gone in the thirties. The interurban pulled into the foot of Columbia Street, so you had all that traffic to weave your way through.

Westminster was another enclave all its own and the cops were murder. They'd go out and pull in every truck going through their town. They'd have some phony pretext for stopping you, then they would poke around 'til they found something wrong. They'd have roadblocks you couldn't get around. That was the price of using Westminster streets. The only traffic fine I ever paid was in Westminster. One day at the foot of Columbia Street, here's a double line around the corner. We'd been swinging wide to get around this tight corner twice a day for years and nobody knew about what this new double line meant. There'd always been a single centre line, which it was legal to cross, but a new bylaw had been passed that if the line was double you couldn't cross it on any excuse. They must have passed the

It was always a challenge to get a truck through Westminster without being ticketed by one of its predatory traffic cops. NEW WESTMINSTER MUSEUM AND ARCHIVES IHP7791

law and painted the line on the same day. You couldn't really get a loaded truck around that corner without getting a wheel over centre, and here's a cop sitting there pinching every goddamn truck.

You could meet any one of the cops in the bootlegging joints down there. There were two or three bootlegging joints that were right in with the establishment. One, I forget the name of it, there was a murder done in there while we there and it was closed up.

Creep up the hill and over to Kingsway and into Vancouver. Kingsway was the only way. Later on they opened up Grandview Highway but it was slower except on holidays when the traffic was bad on Kingsway and you could beat it down Grandview and save some time. The Burnaby section of Kingsway was all dogwood. You never saw so much goddamn dogwood in your life. Dogwood and hazelnuts, all wild. You'd just see the occasional house out in the brush. Then they started catering to tourists and you'd see the odd place changing over to an auto court. Mostly because of Prohibition, they were set up to catch Americans who came up to drink beer. There was big traffic in that. They were largely places of ill repute at the start. Liquor and women. Later it got to be a place where Vancouver businessmen would duck out at lunchtime to fool around with their secretaries. During the Depression it was all too common for bosses to take advantage. It was come across or starve. People today have no idea how bad it was. That's another benefit of unions that people never think about.

Kingsway was narrow. Just two lanes, one each way with a high crown and big humps where the side streets crossed, especially towards the shoulder. You had to watch you didn't get too far to the right and hit one of these intersection humps too hard or they would throw your cans over. One time I was coming back empty and in addition to the usual 120 cans I had the tailgate stacked with 450 cases of empty milk bottles. Milton Nelles's latest get-rich scheme was to cater to the people in Vancouver who had had an objection to pasteurized milk and he was starting to ship in raw milk in bottles from his creamery in Abbotsford. Handling all these bottles was a goddamned nuisance but he was the boss's father-in-law so we had to do it. We hauled his full bottles in, dropped them off at a dairy in Vancouver and took a load of empties back. There was no place to put these cases of bottles inside the truck so I lowered the tailgate so it acted like a four-foot extension of the truck held up by a chain on each side and I stacked these cases as high as they'd go. Well, out near Edmonds a car braked in front of me to make a turn and to avoid a hard stop I swung over out and hit one of these intersection humps so hard one of the chains holding the tailgate snapped. The cases of empty milk bottles dropped onto the road and every bottle broke into a million pieces. To make things worse, it was Labour Day and holiday traffic was piled up for miles. I didn't know what to do—get the hell out of there before the cops came or stop and pick up the cases or what. Well, there were two or three houses there and be damned if people didn't come running out with brooms and pitch in to give me a hand. I was never so glad to see anybody in my life. We swept up the goddamned glass lickety-split, I recovered what cases I could out of the mess, then I headed home and never heard another word about it. Nelles, he squawked, but since we were just hauling his stuff as a favour there wasn't much he could do.

When we reached town we just crawled along. Those first trucks had no goddamn brakes worth the name. It was all mechanical—rods and levers. Hydraulic brakes hadn't come in yet and air was years in the future. When they're just newly set up mechanical brakes worked to a degree. But they wouldn't stay adjusted. The linkage would loosen off, the rods would bend and after a couple of days you couldn't depend on them. Half the time they didn't work worth a damn. You'd brake by gearing down as much as possible. You'd never be able to get away with it today.

We didn't do much maintenance on McGarva's trucks. Occasionally we'd get out a grease gun while we were waiting to pick up cans from the dairy, but that was about it as far as upkeep went. On a regular haul like that there were no terrible great strains. You knew when things were going. Occasionally a universal joint or something. Brakes—you'd get them re-lined at Begg Motors or at the dealer's. Get tuned up. Just what had to be done. Mostly you were trying to get by 'til the truck was traded in. Les's philosophy worked very nicely—he didn't even own the goddamn trucks. The bank did. To him they were just a machine to make money. He didn't take any pride in shining them up or putting on extra lights or any of that bullshit. If it wouldn't answer why, if it wouldn't make money, there was no goddamn use in doing it. He wouldn't even paint his name on it. But he kept them pretty new. If a truck started to give him trouble he'd trade it in. His trucks were always new and sharp-looking. Our competition Parberry's trucks were always old and ratty-looking. But his were bigger. He ran bigger and slower trucks and Les ran smaller and faster trucks that were always overloaded. But Parberry was the same. They wouldn't paint

The Parberrys moved into general freight hauling later—and even put their name on their trucks.
WHITE FAMILY

their name on them or anything else. Later when his son Chip took over, he took the name Sumas Trucking and painted that on some of his rigs, but his old man never bothered that I recall.

There were these bloody horrible fogs. Nobody thinks of that now. Now if it's foggy it only means you can't go sixty clicks. But at that time you couldn't go five. It was a mixture of real fog and smoke from all the beehive burners at the sawmills—there were dozens of mills around Vancouver—as well as a good measure of coal smoke from houses. It was yellow with smoke. I guess it was smog, really. All the traffic came in on Kingsway, and somewhere before Fraser Street you'd start running into low spots where it would collect. Bloody huge fog banks. You'd follow the streetcar tracks right downtown and you'd develop a kind of sense of where you should turn. You could feel your way along the track ruts with your front tires. Any time it was foggy it was always a big worry how to get off Kingsway over onto Fraser without nailing somebody head on. Your horn wasn't any use because nobody would know where it was coming from.

Oldtimers get all sentimental about the old Vancouver streetcars, but they were a menace to traffic. No truck drivers were shedding tears when they disappeared. CITY OF VANCOUVER ARCHIVES 1184-3225

We'd have to hire kids to go in front of us, to lead us through the fog in some of the worst spots. I'm not fooling. Lead us with flashlights and hollering. You couldn't see anything. Up and down Fraser there were these kids with flashlights, they would go out and lead you around for a quarter. You'd snuffle along in low gear with them jogging along in front of you. And sometimes they'd lead you up on the sidewalk or off the road and laugh and laugh and run away. Those fogs have disappeared now, but they were just yellow mud. I ran into a streetcar once and there was absolutely nothing that I saw until I hit it. Oh boy, was there ever a lot of shouting and screaming over that. I just got out of there as fast as I could, glad for once the fog made it easy to disappear.

But what I really remember about those days is not the trucks and the driving so much as the people—the life down on Carrall and around Water Street out along Powell. That's what sticks in my mind. You got to know all sorts of people through there—drivers and shippers, longshoremen and storekeepers, well-known characters working and hanging around down there. We all knew each other, somewhat anyway. It was a smaller city; you could keep it all in your mind.

We had several little calls before we got to Turner's Dairy, then they took forty, fifty cans. Ok, all Turner's cans were in the back. You've delivered to the various little dairies like Avalon out of the side doorway. Then you just slammed Turner's thirty, forty cans out quick. It's done goddamn fast. There's no fooling. You wait your turn to get in, you slam in there, you set those cans off on a roller track. Turner's had a proper loading dock right at the same height as the truck deck and it was equipped with a roller track. Turner's were good people. Sometimes both trucks would stop there if we had to split their fifty cans to balance our loads, but it worked because they were so slick and the wait was so short. National Dairy, the haywire Greek outfit, 1132 Hastings at Glen, was quite a different matter. We had to back up to a little door and lower each can down to the ground and some cocky little Greek rolled them away one at a time, by hand. This was our biggest drop and they'd take up to sixty cans this way. Then everything for the rest of the trip would be geared to when we could get the cans back from National. They had to be weighed, graded, emptied, then washed. The whole issue would come down to who was washing the cans. If it was little Shorty and

Once we reached Vancouver, the first order of business was to make a circuit of all the dairies to deliver our cans. Some, like Turner's Dairy, were a treat to deal with and others, like National Dairy, could be a nightmare. VANCOUVER PUBLIC LIBRARY 81129

you were getting along fine with him, everything would be fine. If it was some sulky relative of Louie Powell the cans wouldn't be ready until four and you'd have to cool your heels for several hours.

You'd bugger off if you had anything to do. If you were getting along with them it'd be all ok. If you're not, it's just shit all the time. I would go storming in and tell Louie we couldn't make it with that bastard… he would tell them to straighten up sometimes. The Greeks were all that way. Dog-eat-dog kind of thing. But this was our biggest dairy and Les didn't want any screw-ups with them, so we'd have to put up with whatever they dished out. Les had a special relationship with Louie Powell, which was aided by the fact Louie was a hard drinker. He downed a quart of whiskey a day. I couldn't believe anybody could even afford to do that. A quart of whiskey was a day's wages for me. Louie loved this contention and stuff, he was really into milk politics. And he made Les. Parberry couldn't haul into his place. Les was willing to sacrifice all his shippers to the mercy of Louie Powell, and for Louie's part Les could do no wrong. This was a case where Les could see and Parberry couldn't. If you threw your shippers on the mercy of Louie Powell who was supplying all the Greek cafés in town, you had what passed for loyalty from Louie Powell. But there was a price to pay. He had to kiss Louie Powell's ass, find him lambs for Easter and cater to every cranky Greek whim. One time Powell was out in the valley with his friends from the White Lunch and he says to me, "Tell that guy of yours I want to see him." I tell Les and he says, "Fuck that lousy Greek! I'm not kissing his ass anymore. I kissed it 'til it's red now." And he made himself unavailable. Louie never forgot it, but they continued to work together. Once Parberry saw what an advantage it was to have a dairy that would more or less do what you wanted, he got in with Crystal Dairy, and that became their dairy.

I played ball with Louie. You could always work out some sort of a deal with him if you had a spill and needed to hide the fact you'd lost a bunch of milk. We were always being approached by some of these small farmers to see if we couldn't get a buyer for their milk, so they could get a little better deal than the FVMPA. At this time a hell of a lot of small farmers shipping milk were near destitute. Farmers stuck without an outlet a lot of times had to give it away for as low as four-bits or a dollar a can—a ten-gallon can. Well, we'd bring them to town and go see Louie Powell about taking some extra milk from a new shipper. You'd go down and have a drink somewhere and Louie'd say, "Well alright, bring it in." Of course he wouldn't pay the regular rate. He didn't expect to do favours for nothing. But these farmers with no place to sell their christly milk, at least you could get them some money. All we got out of that was the haulage charges for bringing it in—and a new shipper that hadn't gone to the opposition.

After seeing Louie it was over to Jersey Farms Dairy to drop off a load and then out to the cheese plant way out at UBC or over to Clark's Dairy. After that I'd beat it down to Gibson's Dairy, that I carefully saved for the last. It'd usually be around lunchtime. Gibson's Dairy was right beside the Rex Theatre on Hastings by Carrall.

A lot of drivers coming into Vancouver had arranged to meet down at the Rainier. You'd go out the back door of Gibson's Dairy and across the alley and head into the Rainier Hotel at 309 Carrall. We all had charge accounts there. That's where we'd have some drinks and arrange who was going to make what pickups around the city. When Les was in town I'd

meet him there and he'd tell us, "You've got this or that pickup to make."
Every couple of weeks he'd go around to the dairies and collect his money
and then we'd get paid. Les'd deal our wages across the table at the Rainier
and we'd settle up our bar bills there. Ernie Clark, who owned the Rainier,
would be around to collect and he'd buy us all a round.

Ernie Clark advertised himself as "The Loggers' Friend." He had some

In the 1930s, Hastings was Vancouver's most vibrant street. It throbbed with life at all hours. CITY
OF VANCOUVER ARCHIVES STR N195.2

money sunk in different logging camps and he staked quite a few loggers over the winter shutdown. We had our own table down there and it was pretty lively. There'd be any number of people hanging around asking if you knew of any jobs out in the valley. There'd usually be some message for me at the Rainier about some little deal I was setting up on the side, without going through Les.

We'd eat at the Baltimore Café across the street or at the White Lunch off the alley on Columbia. At the White Lunch you'd grab a meal for two bits, and if you had to pay thirty-five cents it was pretty luxurious. Or we'd go over to King's. That'd been a famous saloon in its time, a well-known part of the scene. It wasn't a saloon anymore but they had a tremendous buffet laid out—steaks and pork chops and everything, so much a piece.

One thing about Vancouver then was you didn't have to go miles and miles to pick up every load. Everything was concentrated downtown. Our regular pickups were mainly along three blocks of Water Street and out along Powell and from the docks. Arrow Transfer on Granville Island was the other hot spot. Uptown, around Granville, there was nothing much of interest to us going on, although later we got a deal going with the cheese plant out at the University of BC, way out on Point Grey. The other drivers cursed it, though I enjoyed the feeling of being on the university campus and talking to the people there about what they were doing. I always had that fascination and I guess I always felt a little in awe, thinking, "This could have been me."

We spent a lot of time down on Water Street picking up bulk orders from Kelly-Douglas, Malkin's, Swift's and the produce wholesalers for stores in Abbotsford. Three blocks of Water Street was by then a wholesalers' district, so plugged with trucks you could hardly get through at times. You'd hand in the orders to Kelly-Douglas as soon as you got in but there wasn't much point in waiting around because they would never be ready much before five o'clock. So we'd go making freight pickups.

We had to hang around Vancouver 'til at least six anyway for the last dispatches. So it was just some hours in the afternoon you had to yourself. Otherwise it was driving from morning to night. We'd head back and get into Abbotsford about eight, maybe nine, at night. We'd have to drop off the freight and switch around our loads again so we'd have the right milk cans to take out next morning. It might be ten o'clock before you got home. So it was a pretty full day.

Some guys couldn't stand driving in the city, it wore them to a frazzle. But I liked it. It was different from today. The pace was set by the streetcars. In a way it was harder to drive deliveries than now. You had to work your way down alleys and around streetcars. You might get by one, but there'd always be another one ahead and a string of cars and trucks plugged up behind. Slow-moving traffic.

Today traffic is so goddamn adept. People are expert drivers today by comparison. But at the time most people really didn't know how to drive. They drove around the city like they were out on some country road. They hardly obeyed any rules. The few traffic lights in town were only on the main downtown corners. You just buffaloed your way across most corners, tried to get a jump on the other guy or you'd just sit there. With a truck you did a lot of bluffing. You just crawled ahead and hoped that the other guy would stop. You wouldn't dare do that today. The trouble was taxi drivers who wouldn't give anybody the right-of-way. It was like driving in Mexico today, where the guy that makes the biggest noise gets the right-of-way.

I'd often have a delivery down on Pier D, the CPR wharf. That was something, a hell of a big place even by today's standards. It was always busy. You really had to know your way around that pier. Freight for all the places along the coast had their separate locations. Jordan River, Tofino and so forth. You had to know the freight sheds perfect or you'd never come out right. We dropped off quite a few loads over at the Union Steamships dock too, beef and spuds and cattle feed to ship up the coast.

We picked up a lot of stuff from the Mac & Mac warehouse on Columbia and Cordova. It was one of Vancouver's big companies in those days, a hardware and dry goods supply house for the whole province. Its right name was McLennan, McFeely and Prior I think, but nobody called it that. It was always "Mac & Mac." They had a store boat that went up the coast, the *Sunrise*, and later they started opening branches in different towns, including Abbotsford. Then they just disappeared, like all the old Vancouver businesses. After Mac & Mac you'd head out along Powell. That was all part of our beat—but it's kind of hard for me to capture what it was like then. It wasn't a main artery like Hastings or Kingsway. It was

The Vancouver waterfront was a hive of activity in those years and you had to know your way around or you could get really fouled up. A lot of guys hated to take a truck down there but I enjoyed the atmosphere. VANCOUVER PUBLIC LIBRARY 24249

more of a feeder street to the waterfront. It wasn't a truck route like you understand today; it was just an easy street to drive. I once picked up a logging donkey up in Harrison and hauled it in to Arrow Transfer. It was overwidth and overheight and it was miles overweight, so I hauled it down Powell.

Buckerfield's was down there. They were a big distributor of feed for all through the valley. The bigger dairy farmers started using mixed feed instead of growing their own oats. So we hauled a lot of that from the Buckerfield's plant downtown to their warehouse in Abbotsford or direct to the farm. A hundred, a hundred and twenty sacks of mixed feed—five, six tons a load. You had to stack your empties somehow and get these 120 sacks of grain on. They were bastards, Buckerfield's. You'd back under a chute in this shed alongside the elevators. Guys working on the second floor would fire these feed sacks down, and you'd have to throw them into the back of the truck as fast as you could. There was this Alex who was a foreman down there, a miserable old bastard, and he'd dump them down the chute just as fast as he could pick them off the skid and make you pull them out of the way just as fast at your end, except you had a lot further to go than he did, you had to heave them all the way across the truck. You had to try and stay ahead or they'd start to pile up and it would be a hell of a mess. We'd have that hundred sacks stacked away in a few minutes. I had lots of guys say to me, "You can't put up with this!" and holler at them—"You dirty bastards!" But it didn't make any difference. Alex was a limpy guy, one of the most miserable men I ever met. Real hard-time foreman, the kind that was glad there was a depression on so he could treat people like dogs and get away with it. The way they drove men was incredible. If they tried to grab a smoke between trucks, old Alex, he'd be ranting and raving, "Come on, get that truck loaded and out of there. We gotta get trucks in here." I hated him. How I got back at him, he was always in such a sweat he wouldn't count and when he finished, I'd yell, "Five more sacks. Five more sacks. You're short five sacks." By god, we'd get five more. Then I'd have five sacks to sell. I'd drop them off in the garage across the street before I delivered the load and make a nice piece of change at Alex's expense. He wasn't as smart as he was mean.

Trucking was really just getting organized. At first there wasn't any real control of loads. Anybody hauled damn near anything. It was a pretty freebooting situation. Later, when they got these load-licensing regulations and started to make them stick, there was no more room for this jumping around from one thing to another.

For some years we had a lot of hauls taking equipment from logging outfits around Chehalis and Vedder down to the docks to be shipped upcoast somewhere. I always liked a load to the docks, it was always an adventure. We were still experimenting with hauling different loads. You'd have to puzzle out how to get something on or off best. It seemed like we were always trying something for the first time. Now with forklifts and cranes the load's on or off—zip, nothing to it. But then it was all huffing and heaving and back power.

Those longshoremen, they were something. They were union and there weren't many unions around worth the name. Yes, there was a Teamsters union, but they didn't amount to a hill of beans. Us guys were always a little awed by longshoremen who earned real wages and worked eight hours a day. We didn't know what an eight-hour day was.

I enjoyed driving. But the way we worked could be condemned out of hand today. Do our regular hauling, hustle around and beat it back out to pick up an extra load. It often meant that you worked a stretch of thirty hours straight just to get through your work.

There were big labour battles that were going on all around; going on in that part of Vancouver all through these years. I wasn't myself involved. Yet we were right there in the middle of it: the longshoremen's strike and the post office occupation. But we were working and this other stuff was just part of the scene. You'd wish them well and maybe drop some money in the tin can from time to time, but that was about it.

We had different angles of using the truck to make a little money on our own. Once you had covered what loads McGarva had lined up you could try and rake in something on the side for yourself. One thing about it, you'd never know what came next; always something different. We were always looking for a load somewhere without Les finding out, though he usually did. "That Frank, he's got more rackets goin' than Al Capony," he'd say. He didn't object too loudly as long as he thought he was getting the best ones for himself.

There were eight or ten of us drivers working all the angles we could, between all the different trucking outfits. You'd maybe bring in a load for one of the farmers. Or there'd be somebody moving or wanting something hauled cheap—we'd be right in there. What we made on the side might seem like small change today, but it all added up. Mostly all those deals came through our table at the Rainier. It seems strange now, but that's the way trucking was done then.

One deal I had going on the side was with this blacksmith. There were still quite a few blacksmiths around the valley and they used a good deal of coke. Every so often I'd haul coke from the gasworks down by the viaduct out to Harry Williams's blacksmith shop in Aldergrove. You'd duck into the gasworks and throw ten sacks of coke on the tailgate and take it along on the way home. He'd always be in the market for steel in old axles or main springs or something. He turned out wedges and sledges and loading tongs and logging shackles. They were handmade and always sort of expensive. You'd trade this coke or steel for what you could get from him, then take it down to peddle to one of the hardware stores in town that handled that stuff. Whatever you made was velvet for you.

Or another angle was the deal I had with the Mainland Foundry, a black-looking place with flames inside. I was fascinated by it. They would always take some of this special foundry sand that they used as their floor. Just this side of Abbotsford was this bunch of sand that was just right as foundry sand. So if there was nothing else I could run out there and shovel on a load for them.

Other times I'd stop and pick up a load of lumber at the lumberyard on the corner of Wall and Powell. Maybe I'd have a beer with the shipper in the Princeton Hotel, which was around the corner. I'd haul loads of this third-grade lumber out to Abbotsford. It sold for peanuts and people would use it for barns or sheds or whatever.

For awhile we bootlegged spuds. There were a lot of Chinese market gardeners leasing five, ten acres of land on Lulu Island and around Sumas Prairie growing early potatoes. When the Potato Marketing Board was brought in, these Chinese more or less all got frozen out. That was part

Vancouver's gasworks with its trademark tower was long a city landmark. I picked up many a load of coke there for my backhaul to the Fraser Valley. CITY OF VANCOUVER ARCHIVES 99-4979

of the idea behind forming the board. So the only way the Chinese had of selling their spuds was to bootleg them. That must have been before the Pattullo Bridge opened because I remember sneaking across the old railway bridge at night with loads of black market spuds.

Two drivers would go together. With a three-ton truck we could make up to forty bucks a load on these bootleg spuds, which was really big money. My partner would take the milk cans in and pick up the freight and I'd duck into one of these Chinese farms, load up with spuds and run them in at night. We'd sneak the load out of the valley and into town and pull into some café or house off a back alley in Chinatown with this load of illegal spuds. It got to be pretty organized after awhile. You'd pull in and twenty men would appear from nowhere and unload you in no time flat.

That produce was bought by the Chinese wholesaler; a lot of them bankrolled these Chinese farmers, put up the money for renting the land and getting seed and what not. There'd be labour contractors who'd arrange to bring out groups of Chinese women and men to do seasonal work on those Chinese farms. The spuds we brought in would go to the grocery stores or the Chinese peddlers would take them out of town on their black Model T trucks. There must have been quite some mechanics stuck away in Chinatown to keep those old trucks going because they just ran and ran. I didn't understand half the ins and outs of the politicking behind that Potato Marketing Board and the black market trade. Our part of the deal was over when we delivered the spuds.

Our time off, if we didn't spend it in the Rainier, we'd go to the Savoy Hotel or the Columbia or the Stanley. There were a lot of beer parlours clustered downtown. Each one had its own atmosphere and clientele. Everyone you knew was down there. Now I wonder how we had the time to get around to all those deliveries and pickups and still have time to sit in beer parlours—Dutch and old man Parberry, Les Groat and his brother Bob, myself, Les McGarva and a bunch more. They're all gone now. Usually you had a fair amount of booze in you before you left for home.

Around Carrall Street it was sort of the tenderloin district, but different than people can imagine today. There'd always be people around talking. People stopped and talked to each other a hell of a lot more. Sure enough there were alcoholics around. But it was a friendly place, a place where loggers came to spend their stakes after working for two or three months in camp. They came down to Vancouver—which was Carrall Street, "Smokeytown." Even if they were on their way home to Strawberry Hill or somewhere they'd spend a bit of time down at The West or the Rainier on the way.

Some talk about how rough it was, but it was kids' play compared to what you see down on the east side now, and not only there but in Surrey, Abbotsford and all around the Lower Mainland. About the worst you could say was that there were people there who wanted a little excitement and there were others that wanted to get their money. There was drugs, but you heard about it more than saw it. There was prostitution of course, it was an accepted part of the scene. You could get anything and see anything. There used to be a woman there who performed with a donkey. These stiff-necked old farmers from the valley that wouldn't let their daughters wear lipstick, when we brought them into town, that's the first thing they'd want to see. They'd claim to have urgent business when they were hitting you up for the ride but before you crossed the Fraser they'd be starting to hint around about the seedy stuff and where to find it. It's a wonder some of those old rubes ever made it home alive, but the fact is, it wasn't really that dangerous on the skid road then, not by today's standards anyway. If you went down Cordova Street roaring drunk and flashing money I suppose there'd be a good chance you'd get rolled. But with normal care you never had to worry about your safety down there then.

I used to spend so much time down around Carrall and along the waterfront. And yet it's hard for me to come up with a description of what it was really like and how things have changed. It used to be just a lively place where the action was. Today it's sleazy, worse than sleazy. In the last twenty-five years those places have deteriorated so much that even the no-goods don't hang out there anymore. Loggers don't come into town much now. They've got a house in Port Hardy or somewhere. There's no friendliness in any of these places now, even when they take your money.

Coming from a small town to drive truck around the city, well, that was a *living* as far as I was concerned. Hauling into Vancouver, that was real life, I thought. Hell, what does a young fellow want anyway? Just to keep roving and rustling things up. I hauled into Vancouver nine years

The Rainier Hotel on Carrall Street, a legendary hangout for bingeing loggers, was our home away from home at the Vancouver end of the milk run. Carrall was the heart of the tenderloin district where you could get anything and see anything. CITY OF VANCOUVER ARCHIVES 99-3304

steady, 'til '41. Then later off and on to help Les McGarva. I drove half a million miles on that job. To the moon and back. I liked it. But we were pretty hard-driven too. In truth you were driving or picking up all the time and what spare time you had was spent downtown. Of course, after I got married it didn't work out anymore. My wife got me off that job pretty quick.

9

The Fast Lane

So that was the Great Depression for me. I wasn't out of work a single day that I didn't want to be. And I haven't had so much fun since. Sure, there was a lot of suffering and a lot of people out of work, but the majority still had work of some kind and if you had something special to offer or got in on a coming thing like trucking, well there were opportunities to be had, even in the worst of the Depression.

I moved out of my mother's house and boarded at McGarva's soon after I went driving for Les. There was just no way I could make it with Mother, a young guy out discovering the world of real people, then coming back to that confined world of hers where you couldn't be seen with the wrong sort of people and a bit of beer on a man's breath was a major scandal. I kept giving her money but less and less as time went on. Beryl by this time was helping out in a big way. She first went to work for Mrs. Greenwood, the wife of Dad's old policeman friend, working as a housekeeper in the police station where they lived. During those years she had several other jobs, the chief one as cashier at the local movie house. All her wages came home to our mother. Mother was just too busy with her five children to even think of working elsewhere, although she still kept up her social column in the local newspaper.

Sometime about 1933 or '34 Beryl took a job in a small dress shop in town. A while later Beryl told me that the owner wanted to quit and offered to sell the shop to her for $300 down and the stock to be paid for as sold. I was working steady but $300 was still a pretty big chunk of dough for a guy earning $60 a month and I struggled to find it in time for the offer. Finally I got the money and after some negotiation the sale went through. Beryl must have been all of seventeen or eighteen years old, but by God if she didn't dive into that fashion business and make a go of it. She was a born merchant and a real go-getter. Despite the hard times people were doing less sewing at home and wearing more factory-made clothes, so it was the right thing at the right time. The twenties had revolutionized the way women dressed and blown away the old Queen Victoria look with all the ruffles and layers and yards of cloth down to the ground. Women had legs all of a sudden. When we first started to see pictures and movies of modern-looking women with legs and arms people like my mother denounced it as the end of civilization, but within a few years every backward little cowtown in North America had fashion stores selling clothing like that, and my mother and sisters were right in there with them. Not baring quite as much as the flappers, but generally wearing much more practical clothing that revealed they had a body shape more or less like other primates. That's about all I'm going to say about ladies' fashions in this book. As far as I'm concerned, once they got rid of the old sugar-plum look in the twenties they got up to most of the same tricks they have now, except for wearing tight pants and all the things they do to make breasts jump out instead of being pressed flat. If it sounds like I'm complaining about that, I'm not.

A lot of the new store-bought clothes that were becoming popular in the 1930s needed dry cleaning and there was no cleaner in Abbotsford so Beryl went to work and set up an account with Kingsway Cleaners in Vancouver. I was driving by there twice a day so she got me to run the goods back and forth. This turned out to be a great traffic-builder and gave her business a real leg up on the competition. Beryl operated this shop for many years and kept Mother and my sister Gladys busy helping out. They set Mother up with a millinery department and she had her own little business selling hats, which were still a big thing then. Beryl bought a house and car and more or less laughed at the Depression.

One day Beryl told me that a guy I knew named George Anderson had asked her to marry him. I didn't like George and I just couldn't see that he was good enough for her so I condemned the proposal and she backed away from it. But bright and talented as she was, Beryl was one of these women who had no luck when it came to men, and later married a guy that made me wish I'd pushed the George Anderson match with all my might.

I did what I could to help my sisters and my little brother, Wesley. When Hazel graduated she wanted to go to nursing school, and I found money for that. Gladdy got off to a bit of a false start with some hotshot in uniform who gave her the slip, but later got married to Herb Stokes, a fellow who took her up to 100 Mile House where he worked his whole life as bookkeeper at the big sawmill there. He was a drinker but he managed to hold things together and together they raised a fine couple of kids before she fell victim to cancer at an early age. Wesley was five years younger than me and just coming into his teens when I left home. He hadn't been as affected by Father's death as I was because he was only ten and hadn't had the chance to pal around with him like I had, but I worried about him growing up in that henhouse of Mother's with all her church stuff and I tried to get him out and show him the other side of things as much as I could. I had him in the truck every chance I got, switching places and letting him steer just like Dad did with me. I took him into Vancouver so he could meet the men I worked with and I got him involved in the work just like my father did with me. He loved it. We had always treated each other as partners. Our father's influence was strong. We had the example of his relationship with his father and brothers as I can see it now.

I soon realized I didn't have much to worry about as far as Wesley went. He was very bright and did well in school. He had something a bit special that caught people's eye. Mike Shore, the CPR station master, took a real shine to him and put him to work around the station doing odd jobs. One of his tasks was checking the numbers on boxcars that came through. You know, each car has a great big long number on it and that's how it's tracked. Each station master was supposed to watch these numbers and check them against some kind of checklist but I guess it was one of those things they didn't take very seriously or Shore wouldn't have trusted it to a young kid. Well by god if Wesley didn't put his sharp little brain to work on it and start turning up all kinds of anomalies, wrong car on wrong

I worried about my brother, Wesley, after I left home, but he gave me little cause. He got good marks in school, got a job at the CPR station and learned to be an expert telegrapher. We were six years apart in age but could not have been closer. WHITE FAMILY

track, right car going to wrong destination and all this. No doubt this helped the station master earn brownie points with the CPR higher-ups and made him all the more tickled with Wesley.

Of course the big deal in the station those days was the telegraph office, that was the nerve centre of the town and it was the preserve of the telegraph operators, who were considered a cut above the ordinary guy, like computer wizards today. One of Wesley's duties was delivering telegrams and he took a big interest in telegraphy so Shore gave him a spare key to practise with and it wasn't long before he taught himself Morse code. He had a chum named George Grant and Wesley taught him Morse code as well. They set up light bulbs on poles on top of their houses so they could send messages back and forth across town and before long both of them were top-notch telegraphers. I was proud of the smart little guy and tried to be a bit of a father to him.

It was hard for me to spend much time around home once I started driving truck just because it went seven days a week and lasted all hours of the day and night. It also put me into such a different frame of mind it was hard to relate to my mother's way of life. Living at McGarva's put me into a world completely different from anything I'd known or imagined. There was drinking going on at all hours of the day. There was partying, good times, everything was loose and easygoing. There'd be somebody on the sofa groaning and getting over the day before. There'd be any amount of people there. My old high school heartthrob Rita was around quite a bit and I went out with her every chance I got. She became a regular in the truck and we became great pals and had a lot of fun, but she wouldn't give me a tumble, try as I would, and in the end we drifted apart.

Les's house was a hub. People were coming and going all the time, usually with a bottle under their arm, wanting to visit and talk. No religion, no hang-ups, everything was on the line. There would be dogs barking, kids yelling, people laughing all hours of the day and night. People sought Les out for his opinion on things—what do you think about this, what do you think about that? Crops, milk prices, everything. On a Sunday, talking and talking. Farmers are always talking about what they're going to do, how things are going to go, what contracts they're going to get, the price of hay and all this. Les was crude and uneducated but people who knew

When I went driving milk trucks, I started boarding at the home of my boss, Les McGarva and his wife, Florence. The contrast with my mother's quiet, religious home couldn't have been greater—Les's place was a real party palace and the booze was flowing steady. THE REACH P819

him knew he had insight into things and liked to hear what he had to say. Over a bottle of course. He was always very easy to approach and he'd give it to you straight—as long as he wasn't trying to work you over for some scheme of his own. But even when he was working you over, he was never phony. Any pretense just threw him.

His wife, Florence, was pretty steady and managed to keep things more or less together. She'd be up early every morning and have my breakfast cooked. She wasn't lazy. But it was difficult with that wide-open way of living. Most of the time she never knew where Les was or what he was up to. They had some terrible fights, not surprising given his non-stop drinking and womanizing. And there was tragedy. Her father, my old boss Milton Nelles, was a regular visitor. One day he came over in his car, had a coffee, then put on his coat and left. There was some commotion out in the yard and a few minutes later he comes back in carrying Les and Florence's little one-year-old in his outstretched hands. The child was dead. It had crawled out into the driveway and he'd backed over it. Everybody just stood there speechless, with him holding this lifeless little body. I can see it now, plain as day. But that was life at McGarva's, wide open, full throttle all the time and you never knew what was going to happen next, except you knew something damn well was. It was so different from what I'd been used to. I couldn't get enough of it. I thought, wow, how long has this been going on?

I can see now I was looking for somebody to replace my father and Les was the first guy I ran into who really took an interest in me and at the same time was somebody I could look up to. He was seven years older than me. He wasn't the kind of guy the people I grew up among thought much of, but I guess he was what today they might call charismatic. He wasn't flashy at all, certainly not in his way of dressing, though he kept himself clean and neat. He was medium in stature, and had a soft-spoken, hesitant manner that didn't draw much attention when he was sober. When he was drunk it was a different story. Then he could be the most obnoxious sonuvabitch you'd ever seen. Loud, bragging—he turned a lot of people off. Unless you were drinking with him—then you thought he was a hell of a fine fellow. But even when he was sounding like a damn fool, one part of him was calculating. He had the ability to think when he was drunk, in fact that was when he did his best thinking and made his best deals. He could manipulate a situation and not be seen to be doing it until months later you'd realize he knew exactly what he was doing the whole time.

He was anything but sophisticated—he only had a grade four education and could barely sign his name but you'd see him sitting at his table in the beer parlour with a stub of pencil figuring and figuring on the back of an envelope or something, it looked like he was working out the theory of relativity, and guys would say, "There's that sonuvabitch with that pencil again, let's get out of here!" But if you took a closer look he'd be going two plus two and maybe multiplying by four or something. It was the most basic kind of figuring, but he seemed to draw no end of meaning from it. That was all the bookkeeping he had. At certain low times of the year—these figures don't work now—the truck was only earning $12 on a trip to town, gross. He had to pay gas and payments amounting to $30-$40 a month. In the bigger part of the year it was earning more than that. I was working thirty days a month, he paid me $60 and gas was $100 a month. So even in the low season each truck was earning $160–$170 a month profit. The miracle of Les was despite all his drinking and wild behaviour, he kept the money straight. The bills were always paid and every time he spent a dollar he made two back.

Drinking was what that scene was all about. Everybody drank. Les would wake up in the morning and down a couple beers before breakfast. He was no good until he'd had a few drinks, he could barely talk. But after a few drinks the lights would start to come on and he'd start laughing and planning and rallying everybody else for whatever he had on that day. And he'd keep right on drinking, all day and into the night. Every day like that. I'd had a beer or two at Haddrell's hotel but until I started with Les I really hadn't any experience drinking. I soon found I liked it. I'd been awkward socially all my life but sitting around McGarva's kitchen table licking up the beer or over at his table in the pub, I suddenly found I was one of the gang. I learned how to be with men. Drinking solved a big problem for me.

Les started out driving his own truck and that kept a bit of a lid on his drinking but as things built up he found he was better off paying someone else to do the driving while he looked after the business of getting new shippers and keeping things straight with the dairies. After that he would go down to the beer parlour in Abbotsford, which was called the Atangard, and stay there all day. He had a special table there that was his table and the bartenders kept it for him. When they sold the hotel they said this is McGarva's table. He spends fifteen dollars a day here, that is what this table earns. Fifteen dollars a day was a big deal. And over in the opposite corner was another table reserved for Les's arch-enemy and competitor, Irv Parberry. They both ran their competing milk hauling outfits out of the Atangard Hotel and different times of the day there'd be opposing teams of drivers and shippers and camp followers partying it up and yelling back and forth at each other. Generally they kept it pretty friendly on the surface and Les and Irv would make a big show of slapping each other on the back and sitting down for drinks, "How's it going? Made your first million yet? Ha hah ha." Then as soon as they were out of earshot it would be, "That goddamn lying, thieving sonuvabitch, I'm going to have his nuts for a hood ornament..."

Les was a good deal younger than Parberry but he'd got into the milk

The Atangard Hotel on downtown Abbotsford's busiest corner was the unofficial office of both Lester McGarva's and Irv Parberry's trucking operations. They had reserved tables in opposite corners of the beer parlour and would spend most of the day there doing deals and scheming about how to put each other out of business. THE REACH P12427

business first and got the jump on him, so our drivers always figured we were the real thing and Parberry's bunch were the phonies, the claim jumpers. Irv Parberry was one of the valley's colourful characters, a big barrel-chested man probably in his sixties who had a good spread in south Sumas, right up against the border. He had made quite a good thing out of smuggling booze through his back fence during Prohibition and had done a stretch in jail for it. He was a bit of a throwback to the kind of larger-than-life types from the pioneer times and had quite a large brood of sons and daughters, including one I had a pretty good thing going with for awhile.

They had a special way of talking, those oldtimers. It was a type. I think the last of them were up here in Pender Harbour. Free-spending, funny talking, drawling, deliberately mispronouncing words all the time. Always trying to find some weird way to pronounce a word. The whole play is to appear drunk and dumb and be grandstanding all the time, hiding the fact they were very clever, very capable people. These were the characters they developed. There were some early homesteaders in Surrey by the name of Klein, and they moved up to Pender Harbour where some of the descendants carry the tradition on to this day. They knew my father, the Kleins, and the older brothers, John and Charlie, used to call me Si when they met me on the Howe Sound ferry. They had that same gee-whiz, I'm-just-a-dumb-yokel manner that reminded me of Parberry. That fellow down in Oregon almost created a Parberry type in that book, *Sometimes a Great Notion.* Almost. He had to have met one.

Of all those oldtimers, Tom Elliott was my favourite. He was one of the best shippers in that part of the valley. He shipped ten cans, all of it good. Only a few shipped fifteen and that would be in the flush. And the funny part of that is, Tom wasn't really a farmer. He'd only got into dairying late in life, after he'd lost his hotel in Astoria. I guess he was in his sixties or more when I first knew him. He was a compact man always nattily dressed and wearing a big Stetson. He wasn't noisy but he had presence. I loved to hear him talk.

Farmer, bootlegger, trucker, ex-con—Irving Parberry was one of the real characters around the Abbotsford area in the 1930s. There was a grand battle between him and Lester McGarva for the Abbotsford milk hauling business. WHITE FAMILY

He grew up in Ontario. Laura Secord was his great-aunt or some such thing. He went down to the States and just about got his whiskers trimmed. He was boarding on this farm and while the man was out working, the woman was entertaining the neighbour. The guy caught them and killed them. And Tom saw him do it. So he ran away and hid in the attic but the guy saw him and came after him. Tom was cowering down trying to look invisible and listening to this guy coming up the stairs—*thump thump thump*—he was scared to Jesus and the guy came up and grabbed him but instead of killing him he said, "Now you just run along and as long as you mind your own business and don't say anything about what you saw here, you won't get hurt." Just to be good and sure, Tom lit out for the West Coast and landed up living on a Chinook Indian reservation near Astoria, right at the lower end of the Columbia River. Tom always had a good way with Indians and used to converse in Chinook. The Chinook tribe had the best salmon fishing on the coast at The Dalles and used to host a big trading jamboree with Indians from all over, so their language became the one language that was understood throughout the whole Pacific Northwest region, and traders found if they learned Chinook they could communicate with any other tribe, so it grew into a trade language called Chinook Jargon. Tom used to seek out the oldtimers who knew it well and really get into it. *Halo salmon mika?* (Have you any fish?) There was some kind of sign language he used to use, too. My father had that as well. I used to see him out dickering over fish with these guys from the Sumas reserve and they'd be waving their arms around like boy scouts practising semaphore. They were both a bit unusual in that they treated Indians with respect.

While he was living with the Chinooks Tom got a job hauling freight up the river to the road crews that were working on the Great Northern railroad. They made a trip once a week. They'd pole and paddle their way up with a load then enjoy life on the way back down. He kind of made his base there and married a Chinook woman but Tom was a guy who kept moving. He'd been way up the Nass River, just as a roustabout. He'd been over to Siberia. The federal government sent a delegation over to bring reindeer into Alaska hoping they'd become an economic mainstay like they were in Lapland and he was part of that. By 1896 he was up in the Yukon prospecting and heard about a couple of guys finding gold over in the next valley. So he went over there and spent the '97 season digging $10,000 worth of gold out of the Klondike. He went out then and the next year was the Klondike Rush of 1898. So he went back down to Astoria and rounded up a bunch of women from the reservation and took them back to Dawson. He said, "C'mon, you might as well get paid for it," and they were all for it. He set up in business mining the miners, and came out of it with more gold than most of them did. After that died down he went back down to Astoria and bought a hotel. The rumour was that he married one of his working girls, but if that was so, he couldn't have made a better choice. She was half Native American and half Kanaka and a finer person you couldn't want to meet. He wanted to use the savings he'd built up to get into the real big money so he bought a lumber mill. While he was running the hotel he had these guys cutting logs and piling them up along the riverbank, all ready to float down to the mill in the spring freshet. There was a strong market and everything was looking good, but that spring a big high water came and flooded him out. He went out to the mill and here it was just starting to float away. He said, "Jesus Christ, if I'd only thought enough to drop a match in there I would have collected the insurance," but he lost the whole thing, mill, logs, everything.

That left him with a lot of debts but he still had the hotel, so he goes back to town and it's just been announced—Prohibition. No more liquor sales. Among other things he owed the distillery $8,000—a big pile of dough—so he took his bill in to see them and he tells the head man, "Jesus, you know, there's just no way I can pay this now." The distillery boss says, "Let me see that bill." So Tom hands it to him and the guy scribbles across it, "Paid in full" and throws it back to him. And he says, "By the way, I got 200 cases of liquor in a warehouse downtown. I'm under orders to destroy it and I'd be obliged if you'd take care of it for me." So Tom got to bootleg the last big bunch of whiskey in Astoria and got together enough of a stake to move out. When he was digging around in his things he found a deed his brother had somehow acquired for land up on Sumas Prairie. So Tom went up to look at this land right at the start of Prohibition and set to work creating a dairy farm—that would be the same year we moved to Abbotsford, 1919. I can't tell it like Tom, he would have us just riveted in our chairs as he told us all this. How he went about learning how to build up his herd, manage his hay crop and all that goes into developing a first-class dairy farm I don't know, but he must have read the right books because by the time I was hauling milk he was one of the best producers in the valley. But it was his good humour and love of life I remember.

You end up writing about all these deeds, all these trucks and cans of milk and deals because that is what's easiest, but really it's not the real story, the real story is what gets you through the day and Tom was a beacon for me in those days, an older guy who'd seen it all and wasn't afraid to reach out a steadying hand to a wild young kid. But he didn't do it in any preachy way. He just did it by being there and being a friend and an example of how a man could go through all this crap a life throws at you and still keep smiling and laughing and be entertained by it all, as if it was a huge show put on just for our personal entertainment. He inspired me. He still inspires me. Not a week goes by but I think of his great zest for life and his wonderful spirit and ask myself, "I wonder what old Tom would have to say about this?" And I can almost hear him saying what he would say.

I think of my father that way too. In that way the dead don't die, they stay alive and keep you company as long as you remember them. And that's what makes up a life, these other people you run into who become part of you. I kind of like this idea the Mexicans have, of having a day when you invite all your dead relatives and friends to come back and you set a place at the table for them and get out their favourite things and give over a special time to bringing them back into your life. It's damn civilized.

10

Milk Wars

With Parberry in the business, it put a lot of pressure on Les's outfit to give good service so farmers wouldn't be tempted away for a few cents' cheaper freight, better milk prices or some other perk, like a free trip down to the Vancouver skid road. Les and Parberry sat up nights scheming to steal business from each other and some of the farmers were pretty fickle.

We were one hundred percent out for new customers. It was more work, I don't know why a guy would do it. Today you wouldn't be so stupid. It was just part of the game. It made the difference between being real wage slaves and being independent entrepreneurs, sort of. I guess that was the psychology of it. McGarva would play it up; it's not that hard to work people over on that basis, I realize now. Today, you can see all these guys driving truck and selling off it even more. Driver-salesmen. They're all for their company, pushing Coca-Cola over Pepsi. It's funny how it works. Whatever you get for it. In those days you got the right to climb in at the bosses' table and sound off like you knew something.

In a lot of ways it was counterproductive because a lot of the scratch farmers we picked up weren't worth the trouble. One good shipper like Tom Elliott was worth ten poor ones like Howard Boley—except Howard had better-looking daughters. Old Tom shipped ten cans and they'd always be in good shape. He'd get up in time to get all his cows milked early so there was plenty of time to cool the cans before you came by. The milk

Sumas Prairie dairy farmer Howard Boley wasn't our best milk shipper but he sure had the best-looking daughters. This is Kathleen and Jean dressed up in town clothes. WHITE FAMILY

had to be cooled otherwise it would deteriorate on the trip into town, especially in summer, so they had these big wooden tanks with cold water running through them, and all the cans had to go into that for an hour or so before we came. Then they were supposed to have the cooled milk set up on a stand and waiting for us so we could just pull the truck up alongside and roll them in. The better shippers always did this, but some guys like Howard just never could get out of bed in time and their cans would still be in the tank, barely cool enough to travel. We would have to walk over and pull them out of the water ourselves then hump them up onto the truck. It was a lot of extra work and it put you behind schedule but there wasn't much you could do except curse under your breath.

One thing about Howard, he was an easygoing guy who never complained, but a lot of the poorer grade of farmers not only caused extra work, they were the ones who gave you the most grief, too, because they were always unhappy with their dairy, wherever they shipped. Their milk would have problems and the dairy wouldn't pay them the full rate, but of course they would see it that the dairy was cheating. They were right about that sometimes, which made it all the more complicated to be the go-between. We would hear all the farmers' bitches against the dairy, then at the other end we would hear all the dairy's bitches against the farmer. And here we are, just a bunch of young kids who don't know what to say to all these cranky old bastards, except we know our boss will take it hard if we lose a shipper of any description.

The dairies and the farmers and the truckers had quite an involved relationship and a lot of it had to be based on trust. Many of the farmers weren't very sophisticated. They'd started out with stump ranches—land that had been logged but not cleared of the huge old stumps that grew so thick in the valley, so the farming was done in the spaces in between and these old farms were more on the subsistence level. They weren't committed to one crop, they didn't know that chickens didn't pay and beef didn't pay so they had chickens and cows and pigs and goats, well not many goats, but sheep—they had a little of everything. They didn't know that it wasn't good business—they were thinking survival, not profit. And that was a stump ranch. Usually the farmer would be earning part of his living at something else like logging or fishing, so there might be an old boat up on blocks and a few pieces of rusty logging machinery—they were half farm and half junkyard. A friend of ours, Tom Haines, and his family had one of the classic old stump ranches on Otter Road right up until the 1970s, my god, it should have been turned into a museum. It represented a forgotten phase of BC history. When the First World War came along all of a sudden there's money to be made selling milk so these guys started blasting out the stumps and running a few more cows and concentrating on the dairy business. But there was a lot to running a good dairy farm they had to learn, and some never did.

The FVMPA was stuck with the lardasses. Miss the truck today and ship tomorrow and all the horrible things. Their milk would be rotten, low grade, dirty and the bull would break through the fence and breed all the cows at the wrong time. If you left it to the cows, they'd calve in the spring and milk though the summer then dry up in the winter. You'd have milk when there was a glut and no price, then when milk became scarce and the price went up, you wouldn't have any to sell. That was the old breed of farmer, that was the way it always had been done. Let nature take its course. Every guy had his own ratty old bull then and you'd just hope they

Milking was a job reserved for the low man on the totem pole. HARBOUR PUBLISHING

didn't keep them so long that they were breeding their own daughters, but often they were. One guy out at Clayburn had a herd that was all deformed, their feet were all in toes and everything else. The good farmers got good bulls and held back on the breeding so they had cows coming fresh later in the year and milking through the low season when the price was good, but to do this you had to put up extra feed or buy feed because the grass wasn't growing, so the hand-to-mouth guys couldn't manage it.

The brighter farmers went in and made their own arrangements with the dairies. But a lot of the farmers were after you to get them a dairy or get them a better dairy than the one they had. Sometimes the shoe would be on the other foot and you'd be after a specific farmer to change over to an independent, because he produced good milk or because he was in a location where you needed another pickup. Dairies, too, were getting new business or losing it and they would be wanting to get more milk or drop some of the less desirable shippers. They'd talk to Les if he was there but if he wasn't, they'd be out to the truck to tell us they could handle some more milk. We knew what was going on at the dairy too, largely. We were always talking to the guys.

The dairyman was the head man at the dairy. He'd tell us that so-and-so was getting pretty haywire in the milk. What that really meant most times was that they had too much goddamned milk and they wanted to get out of their obligations to some of the less desirable farmers. Ernie Cook was the dairyman at National Dairy and he was an alcoholic. He'd say, oh that guy, he's getting pretty bad in the milk. And that guy would catch shit. Ship and ship and ship and get nothing for his milk. Until you could move him somewhere else. But then of course when they wanted milk, it was a different story. Like when the hospital contract was knocked back and forth and around and around. Okay, it was up for tender. The Greeks were great on the bidding stuff. No matter how cheap they bid it, they could always make up by stealing some milk off the shippers. They'd steal on grade, you see. They'd claim a shipment was only three percent butterfat when it was really four. Each shipment was tested to measure the butterfat content. They had to do it that way because otherwise the farmer might just take five cans of milk, add a can of water and claim he had six cans. But there was no way of cheating on the butterfat so that became the standard of measure. Then they might also say the milk was too sour, or too contaminated for the fluid market, and had to go for industrial or manufactured milk, all lower grades with lower prices.

The Greeks could underbid their competition for something like the hospital contract knowing they could always take it out of the farmer's hide. So they land this huge contract and suddenly they need to increase production by 500 pounds a day right now. So they're after us to get back some of those guys they were saying were no good just the week before.

See, the dairyman opens the can and he sniffs and then he cocks the can—leaves the lid cocked up a bit, meaning he's officially inspected that can and he's letting it ventilate before it's emptied. But that first sniff is vitally important. It tells him everything he wants to know about that can of milk. Right there, a hundred pounds of milk that's been sealed for three or four hours, the gas in there tells the whole story to a trained person. That and the colour of the milk. He could sniff it, then look at it, judge its colour, and he could tell you what farm that milk came from. In fact sometimes if you got the cans mixed up he could straighten them up for you. He could tell you the goddamn milker was using liniment on his hands. If he wasn't too drunk to smell at all, Ernie could tell you most anything. "He's gotta cut that out, he's gotta wash those tits off better" and all this stuff. Sometimes a cow would be getting medication and he could tell that. "Get that cow out of here." And the farmer had to do it, because otherwise he was going to get nothing for his milk. The dairyman's word was law.

It had to be that way, because milk, my god, it's the perfect medium for bacteria to grow in and you couldn't have some unsanitary bastard out in the sticks infecting half

A dairy hand dumps a can of milk into the dairy's reservoir while emptied cans are placed in a washing machine. In my day the washing was done by hand and we sometimes had to wait hours, which meant good business for nearby beer parlours. CITY OF VANCOUVER ARCHIVES 1184-1856

the population of Vancouver. Mostly our shippers put out quality product but there were some awful bastards who never should have been allowed to ship. It started with the milker. The job of milker was the lowest of the low. For a working man that was the last resort. Unless the farmer's daughter did it or the farmer himself, but if he got a little better fixed he got some cheap help to do it. There was a guy named Harvey Parks who was all crippled up with syphilis and worked as a hired man all around the valley milking cows. Old Hari Singh had a crew of crippled-up old Hindus there that couldn't make it anywhere else doing his milking, they had pulmonary diseases and things, coughing and spitting all the time. You'd see the milk mixing with the dirt on their hands and this grey gunk would ooze out between their fingers and drip down into the pail. I'd loved milk as a kid and never got enough but after I'd been on the trucks for awhile I couldn't bear the thought of drinking it anymore, and I've never been able to get over that to this day, even though it's supposedly all perfect now.

If you had milk that was contaminated to start with, if the farmer hadn't got it cooled well enough or if he'd tried to pass off some day-old milk by mixing it in with fresh stuff, well it would be positively putrid by the time the dairyman opened the can. Even good milk you had to get into town as damn well fast as you could or it would start to go down in grade and there would be hell to pay. Speed was a big thing. There was no time to waste. We always said we delivered milk faster than Parberry and Parberry said he delivered milk faster than we did. Hot weather was a real bugger. You had to keep it under fifty-five degrees. It fell on the shoulders of the dairyman to watch over the incoming shipments and use his skill to sniff out any bad milk before it was allowed to be poured into the dairy's main reservoir. So the dairyman needed to be in charge, but it was cruel to watch how he used his position to take advantage of shippers sometimes.

By the same token, if I spilled half a load of milk coming in, which I did sometimes, they would make it up for us. If you'd been playing ball with them, and you made sure you were if you had any brains, they'd even it out over a couple of days, short the farmer on his tally by a couple of cans each day until the loss was made up. So in turn if you caught the dairy cheating the shipper for their own reasons, you had to keep your mouth shut. You had no choice. The farmer was the one who was paying you but the dairies were the ones who had all the power. Your business depended on keeping in their good books.

We had some spills. You couldn't haul milk in cans and not spill some. You were spilling a little bit all the time, from loose lids mostly—you'd heave a can up onto the truck and a splash would go right down your shirt front. By the end of the day you'd smell like a dairy. That smell of sour milk would cling to you, you couldn't wash it off. Going into a pub or restaurant or anything, you'd always be self-conscious about it, the same way roofers must worry about their tar smell and fishermen worry about their fish smell. You get so you can't smell it anymore yourself and you forget until you see the waitresses wrinkling up their noses. They used to say that's how you tell you're with the wrong kind of girl. If she can smell fish she's from the wrong background, and if you marry her she will fool around on you when you're out fishing. Same for dairy farmers, I guess. It was always good to be back drinking in a Fraser Valley beer parlour where essence of rancid milk was an honourable scent.

I spilled a lot of milk down on Carrall Street one time. This particular truck had open doors, we just used chains, and I hadn't blocked the cans up like we did on the long haul because I was just going across town. A taxi swung out and to miss him I swung around and slammed on the brakes and the whole back load tipped over and went out that goddamned door. There were cans and milk right across Carrall and Hastings. Washing around there, it just seemed like The Flood. You never saw so much milk in your life. Once it dumps on the pavement, it just goes, it never absorbs. Jesus Christ there was a lot of milk. People howling and crying. It seemed like the end of the world to me, waiting for the cops to show up and do whatever they would do to me. Anyway I got busy and grabbed all the cans and threw them back up there as fast as I could and soon as I got the last can on and the chain on, away I went. The cops never did show up. But you could smell it for days. It stunk up the whole downtown of Vancouver. I was taking people around on tours to see where I spilled all the milk.

The same thing in Langley: I swung around the corner and the rope let go and the side of the truck went out. The milk went all over, washed across the street, up the wall of the building on the other side and back, you know. I don't think either of those spills resulted in an insurance claim. You couldn't hit the insurance too often so you saved it for when you really needed it. Instead you shuffled the cans around hoping each farmer wouldn't miss one or two hundred pounds in a month and with the cooperation of the dairyman you'd probably get away with it. Somebody might be squealing but at the end of a month it didn't make all that much difference. Jesus Christ, with the money we were getting, we couldn't pay for it.

Another time I was somewhere down on Powell. This was later on at night and I'd had a few beers. I had Rita McGarva with me and we were going to do something. Anyway I went to back up to get room to get out and there was the goddamnedest crash behind and I looked behind and there was one of the big concrete light poles lying across the street. We knocked it right over. Funny thing is, the city can be deserted as a tomb and soon as anything happens, there's a crowd. I don't know where they all come from. But we got back in the truck and got the hell out of there and never heard any more about that either.

Even now if I go back over the Pacific Highway in my mind, every mile reminds me of a story. One night I was going back late with John McGarva, Les's brother. We'd been whooping it up and making a few stops at pubs along the way and it was foggy as a sonuvabitch. All the way out we had been following this beer truck but you couldn't dare pass because of the fog. Going up Clayton Hill, a long pull outside Langley, this other truck had a full load so he's put her in the basement and we were chugging along just twenty feet behind him about as fast as you could walk and we could see he had six beer kegs lashed on his tailgate. So I said to John, "Jesus Christ, we should have one of those." So John says, "Jesus Christ, we could do it y'know." So I nosed up right tight behind this beer truck and John crawled out over the hood and stood on the bumper, got up on the guy's tailgate and untied the rope and threw off one of these nice big beer barrels. So he crawls back and we go back and get the goddamned beer. The other driver never knew a thing, sitting there in his cab pounding along in the fog.

We called the troops in that time. John took the keg over to his place and the gang rallied round and they were up all night with it. I had to go

Winters can be harsh in the Fraser Valley but no matter what the weather, the milk had to be picked up. THE REACH P494

switch cans with the other truck when we got home and by the time I caught up with him the next day the beer was all gone. Typical John.

Driving back and forth every damn day of the week, you got to know every bump in that road, every mood of landscape in different lights and weathers and seasons. I remember one place just by Otter Road, when you go over that hill the late afternoon sun would go down to just where it kissed the horizon, then it would rise up again as you went on. I watched it a thousand times, plugging along going home because I was there at that same place that same time and on that same date over so many different years, covering the same piece of road, doing the same work, watching my life fall into a recognizable pattern.

In that sense it was a typical milk run, because so much of it was repetitive and predictable, even though it had seemed completely chaotic at first. I thought I was in a groove and nothing was going to change for a long time, but of course looking back I see my life as constant change with hardly a static place anywhere along its length. And it's still going on. Even now at ninety-nine I get up and wonder what new challenge I will have to deal with, if some formerly natural function, like holding food on a fork, will suddenly have become beyond me, or my wife, who was so admired for her intellect, will reach the point where she can't remember my name. From this vantage point life is just a constant churn, not so much like a placid river as a churning, roiling, writhing one with random whirlpools popping up just when you think you've reached smooth sailing.

11

Life in the Dirty Thirties

I can see now I was riding pretty high through the mid-thirties. I was one of the gang in a way I'd never been before and really never was again. I had a good job doing something that was pretty new and exciting. I enjoyed some of the advantage of the early truck drivers like Herb Wareing in that I was in daily touch with the big city and the life of the broader Fraser Valley outside of Abbotsford, as I saw it every day from the road. The crowd I travelled in was a beer parlour crowd, but beer parlours were where the action was in those days. Not that it bore any resemblance to the pubs of today, it was primitive and straitjacketed by comparison. The beer parlours were huge barns of places and of course they had a partition down the middle dividing the men's side from the "Ladies and Escorts." You couldn't walk from one side to the other, you had to go outside, get invited back in by a "lady" and then go in with her. It was tough on our girlfriends, because most of the time it meant they were off by themselves and you'd be ducking over to buy them a drink and chat them up just enough to keep them from going home and taking away the chance you might get somewhere with them later on, but really wanting to be back in the men's side with the gang. It made for a lot of tension to be truthful, it was goddamned stupid. You couldn't have food in those places, you couldn't sing—that was instant expulsion—you couldn't even laugh too loud or the barkeep would cut you off. The only sound they liked to hear was the slurping sound of beer going down your gullet. But just make sure your table never has more than two glasses per person on it. And just picture this: two or three times a night the cops would come around checking every table. For what? It's hard to explain now why a thing like that would ever be, but of course then it was quite different.

Someone like my mother, if she heard a woman had been seen in a beer parlour, that would finish her. That would be it. That woman was never to be spoken to again, never to be acknowledged on the street. No second chance. And Mother wasn't alone. She was the norm, at least among her generation. And that was the world I came from. But here I was now in a different world. We had a lot more freedom than people of the generation just before us. I guess we had WWI to thank for that. There was nothing you couldn't do then you can do now, as far as I know, in private. But what you could do in public was really limited. You couldn't go live with a woman. Young people didn't have the freedom they have today. We were always under the thumb of other people's morals. Always really screwed down.

I don't think young people were any different than they were at any time. Of course contraception was a big part of it—there wasn't any that was worth a damn. Condoms, which we called Frenchies or safes, never

The old style beer parlours didn't permit food, singing, mixing of the sexes or much of anything except beer, but we did our best. CITY OF VANCOUVER ARCHIVES 1184-1018

condoms, were around but they were against the law, you had to go to some sleazy place like Bud Haddrell's to get them. They were expensive too—a lot of people couldn't afford them, the people who really needed them. You could get them from the drugstore on prescription but I never heard of a doctor issuing a prescription for them. It was against the law even to disseminate information on birth control. I know now those old safes were the worst thing in the world. The goddamn things would break. They were made out of sheep gut or poor-grade rubber and they weren't reliable. If you were married you'd break them often enough that your wife would be constantly pregnant.

I remember old Hari Singh, one of our shippers, saying, "Frank, I don't know what to do. The doctor says my wife will die if she has another baby." But that's all the doctor told him. All they would do for him. And his wife did die with another baby in a couple of years. Poor damn people. Hari was a good old guy. Big tall man. He was a radical. He knew Gandhi. He came to their village. Hari and his brother were fighting on Gandhi's side in the struggle for Indian independence. Hari's brother was a radical and a British soldier came into town and shot him dead. Just left him lying on the ground in front of their home. I don't know how Hari got out. I knew afterwards that Hari was a special guy alright. He must have been a Sikh. But no matter what their history, when they got here they were just "Hindus."

Women in those days had it far worse than men. When a single girl got caught she was really a lost cause. No way she could face it down. A lot killed themselves. Or—this is something you no longer hear about—women were always having these mysterious infections and dying or just pulling through after having a terrible time. Nobody would explain why, except maybe to say it was "women's trouble." I remember one of my wild cousins talking about one of the girls who got pregnant, saying, "I could have fixed her up with my fingernail." They didn't understand infection and when it happened, they didn't have the money to go to a doctor and didn't have the nerve to go to a doctor so they would lie at home and die. You don't hear about those now, and there were lots of them.

All I ever did was dump it on the ground. Pull it out. But it seems most people can't do that. And I'm sure that it buggered me up a lot too. In the way that it takes the best part of it away. The best part of your life. It's something that hangs on. But what else were we going to do, for chrissake? If what they tell us now is true, it was no way to live, but that's the way it had to be. But not everybody did that. Not everybody would go for that. It was against a religious principle for one thing.

Among the people I was raised with, you couldn't live with sex openly. There were French and Europeans who were much more down to earth, even my old man had a more accepting attitude toward sex, he was not puritanical in the least, but he was married to an extremely puritanical woman and we both suffered for it. Young people had it bad, no use fooling about it. If you were a young person doing what you were supposed to be doing, living in denial and going to church, well you had to be really weird. And some of those righteous, bible-thumping bastards were really twisted. You could see it in their faces, those bitter old Calvinists and Presbyterians all fouled up with their own hang-ups and dying to take out their misery on anybody who showed a little spark.

But I didn't understand that at that time, I fell for that righteous, straight and narrow stuff of my mother's and felt there was something terribly wrong with me that I wasn't able to toe the line, even as I rebelled. Always you could fall back on righteousness and condemn somebody else, which everybody did. Makes you wonder if any society is true to its morality. Never! Now that we've largely got rid of all that crap, I wonder if they'll develop the real crowd of weirdos now that they did then. I would like to think it's making for a more healthy world but I still see some of that old weirdness when I see these moralists on TV, protesting against abortion and gay marriage. I can always tell which ones the right-to-lifers are, just by the weird look in their eyes and the hard cast to their mouths. I recognize it, that look.

In the thirties more people were susceptible to that way of thinking. Even a bunch of young badasses like us could get indignant if we saw one of the older people not toeing the line. The idea that older people could impose what they thought was good yet get away with what they felt like was maddening. I even got into a tar and feathering there one time. Here was a friend of ours, old Porter, catching hell. The Porters were a great old family that had been there since pioneer days running a famous old store down at the Five Corners in Langley. It's a museum now. They were in the valley since the beginning of time. This member of the family had his own farm and was a good guy but he'd developed a big hernia. I can't remember his first name now. I'll call him George.

George's wife had no more use for him. She was giving him shit. This all came out through this hired man, this guy who worked for him and married his daughter. He told us and after a couple sessions in the beer parlour it got to be a cause, you see.

There was this cop, Bill Moore, a big swashbuckling kind of guy. English. Red face. He played the role to the hilt. He was into all the politics in the country. A real shit. He was on commission—he worked for a share of his fines. They all did that then. There was this cop in Langley, he had this crazy little motorcycle, he putted up and down the highway and hit all the trucks. He'd be sitting at the city limits, and he'd tag you right through town then turn around and tag somebody else back, hoping you'd go two miles per hour over the limit down a hill, get a rear wheel over the line going round a tight corner or break some bylaw only he knew about. He got beat up a couple times and one guy ploughed into him with a truck, but in the end he was just trying to make a living and he wasn't worse than the men who hired him. It was a real peril in these days, every little town had its cop out to pay his wages by picking on the out-of-town traffic. I knew one of them later, he said come the end of the month the city manager would be short to cover payroll so he'd come down the hall hollering at them to get out on the goddamn road and "make 'er pay." People complain about how

Up until 1950 we had three levels of police in Abbotsford: the RCMP, who at that time only enforced federal laws; the BC Provincial Police (above) who looked after provincial law and local cops, who worked for the municipality. HARBOUR PUBLISHING

the RCMP do it all today because they're a national force and not responsible at a local level, but the other way was worse, when you had the local cop in with the local ruling clique. The provincial police weren't much better. They were a bunch of low-lifes, mostly.

Anyway, this goddamned Moore would come to Porter's farm in broad daylight and take the old lady upstairs right in front of George, dare him to do anything about it, according to the hired man. All of us young guys hated Moore to start with and got all sweated up about this situation and talked ourselves into coming to old Porter's rescue. It was just drunken indignation brewed on the spot. Very ad hoc. One thing led to another and somebody came up with the idea of a tarring and feathering. Where the hell we got that I don't know to this day. Somebody must have seen it in a movie or a comic book. So somebody rounded up a couple of pillows but we couldn't figure out how to do tar—you'd have to melt it, and then it would burn him and kill him probably—so we came up with the idea of using molasses and somebody went out and bought a couple cans of molasses.

We decided to wait until Moore was coming back in the middle of the night after one of his sessions with Mrs. Porter. To make sure he stopped and got out of his car somebody came up with the idea of dropping a bale of hay on the road. That would probably be McGarva's touch. So we all crawled into the bush and waited. There must have been about ten of us and of course we were all liquored up. The first night nothing happened but we went out again and by God, old Moore comes along right on schedule, sees this good bale of hay on the road, stops, gets out, walks back, bends over to pick it up—and that's when we come pouring out of the bush and surround him.

Well, what a goddamned joke! It wasn't until we were right there facing him we realized we didn't have a goddamned clue what we were doing. Here's this ragtag bunch of drunks standing out in the road armed with pillows and a few cans of molasses facing the town policeman feeling just about as silly as you can possibly imagine. It looked like we were maybe intending a pillow fight. Moore was a big man, and he had never looked as big as he did right then. Nobody wanted to make the first move. What the hell were you going to do anyway, walk up and start dabbing his jacket with molasses? Say "Would you mind standing still while I pour this over your head, Bill?" In our beer parlour conversations we'd turned him into some kind of make-believe villain, now here he was big as life wanting to know what the hell was up. He didn't know if it was some kind of prank or highway robbery or what.

God, I was embarrassed. I was afraid, too. If we touched him, well hell, we would be sitting ducks for an assault charge. Assaulting a peace officer. This had somehow never occurred to us. But we had to do something, we couldn't just make conversation about the weather or say "Sorry, we thought you were somebody else," so one of the drunker, stupider members of the party started cursing him out and announcing we were there to teach him a lesson and that gave some of the others the nerve to start grappling him, but he was a big, strong guy and he wasn't about to take anything lying down. "I know who you bastards are, every damn one of you!" he roared, "I'm going to have the whole damned works of you in jail for this!" He put up a hell of a struggle, which was good, because it gave us something to do after all, and we all piled on and rolled around making a bunch of racket. Some molasses did get smeared around and eventually the pillows did get broken open though I think we got more feathers and molasses on ourselves than on him. I also think he did more damage to us than we did to him. Several guys were rolling around moaning and holding their crotch or their gut. Eventually we ran out of molasses and feathers and beat a retreat.

I lived in terror for weeks after, expecting a summons every time somebody came to the door. But we never heard any more about it. I think we were all equally embarrassed, including him. The funny thing is, it kind of worked. He stopped coming around and sparking Mrs. Porter, at least in broad daylight. More to the point, we stopped talking about it at the beer parlour.

Les lived kind of a charmed life as far as trouble with officials went. One time I remember he got in trouble with the tax people. He didn't keep any books to speak of. Florence tried to do some minimal record keeping but it was a losing battle, the way Les operated. So finally the tax people catch up to him and there's a bit of going back and forth and they notify him they're going to send out an inspector to audit his books of account. Well, he didn't have any books of account but they scrambled some phony paperwork together and scrounged up all the paycheque stubs and gas bills they could find but it was nowhere near what was needed. So this inspector shows up and looks at this miserable bit of paperwork and says, "Well, Mr. McGarva, I'm afraid this is just not adequate, you see…" and he attempts to explain things to Les but Les is putting on his dumbbell act and keeps saying he wants to show him the operation, show him that it's all good honest hard work and he has nothing to hide, he's just trying to provide jobs for local folks and all this BS. So eventually this guy agrees to go out for a drive with Les and Florence and they take him on the goddamnedest tour of the valley you ever saw. They have some friends all ready with a big barbecue and music and dancing and beer and girls and this guy has never had such a great time in his life. They send him off with his car all loaded down with racks of lamb, boxes of cheese and butter, chickens, you name it. And that's the last they hear of the audit.

That was Les's method of dealing with anybody above him in the social scale—which was almost everybody—he would adopt a bullshit-baffles-brains strategy and it usually worked like a damn. There was a prominent Vancouver lawyer bought a summer place near town and who used to drink with Les. There were two brothers, both top lawyers. I forget their names now. It was Scotch, let's say Stuart. Ian Stuart and Hamish Stuart. They were heavyweights. One had been in line for Attorney General but somehow blew it. The one with the place in Abbotsford—Hamish, I'll call him—was kind of a lost soul, a man with a horrible drinking problem. I guess he came out there to have a safe place to drink. A lot of them used to do that. McGavin, the founder of the big bread company, used to come out there to party. A lot of Vancouver high rollers did. Anybody who did much drinking in Abbotsford soon crossed paths with Les, and this Stuart and his wife were fascinated by him. I remember this one evening Mrs. Stuart was trying to make conversation and asked, "Do you read very much, Les?"

"Oh yeah, I like reading." I'm almost ready to cry, I'm so embarrassed.

"Really! What kind of literature do you prefer?"

"Oh lots of stuff—*True Detective, True Crime…* I'm reading all the time." Which was true. He would get onto one detective story and read it for about a month.

They thought he was great. He was a captivating guy.

We used to get away on the odd junket, the bunch of us. One time Les decided we should all go hunting, go up country and shoot a moose. There was half a dozen of us—Les, his brother John, Parberry, his son Dutch, myself and somebody else, I forget who. We spent a couple days up above Clinton and hadn't shot anything—I'd shot a couple geese, but that was all—and they all wanted to go home. John and I were in one car coming back by Spences Bridge and we weren't in as much hurry and the country looked interesting so we said, "Let's go up the hill here and see if we can find a deer." I never liked working with John much. He was a cranky bugger and never seemed to be in tune with what other people were thinking. A deer jumped in front of us and he shot right over my head at this fucking deer. No harm came of it, but I thought, what kind of an asshole am I dealing with here? You just don't do a thing like that. All that has to happen is you slip or the other guy bobs unexpectedly, and somebody's dead. But as I came to know John better I would see this as par for the course. He wasn't exactly stupid, but he was on a different wavelength to most people. It's funny how some people are like that, it's like they were born missing one of the seven senses. I'm sure by now there's a five-dollar name for it but in our day we just said knucklehead.

We went up the hill and up on top of the hill and it levelled out there, it was grand country, open parkland with well-spaced pine and high grass in between like wheat. And all these pine trees had rings of horseshit around them. Piled high and in a perfect circle like you'd laid it with a compass, about twenty feet in diameter. I couldn't make that out. We went on and down the valley was something that looked like a big white tent. We kept on going until we reached it and it turned out this was a big pile of crispy white stuff like snow except not cold and not melting. Actually it was melting but very slowly. One end was fresh and square and the other end, about seventy-five feet away, was sagging and tipping into the ground. We had no idea what it was, except it appeared to me made up out of squared blocks that had been piled by hand. There was a cabin nearby with a hell of a stink coming out of it. We had to spend the night there and the stink was too bad to think about using the cabin so we bedded down in the woodshed, which had a pretty good stink of its own.

At dark along came an old guy with a pack on his back and a dog with a pack on its back. He's been down to Merritt to get groceries and he smelled just like the cabin. We asked him about the mysterious pile of white stuff and he told us the story. He'd been there since the beginning of the First World War and this white stuff was soda that he'd been cutting from a nearby soda lake that dried up and went solid in the hot months of the summer. There are a number of small lakes like that in the Interior, that have so much mineral and alkali in them that when the water evaporates in the hot weather it congeals. When he started out the soda had a value as a cleaning agent so he'd placed a mineral claim on this lake and was hauling small amounts down to trade in Merritt. When WWI came, cleaning soda came into high demand and some businessmen offered to buy the property off him. They gave a $500 deposit and told him they would be back to pay the remainder and told him in the meantime they would pay him for any soda he cut and piled. He'd spent every year since patiently waiting for them to come back and pay the rest of the money and pay him for all the soda he'd piled. He cut it with a handsaw when the lake was solid and packed it up to dry ground so one end of his pile was fresh and square and the other end was melting down and running back into the lake. I didn't have the heart to tell him that synthetic soda had long replaced the natural kind and his buyers were never going to come back.

We asked him about the circles of manure around the pine trees and he said, "Oh, that's the horses." There was a big population of wild horses on the mountain and during the winter when it started to snow they'd each pick a tree and walk up to it so their heads were protected by the branches. As the snow piled up they would tramp it down by shuffling their hind ends around, keeping their heads into the tree under cover of the branches. They'd spend all winter like that, crapping as they moved, so the manure built up in a circle one horse-length out from the tree. I've often had occasion to think of that old fella up there on the mountain endlessly piling up his soda new and fresh at one end and melting away at the other without ever stopping to think why. I thought the old boy was nuts at the time; now I feel a lot in common with him.

Every once in awhile I tried to get Les interested in branching out, starting a freight service up to the Interior or over to the Island where they had dairy farms, but he wouldn't have it. "I've heard its all just brush and boulders," he'd say. "The only part of BC that's worth a goddamn is right here." But one time we got a chance to move someone's hired man to Port Alberni, and Les let me talk him into doing it. Alberni was just getting going then. I'd never been on the Island and Les had never been on the Island so this was a big excursion. He figured and figured—he didn't know what he was figuring, he got a map, some squiggly little thing from the gas station that was all you could get for a map then, and he was figuring out the miles and the time, and finally he came up with a price. This guy was real down and out broke so it didn't matter anyway.

So we threw all his goods on the truck and the man and his wife and baby sat up front with Les and I went out in the back. And we set out. Of course we got drunk before we set out. So we get down to Vancouver and we couldn't get the sonuvabitch on the ferry no how. The old CPR ferry to Victoria. They didn't cater to trucks. There were very few trucks anyway, and any freight hauling there was they had corralled for themselves, hauling trucks and railcars on barges. They only had a little hole in the side of the ferry and the truck was too high and too wide to squeeze through it. So we had to go back and have somebody bring down the other truck, which was smaller. Even then it wouldn't go in the door until I took the duals off, the dual rear tires, so I'm doing that while they're transferring all the stuff and everybody is drinking and making a lot of noise, it's a big party. Les was trying to get the woman to go in the back with him and eventually we get it all stowed away and get the goddamn truck loaded aboard and Les rounded up some of the sailors and started feeding them beer and talking to them—everything is a great big adventure.

We get over to the Island and I take over driving and Les is out back and we're going down the highway and the baby's crying and the guy is getting mad and the woman says, "I smell something burning." I stop and go back and here the mattress is on fire. Les passed out with a smoke and set it on fire. Here he is beating away on it saying, "I pissed on this goddamn thing until I can't piss anymore but I cain't get it out no how!" With the mood the guy is in I don't want him to find out we've ruined his bed so I say to Les, "Alright, I'll get going and you throw the sonuvabitch off." So I get back in the cab and start up and this woman is saying, "I smell something burning. What is that?" "I don't know, something underneath," I say. Then there's this big flare of light as the mattress goes overboard and she says, "What was that?"

"What? I didn't see nothing," I say.

We got them over to Alberni and of course we couldn't get all the money out of him—plus the mattress was gone. Nobody claimed to know what happened to it, but they knew alright. They had been drinking right along with us. Anyhow, we got back to Vancouver and we realized in all the bollocks over loading, the ferry guys had forgotten to take our tickets. So we go into the office and claim we bought these tickets by mistake and by god they let us turn them in for cash, which means down to the nearest beer parlour we go and we get drunk all over again. Lucky we were both used to driving the Pacific Highway dead drunk and sometime in the middle of the night we crawl into Abbotsford. You could hear Les for weeks after that talking about Vancouver Island. "There's nothing there at all. Just a bunch of fucken brush and boulders. Just what I thought all the time."

As time went on I began to see more of Kathleen Boley, or Kay as she was usually called. I had dealt with her father, Howard Boley, since I went out to butcher one of his cows with my father back in the twenties and when I found myself on the milk haul I got him as a shipper. When my dad and I first dealt with him, Howard had been on what we called the Old York Place, one of the big old farms close to Abbotsford with quite a history—the original owner pre-empted it in 1865 and their son, Fraser York, had been the first white child born in the colony of British Columbia after it was created in 1858. Howard was just renting and he hadn't been able to hang on to it—it was too much for him and his old lady couldn't get along with the in-laws. The Boleys were another pioneer family from the 1880s who owned a big old farm nearby and they had a whole bunch of sons—Lester, Howard, Edgar, Theron—I can't remember them all. Howard then rented over in the Rosedale area on the other side of the valley for a number of years and I didn't see any more of Kay but sometime in the late twenties or early thirties he managed to buy a nice piece of marginal land back on Sumas Prairie south of Vye Road.

Kathleen (Kay) Boley, the farmer's daughter from Sumas Prairie who kept catching my eye. WHITE FAMILY

I liked Howard. He was a slow-talking, slow-moving, easy-living guy, a real old-style farmer who knew everything there was to know about soil and crops and weather but was no kind of a hustler. His farm was rundown and he couldn't get his milk out on time and would be shipping it warm or holding it over and shipping it the next day and never getting top price. The driving force in the family was the old lady, who handled all the money and gave all the orders but seldom appeared outside the house. In fact I got the impression she spent long periods in bed afflicted with some mysterious ailment, and ran everything by bellowing orders from her bedroom in a grating voice strongly accented by her native Hebrides Gaelic. She also thundered out Gaelic prayers and direct conversations with her maker, which I gather is something of a national pastime in the Hebrides. God apparently paid close attention to her input because He took her side in every argument with her in-laws and supported every demand she made on her children, and the proof was that she said He did. When she did appear out of doors, look out! It usually meant she was on a holy rampage, like the time she clubbed a bill collector over the head with a two-by-four, an incident she often recounted with relish. She had her whole family cowed, especially Howard, who spent most of his time in the barn and only ventured into the house when he had to. They had four good-looking daughters and one young son who all worked like slaves. Kay took care of the house and looked after the younger kids while Jean served in the place of a hired man out in the barn. I used to feel sorry for her, always dressed in old trousers and stinking of cowshit, it must have been a hell of a way for a young woman to grow up.

Kay was bookish and artistic and loved school but the old lady browbeat her into dropping out in grade eleven with the solemn promise that she would reward her by buying her a house when she got married. Kay desperately wanted to stay in school but couldn't stand up to the old lady. She had the soft, giving personality of her father. She was the real mother to her sisters and brother and they loved her and looked up to her. But after five or six years of slaving away in the house with no end in sight, she was starting to get a little desperate as I see it now. Even a milk-truck driver with sticky-up hair and a bad reputation for drinking and fighting must have started to look okay and she managed to put herself in my path surprisingly often.

She didn't have to try very hard to get my attention. The years had done nothing to take the edge off the beauty that had burnt itself into my memory ten or twelve years before. She had the looks of a model or a film star. In fact one of the local photography studios had come out to do a photo shoot with her, which they used to decorate their showroom. But it was all going to waste because she seldom got off the farm and when she did she was so shy she stayed in the shadows. I was very surprised when she shyly approached me about getting a ride to Vancouver one morning and of course jumped at the chance to take her.

I found her very stiff and awkward compared to the fast crowd I was running with but there was something so good and wholesome and capable about her I couldn't help thinking she would make a hell of a wife. It wasn't long before we were making a fairly regular thing of it and managing to fit in a few side trips to the ice cream bar, then the restaurants and the movies, but it was slow going with the old lady hovering in the background with her two-by-four and it didn't help that Kay was completely turned off by my drinking buddies and the whole beer parlour scene. And as far as anything physical went she was untouchable. It took me months before I could hold her hand, and months more to get a kiss. I found her pretty frustrating and spent more of my time with the McGarva and Parberry girls, who were game for anything in the name of a good time. There was a bunch of us went over to Sumas all the time. The bars across the line, now that they were back in business, were more lively than the Canadian beer parlours with all their fun-killing rules. The American bars had music and you could sing and dance in them. I had this friend, Scotty Grant, who worked in a bike shop. He had a nice voice and used to sing to beat hell. So we'd go over to the tavern and say, "Hey Scotty, sing us a song." He wouldn't do nothing until he'd had six, eight beers, then he'd grab the mike and he'd sing like hell. That was the start. We'd sit there all night with beer all over the place, he'd sing once in awhile and the girls would be dancing—we figured we were really living.

12

The Great Lawsuit

As time went on I had the milk business pretty well figured out and Les didn't need to spend as much time running things, although he was always rattling up new shippers. He had lots of other irons in the fire, always. He got hold of a farm somehow, by trading back and forth and promising this and that, then he built up a good herd the same way, renewed the fencing with free bobwire he traded scrap irrigation pipe for at a Vancouver scrap metal place, fixed the barn with lumber he got in payment for doing some hauling for a local mill—in time he had a first-class farm that he'd barely paid a cent of cash money for. He then went ahead and built himself a big new house on the same basis, hardly spending a dollar of his own money. This was how he worked and there was no end to the schemes he would come up with on a daily basis. Before long he had a second dairy farm and was shipping a lot of milk himself. In his drunken, disorganized way he had made himself into one of Abbotsford's most successful businessmen, a feat all the more remarkable considering economic conditions that were causing many of the established businesses to go bankrupt and lose everything.

When we were drinking together he often hinted that he planned to make me a partner in the trucks. It made sense because by this time, 1936 or '7, I was running the day-to-day stuff more than he was and he was already starting to experience some health problems. He was drinking too much and his heart was going. It was all getting a bit too much for him.

There was no way he could go back to running it all by himself. He had other drivers, mainly George Grohnert, but they came and went and didn't have the experience or dedication I did. To them it was just a job. I put a lot more into it because I figured I was laying the groundwork for a future in the trucking business. I often fantasized about expanding into the Interior and Vancouver Island and owning a fleet of general freight trucks. Sometimes I imagined I could see my future stretching out before me like a clear stretch of highway, beautiful Kathleen Boley at my side.

There wasn't much I wouldn't have done for Les at that point. I remember one time the guys spent the day getting all steamed up about the competition. Not Parberry or McGarva; this time the two of them were drinking together and directing their anger toward a new trucker that started up by the name of Bill Coombes. He had been driving for Nelles but then he got hold of a few hundred dollars and he and his brother bought a '35 Ford three-ton and got into the milk business. Always somebody was going to show Les and Parberry how to do it.

So the Coombes boys started in hauling freight and hauling milk. You still didn't need a licence at that time, although shortly after they started bringing them in and Les and Parberry both got them. But at this stage anybody could scrape up a down payment on a truck and go around offering to haul milk ten cents a can cheaper. The Coombeses were working like hell and just about making it I guess. Well, Les and Parberry put their heads together and started figuring out what they were going to do about this. They figured there wasn't enough room for three outfits in Abbotsford and they thought this price cutting was just the worst crime in the world, never mind it was exactly what they'd done to get business away from the FVMPA. It offended their business principles. Cutting prices was about the only way anybody got any work during the Depression, yet there was this edict going around, from the government or board of trade or who all I don't know, that it was the worst thing you could do for the economy. To hear Les and Parberry you'd think they were personally charged with the responsibility of protecting the Canadian economy by doing something about these unprincipled bastards who were cutting the milk hauling price.

When we got back from Vancouver they were well into it. I think

Parberry's son Dutch was there. Dutch wasn't like his old man at all, he was a decent, quiet sort of a guy with a very dark complexion. It wasn't like him to be mixed up in something like this. Anyway there was him and me and Rendall McKinnon, I guess. We got back from the day's haul and we were buying beer and talking about our adventures and Les and Parberry were really getting into their beef with these Coombes boys. And really into their cups. "Those dirty cocksuckers… rotten bastards…" Well, by Jesus, first thing you know we're staggering up the road to where Bill's truck is parked, Parberry lifts up the hood, starts banging away at this fucking thing, cursing away, "dirty rotten cocksuckers…" And we wreck these poor guys' truck. Busted everything we could bust.

Today I just can't feature it. I can't believe I was ever party to something like that. But there we were. It was a mob kind of thing, you get sucked in. Up to that time these guys had been friends of mine and that truck was all they had. I felt damn bad about it, and damn scared. Driving out past the wreck the next day. I couldn't bear to look at it. I figured, "I'm about two hours away from the penitentiary right now." But we got away with that one, too. The Coombes boys took the hint and got out of the milk business. It went against just about everything I was raised to believe in, but I figured I was proving something, I was showing Les I was the guy he could really count on when the good of the company was on the line. I kept my truck parked right by my bedroom window for a long time after that.

It was quite a life, honest to Christ.

This was getting on late in the thirties. About 1938, I guess. One day I heard a rumour Les was taking his brother John in as a partner in the trucking business. I heard hints about it around the beer parlour and didn't believe it. John was older than Les and had all of Les's faults but none of his abilities. Les's mother was a big influence in this, she was after Les to help John out because John had lost his job in the mine up at Kilgard and was living in a shack on this little stump ranch. Les and John were always rowing; the first time I ever met them they were having a big row, a real hollering, cursing, chair-throwing affair. Normally Les had an infallible memory for anybody who crossed him, and that person was on his shit-list for life. John was the only one who could screw Les over and come back for more. Still, I couldn't believe Les would go so far as to actually put him in charge of his precious trucking business. I confronted him the first chance I got him alone and I could see he didn't want to discuss it straight out, he kept muttering about John being his brother and just because he was giving John a little break didn't change anything between us and all this. I tried to feel reassured but it was just such a damned bitter pill considering everything I had put into building the business up, working all hours and sticking my neck out, while John had never done a damn thing and didn't know a thing about it. Anyway, I was getting serious about Kay and didn't want to lose my job with the Depression still hanging on, so I decided to ride it out and see how it went.

It was worse than I feared. The way Les explained it to me, John was only going to be involved in running one of the trucks and he and I would run the other one, but John was a pushy guy with no sense of caution, and before I knew it he was calling all the shots and Les was completely in the background. He brought in a friend of his to drive the other truck, a hopeless guy named Freddy Thompson who promptly got in a bad accident. He was sailing past Victoria Drive in the fog and swung out to

The trucks were underpowered and slow but we still managed to get into some impressive smash-ups. VANCOUVER PUBLIC LIBRARY 84844A

pass a line of cars and ploughed into a flatbed loaded with steel and ripped his truck all apart. Just pure stupidity. It cut the body right off the truck. He didn't get hurt but he sure fucked everything up. I had to work thirty-six hours straight doing extra hauls before they got another truck up and running. But Freddy was just as cocky as ever, he didn't learn a thing. John was swaggering around the place barking senseless orders and bragging about all the money he was worth and making threats and everything—he's a big trucking operator now. And immediately he starts building a fancy big house to go Les one better.

Well, one day a few months in Les gets a call from the finance company and he finds John hasn't been making the truck payments. They're behind and the trucks are due to be repossessed, but they want to talk to Les before they do anything because he has always been such a good customer. He was religious about that. Even when he had no money for anything else he always found money for the payments and the gas bill. So then he hears from the gas dealer and the gas bill is in trouble too, because John hasn't been paying it, either. It turns out the silly ass has just been scooping all the money the trucks brought in and using it to pay for this house he's building. He doesn't have Les's talent for getting things done on the cheap and he's paying top dollar with money that isn't his. So, another big row between Les and John with shouting and yelling and every foul name in the book. When the dust clears Les has paid all the bills and taken back control of the business, although he leaves the partnership intact and lets John continue running the second truck.

So we go on for awhile and Les is trying to make this hopeless partnership work but John's unhappy because he's had his money cut off and he's accusing Les of stealing his share while Les and I are working like hell trying to bail ourselves out of the hole John dug us into. One night when Les and I have both been in town working late we come back to the Atangard and here's John, Parberry and Hamish Stuart, the lawyer, all sitting together and just as drunk as skunks, bombed right out of their bloody minds and ho-ho-hoing about this big deal going on.

John has sold his truck to Parberry.

Well, that washed Les's end of it right out. That was half of his business gone to the opposition. After screwing the company out of all its money,

John had turned around and sold it out from under Les—truck, shippers and licence. It wasn't his to sell—he was just a partner and couldn't legally sell without Les's consent, but they had got Stuart over and drawn up papers and it was going to be hard to undo. They keep drinking toasts to this agreement and Stuart keeps patting this briefcase in his lap where it's obvious the papers are stashed, but he makes no attempt to show them to Les, despite the fact he would have to sign off on them to make them truly binding, or so we thought. Les was stunned. We ducked into the can to talk it over and decided to play dumb and keep the party going. So we got some beer and went out to Stuart's place. Big party. Everybody's so goddamn drunk nobody can see straight but I've been keeping my eye on Stuart's briefcase and when the coast is clear I slide over and slip the papers out of it. I give Les the high sign and we beat it. Once we're out on the road I show him the papers and he's tickled out of his skin. He figures we've saved the ranch.

Well, all hell breaks loose. Where are these papers, you see? They figure right away we scooped them but they have no proof. Les gets John in a corner and tongue-lashes him over until he's got him backpedalling and denying the deal. Oh, they're howling and Stuart is threatening to put us all behind bars, but without the papers they're stuck. It turns out this is an option agreement that I've taken and they'd given John $1,500 for an option on his half of the business. He was really hurting for money and when they waved $1,500 cash under his nose, he went for it. Sold out his brother. Sold out the guy who was sticking his neck out to give him a break.

They file for an injunction to enforce the option and force us to turn over John's truck and all the shippers that go with it but Les gets his own big-name lawyer, a guy called Costilleou, a great guy, and he turns the injunction back. But it's all very confused because John still has this $1,500 and refuses to give it back. That places us all in a very awkward spot, and it also gives substance to Parberry's claim.

We go out on the haul the next day as usual and as Freddy is driving past Parberry's farm, Parberry backs a load of hay across the road. Freddy has to stop, and one of Parberry's sons jumps into the cab and takes control. So I'm at Slim Webb's waiting to switch cans and here comes our truck with Parberry's son at the wheel. I forget which one it was. Not Dutch. Parberry pulls up in his car and demands we turn over all the cans that normally go with the other truck, because these are for the shippers John signed over to him and of course the shippers are the most valuable part of the deal. I say to hell with that, and phone Les. He's all hopped up and calls the cops. The Parberry bunch is moving toward my truck, they're making to take the cans themselves, so I grab the jack handle and start waving it at them, warning them to keep their distance, and that's when the cops come up.

Well by god, we stopped 'er there. The cops said, nope, you can't just hijack McGarva's truck like that. If you have a claim to it, go to court and prove it, then we'll make sure the truck and the cans are all handed over.

So they launched a suit. It went to trial and came up before Judge A.M. Manson, the so-called hanging judge. Parberry was represented by Ian Stuart, Hamish's brother. Hamish couldn't handle it because he'd become personally tangled up in the case and they needed him as a witness. But this was a mistake on their part, going to the brother. They would have been better to call in another partner and get it out of the family, as things turned out. Oh, they had every farmer on Sumas Prairie down there witnessing for one side or the other. When Manson walks in he looks around at the crowd and says, "Well now, what mighty battle do we have here?" He was kind of an informal old bastard. He kept a spittoon beside the bench and made regular use of it.

It dragged on and dragged on and I got put on the stand. I was scared shitless. Manson declared me a hostile witness, and then I got cross-examined by both sides. Costilleou briefed you, you know—what you're going to say and what you're not going to say and what they're going to say. But it didn't go according to plan and the roof fell in on me. I don't know to this day what all I said. I remember the sensation of feeling like someone else was talking and I had no idea what he was saying. I ended up telling the truth pretty much, I think, except about stealing the papers. I managed to avoid admitting that, although I might as well have by the time Stuart was done with me. I figured I'd blown the whole case and maybe that should have happened but it turned out to be lucky for us that we were before Manson. He was notorious for his moralistic opinions and became fixated on the fact that these two Stuart brothers were involved in what he saw as unbecoming conduct for prominent members of the bar, what with all the evidence of excessive drinking, lost documents and consorting with rabble. He gave the case entirely to the McGarvas. Parberry appealed but lost that, too.

Les thanked me for saving the company and renewed his vague promises that I wouldn't be sorry and I'd get my reward but in the meantime nothing changed. John kept his nose out of our side of the business but he kept Freddy Thompson on his truck and Freddy continued to be a pain in the ass. He couldn't do anything right. Among other things he was always late for our meetings to switch cans. We'd agree to be at Slim Webb's at a certain time in the morning to switch the full cans and then again in the afternoon to switch the empties back again. The mornings were straightforward, but on the way home he'd get wandering around visiting and stopping in beer parlours and I'd be cooling my heels for hours. Then he'd show up cocky as hell, making no apologies. Finally one night I'd had enough and I told him I had better things to do than wait around for him half the night and this bullshit had to stop.

"Fock you," he says.

I whapped him.

He didn't have much fight-back and I dressed him down pretty good. He took off down the road like a goddamned jackrabbit. I was afraid he'd call the cops—that would be his style. If the cops did get into it, it wouldn't look too good because he was pretty munched up and I didn't have a mark on me. I got out the tire iron and worked myself over a bit, gave myself some lumps so I could claim it was more of a two-sided fight, but I could have saved myself the trouble. I had no problem with Freddy from that day on. There was a fair amount of squawking from John but I was used to that.

We kept on trucking. That's one thing about the milk business: the cows keep milking. You don't have the luxury of stopping to think about what you're doing or whether it's what you want to do that day because the cows are bawling with bulging udders and you gotta get out there and milk them, and the trucker has to get around and pick up the milk before it spoils and the dairy has to get it into bottles and out on the doorstep while it's still fresh. There's no let-up, no days off, no weekends. It goes 365 days a year with no breaks. The only break a guy got on that job was in Vancouver after the milk was all delivered and we were in the beer parlour waiting for the lardasses at National Dairy to finish cleaning our cans.

There was a crowd I was in made up of other drivers, people from the valley we'd brought in and local skid-road denizens. Then at the other end I had the Abbotsford gang at the Atangard, and I'd go there and hang out until closing time. I would go to bed every night drunk. In fact I'd often be drunk before I left Vancouver. One day as I was ploughing up the highway watching the sun dip below the horizon at Otter Road I realized I had driven home drunk every day for a solid month. It didn't bother me because everybody I knew at that stage was drinking just as much or more than I was. It was a way of life. I was young and in good health and I could take on quite a load and still function. The men in our group were judged by how much beer they could hold and still navigate and I could hold my own with any of them. I don't know if it worried my family but if it did they didn't say anything. Except my mother of course, but I had long ago closed my ears to her complaints, which seemed constant and endless.

The one person whose disapproval gave me pause was Kathleen Boley. I was seeing more and more of her and at first I figured her disapproval of the drinking crowd was just due to her sheltered upbringing, and thought I could educate her to enjoy it, just as I had learned to myself. But it didn't work. She didn't like drinking and she didn't like the drinking crowd. She had every reason not to, now that I look back, but at the time I couldn't see it. Drinking had opened the world to me and brought me the first real friends I ever had, and I thought it could do the same for her. I was anxious to make my friends her friends. I didn't want anything to come between me and the only social life I'd ever had.

This was the shadow hanging over us and it slowed us down but it didn't stop us. I would always go back to her and she would always be there. After a number of years of this we simply came to understand that we were going to spend our lives together. There was no dramatic breakthrough or anything, the realization just grew of itself. With other girls, there were always things that came up that wedged us apart. With Kay and me, it was the opposite. We started distant from each other and grew together.

Two milk trucks parked side by side for the twice-daily workout known as switching cans. Each truck delivered to different dairies, so we had to move all the cans for Turner's Dairy into one truck and all the cans for National Dairy into the other truck, and so on. We went through trucks so fast we didn't even bother painting our names on the door. WHITE FAMILY

We found we were compatible. Of course once the old lady got wind that we were serious she had a fit. Kay had been doing all the housework and cooking and gardening and mothering for years and the thought of having to leave her bedroom and start doing all that herself threw the old woman into a rage. At one point Kay arranged to have me come over for dinner in the hopes of showing I didn't have horns and a pointed tail but it was a disaster. The old lady started riding me about drinking and fighting and running with loose women from the time I came in the door and didn't let up until I left, which was as soon as I could make it. I never set foot in that house again, although I spent lots of happy hours in the barn with Howard. He went out of his way to show me a friendly face, as long as we were out of the old lady's line of sight, and I coddled him a bit with his milk. He was one of the few guys I'd occasionally lift a lid for—pull the cap off and on cans of day-old milk to the let the rank gases out before the dairyman gave it the sniff test. You could also switch cans from a better batch—there were lots of ways you could help a guy if you knew the ropes. It wouldn't fool the dairyman, but if you were playing ball with him he'd let you get away with it. I gave Howard lots of reasons to be thankful he had a pretty daughter.

Once Kay decided to go with me there was no holding her back. The old lady just about went into orbit. It was tough for Kay because she'd never disobeyed the old dragon before, no one in the family had, but she faced her down. I wondered where this innocent twenty-two-year-old found the courage and felt a heavy load of responsibility descending onto my shoulders. We didn't have a wedding. One day in 1939 we just went to city hall and got the five-dollar rubber-stamp job. She didn't want anything else. She had no use for frills or ceremony, she was completely down to earth and ready to get down to business. Here one day she was an untouchable ice queen, now suddenly the door's wide open. Apart from an occasional lucky break I'd been pretty much on the outside looking in at the world of women and sex up to this time and wow, here your life is suddenly flooded with it, it kind of took your breath away, but you don't dare show any ambivalence. It's weird to be talking about it like this because it was the greatest thing that ever happened to me, though I'm not sure a guy fully understood that at the time. The great parts were as great as they could be. Here was this absolutely wonderful person, and she was willing to throw everything over, devote everything that was going to be her life, to me. A guy couldn't help feeling he didn't deserve it, but there it was. It made you think you must amount to something after all, or at least in the eyes of this one other person, and at times that was all you needed. It's a bit like waking up and finding you've inherited a great estate from some relative you didn't know you had, or have been declared king of some foreign kingdom you didn't know existed. And there's just nothing like being young and in love, going back every day and it's still there, bigger and better, there's no end to it. It was all the better that it wasn't an overnight thing with us, it was a tide that rose gradually and carried us away and that made it feel less like a dream that might pop and disappear. It was wonderful beyond description. But in some ways I wasn't ready to deal with the practical side of marriage and there were stresses and strains that put kind of a crimp on it.

I managed to wrangle a week off from Les and we went on a driving honeymoon in a borrowed car. We headed down into eastern Washington state and toured the Columbia Basin where the Grand Coulee Dam was under construction. We were both fascinated by the dry belt scenery, such a different world from the lush coastal landscape where we'd both grown up, and we continued up through the Okanagan Valley and into the Cariboo, where I realized I had just enough cash left to get home. It was a wonderful break and a great way to start married life. Unfortunately it would be the last actual holiday we would take for almost twenty years.

Kay and I honeymooning in Grand Coulee country, Washington state. WHITE FAMILY

13

Married With Pigs

We rented a little house out toward Musselwhite east of town and moved in together. It was awkward at first. I think any newly married couple must find it strange and hard to get used to, and we didn't have any family support. The only one who tried to do anything for us was Florence McGarva, who gave us a big shower. She rounded up a bunch of people and said "you bring this and you bring that and you bring the other" and by the time she was done all we had to do was buy a wash basin and a cloth. When Florence got busy, there was no stopping her. Another attempt to mark the occasion didn't work so well. A couple of my drunkard friends, including Les and Tom Elliott, decided to show up in the night and treat us to a chivaree. They snuck up outside our bedroom window and started banging on empty milk cans and yelling out a bunch of lewd comments. Once I realized what it was I was kind of tickled but Kay wasn't having any of it. She hoisted up the window and really let those poor buggers have it: "You people get out of here and leave us alone! You're not funny and we don't want you here! Now go home!" She was steaming. I was surprised. This was a side of her I hadn't seen before and I didn't know what to make of it.

I started missing my regular sessions at the beer parlour to be with Kay but it was hard for me. This was my crowd. This was who I'd become. They rode me a bit about being pussy-whipped and one night old Tom and them got full of booze and came banging into the house. "Get up, ya silly bastard,

Kay Boley and I got married in a civil ceremony in 1939 and rented a little place out in Musselwhite three miles east of Abbotsford, where we got busy raising pigs. WHITE FAMILY

get up and have a drink." We were in bed asleep and they barged right into the bedroom and started shaking me, reaching over Kay. Well by God, she blew up and she hit them and Les fell back overtop of Tom and they were both rolling on the floor and Les said, "Look out, look out! She'll kill ya!" She picked up a big book and *whap! Whap! Whap! Whap!* They both got out of there. I was as amazed as they were. Normally Kay was the quietest, mildest little thing you could hope to meet, but I had to hold her back: "Hold it, don't do that!" Oh, I think she just might have killed them if she'd had anything better than a book. "Get out! Get out!" she was screaming. They didn't know what hit them. The kind of women they were used to—and the kind I'd gotten used to—would have laughed, got up and gotten them all beers and had one herself. But Kay wasn't that kind of a girl.

That changed my life right there.

I'd got in the habit of bringing the guys over to our place to drink—I guess maybe I thought this would be better than just being away at the beer parlour all the time and sometimes we'd keep at it until we were pretty blotto. I knew Kay didn't like it but she wasn't one to argue a point, she'd mostly just disappear into the bedroom and sulk. But one day when I brought the boys over she met us at the door with a big hello! And I couldn't believe my eyes. Kay, who normally never finished a single beer, was bombed out of her mind. She was kissing the guys and carrying on something awful. I don't know if she actually said to me, "Is this the kind of woman you want me to be?" but that was the idea. She was giving me a dose of my own medicine, or trying to. She didn't make a very convincing drunk.

It was goddamned embarrassing for me, but I couldn't talk to her about it at all. She was putting me in the position where I had to choose between her and my friends, between her and the only real sense of belonging in the world I'd ever felt, and I didn't want to make the choice. It was unbelievably stressful and I just didn't know what to do. I just kept hoping things would get sorted out.

Kay was always a great gardener and it wasn't long before she had a little vegetable patch going in the backyard and one day I ran into this guy with about ten weaner pigs to get rid of. He was practically giving them away so I grabbed them and took them home. At first Kay was appalled; she had raised pigs and knew what a project it was, how much they stunk and most of all how much they ate. "We have no garden waste," she said. "It will cost us more than we have to feed them." But I had an idea. There was this guy making puffed wheat in a shed on First Avenue in Vancouver. First Avenue only went out a short way then and it was all brush and this guy got this big gun for puffing wheat up. Melograin something they called it—that was where Melograin got started. And the man running it was a nice guy. Puffed wheat has to be screened out because quite a bit of the wheat doesn't puff completely and he would build up quite a pile of these culls. He agreed to sell me a few barrels a week for practically nothing and I knew I could go down to the dairies and buy skimmed milk for ten cents a hundredweight, so that's what I did. Once Kay saw the possibilities, she got right into raising these pigs. Well, these pigs just swelled up on this diet of puffed wheat and milk and did they ever make a mess of that little yard, but when they got about half grown we turned around and sold them for $300. That was the most money we'd ever had.

Meanwhile things were getting worse for Les. His health was going downhill fast and he was having a harder and harder time holding things together. I had told Kay I was in line to become a part owner in the trucks and used that as an excuse for keeping on with the seven-day-a-week work and all the other bullshit involving Les, but Les kept dodging making a commitment. One day he said to me, "Hey, how'd you like to set that little hellcat of yours up with a nice farm?"

Kay and I had actually talked about raising more pigs and saving up to do just that, and I knew there was nothing she'd like better. She didn't like the trucks because she associated them with my drinking.

"How would I ever do that on what you pay me?" I said. I was still only making sixty a month.

"An old farmer I know died and his widow's selling his place. She's sick too and I think you could get it pretty cheap," he said. I knew this place and it was a beautiful little farm, eighty acres of prime bottom land with a good herd and decent fixtures.

"That would be nice, but I doubt the price would ever come low enough to be in my reach," I said.

"You go check it out and see what kind of a deal you can get. If it's what I think, let's talk. I think we could probably work something out."

"You mean you'd back me?"

"If it looked good, yeah, I'd do that."

Well this was like a dream come true. I couldn't wait to get home and tell Kay. Partly because I knew she'd love it and partly because she might see this Les McGarva she was so sure was just playing me for a sucker wasn't such a bastard as she thought. I was hoping he would turn out to be not quite so much of a bastard as he sometimes seemed to me, too.

Meanwhile I kept driving and drinking and spending a lot of time with my beer parlour buddies. I knew Kay wasn't happy with that side of things, but I didn't know what else to do, and like I said, I didn't see anything wrong with it. I thought she was the one who had to change. One day when Les was in town with me we got drinking late at the Princeton and closed the place down. We were pretty loaded, and Les started wrangling with some guy outside the pub. I slid over to head off trouble and the guy took a swing at me. Next thing, a full-scale donnybrook. There were guys climbing on my back, guys charging me from the front, guys coming from all angles and I was doing my best to beat them back. One guy put his arm around my neck from behind so I turned and landed a haymaker into his gut. As he went down I saw a flash of blue. It was a Vancouver city cop. If I hadn't been quite so drunk and hadn't had Les to look after, I think I would have had sense enough to get the hell out of there right fast. But I kept battling, and the first thing I know about six cops have me pinned to the asphalt and I'm off to the slammer.

In one way I was lucky. I could have been charged with assaulting an officer and put away for six months. Instead, the cops decided to treat me to their own brand of justice. They got me in a cell and took turns beating on me until I was an unconscious bloody pulp. At one point after I was totally helpless I remember the cop I'd accidentally walloped jamming his thumbs in my mouth and breaking my palate. When I woke up I couldn't see and couldn't talk. Les got Costilleou and he sprung me and created such a fuss about the beating the cops backed down and let me go without laying charges.

It wasn't a lesson I needed. I had known for a long time most cops are out looking for trouble if they can get it, but the stupid bastard came up behind me. You come up behind a guy in a fight, you know he's going to defend himself first and ask questions later. Anyway, I was a mess. I had to have my mouth reconstructed and was damn lucky the damage wasn't worse or I might have gone through life sounding like a harelip. But it was bad enough. Kay was horrified. It confirmed every bad thing she'd thought about my drinking and my friends. She must have been really wondering what she'd got into and wishing she'd listened to her mother's warnings. But she stood by me and nursed me and I didn't miss more than a couple days of work.

It was becoming clearer things were not well in the McGarva world. Les was really starting to show signs of coming apart at the seams. He had the shakes something terrible and he was losing weight to beat hell although at the same time his face had gone all puffy. He never ate properly anymore and couldn't hold his liquor worth a damn—a couple drinks and he'd be right out of it. There was something wrong with his skin, too, he was getting sores and bruises all over. I realize now his liver was shot. You had to wonder how long he could keep things together. Then there was John always in the background. He was still fucking things up on a regular basis and constantly whining away about this or that. He hated me because he saw me as competition for Les's favour and in his warped way of seeing things he had it that I made him look bad in the Parberry debacle although in truth I'd saved his ass. Having to deal with him as a partner in the trucking business, supposing I ever did get brought in as a part owner, was not appealing. No way I wanted to be shackled to that miserable sonuvabitch. That made the idea of the farm all the more attractive.

I took Kay out to the widow's place and she just went head over heels. It was first class and she was just in ecstasies at the thought of making it ours. Just as Les said, the old widow was desperate to sell. She was asking around $2,000—a steal even in those times, but it sounded like she was ready to go even lower. I told Les it was a go from our side and he said great, that was just great. I asked him what we needed to do to set the deal up and he said he would get back to me. Weeks passed. Kay got impatient. She couldn't understand it. Les had said, "I'll buy you guys that farm, I'll back you on that farm." And then for some reason started to renege after. He'd got drunk and told people and they were saying, "You're a goddamn fool. Don't do that." He'd made money on the farms he bought and couldn't see why it wasn't a good deal. Which it was. This was an incredible thing. Eighty acres, house, barn, good soil right on Sumas Prairie. I had to get Les to put up $1,700, that was what it came to. Either guarantee it at the bank, which he could do without costing him a nickel, or by taking the mortgage himself, which would let him make money on it. Either way there was no risk because the value was there. I couldn't understand his reluctance. It was Les who came to me with that deal: "Hey, real deal here." But after he got all hotted up about it, he started to back off. People around him, principally John and his mother, were dead set against him helping us and harangued him no end. "What do you want to stick your neck out for Frank for? You don't owe him anything. If you have money to throw away, you should help your own brother. He wouldn't be in the trouble he's in if it wasn't for you." And so on. Les started to change his tune, saying, "What do you want a farm for? You're not a farmer. That farm is too small anyway, we'll find a better one…" Eventually we realized Les was not going to come through for us. Kay was beside herself. I was right out of my tree.

The widow kept lowering her price. She really wanted us to have it. Eventually it was down to $1,500, just a crazy price for what she had, but we only had the $300 in savings. We could only get a mortgage if somebody would sign for us at the bank.

In desperation, Kay went to her mother. The old lady was still pretty hostile but the fact remained that she had solemnly promised to buy Kay a house if she would quit school and look after the farmhouse, and Kay had more than fulfilled her part of the bargain. Now we only needed her to back a note for $1,200. No actual money involved. Tons of collateral. Today that same farm is worth $5 million. But no dice. The old lady denied ever making any promise to Kay and told her anything she had coming went out the window when she ran off with that no-good SOB Frank White. "God does not forgive the child that defies the parent! There is no sin more foul!" she roared. "You made your bed, now go lie in it."

That was the end of our dream of owning a farm. The widow finally had to sell her place for even less than she was asking us, some stupid sum for eighty acres, house, beautiful land right on Sumas Prairie.

It was a crushing disappointment for both of us, but even more for Kay. She cried like a child. My heart bled for her, but there was nothing

I could do. I had nobody else to turn to. I was furious with Les, and Kay was furious with her mother and resolved never to have another thing to do with her. That was a bit of a blessing in disguise. Her mother still had quite a strong hold over her up to that point, but that tore it. She saw her for the heartless monster she was then and never forgot it. I don't think old lady Boley ever set foot in any house of ours as long as she lived, at least not while I was around. I had a small amount of revenge when I ran into her son Donald a few months later and aided and abetted his escape from the old lady's clutches by driving him down to Bellingham so he could join the US Navy. He was stationed in Pearl Harbor during the Japanese raid on December 7, 1941, and stayed in the US for the rest of his life. The joke on him was he ended up married to a woman almost as sharp-edged as his mother and spent most of his life working deep sea.

The whole farm fiasco was the final thing I'd ever trust Les on, the last time he could ever screw me around. I told him he better find another driver because I'd had enough. He just nodded and said, "I thought you might be coming to tell me that." He knew better than to say anything more. We shook hands. He looked forlorn and old beyond his years. I felt kind of sorry for him but I actually felt relieved to be getting off the trucks. I'd been in more than one spot where it was a toss-up whether I got out

That's my brother Wesley in his army uniform, likely my mother in the rocking chair and my sister Gladys on the right. I have no idea what I'm doing on that table. WHITE FAMILY

with my skin intact and for some time I'd had a growing feeling my luck must be just about used up.

I had no idea how we were going to live and I never would have had the nerve to chuck a steady job without our little $300 nest egg, but I went over to Buckerfield's and old Bill Stewart put me right to work at good money. This was at the Abbotsford plant, not the Vancouver one, and it was a great place to work. It turned out I had a good reputation I didn't know about and immediately everything was better. This was 1939 by now and things were starting to move.

With me just working regular hours we finally had a chance to relax and spend some time together free of the stress caused by the crazy hours on the trucks and the drinking. I had an old rattletrap car and we went for drives, often taking Wesley with us. He loved Kay. She got on well with all of my family, except my mother, who seemed intent on doing the typical mother-in-law thing and sticking her nose in where it wasn't wanted. But it was a pleasant interlude marred only by the declaration of war in September 1939.

Before I could get a chance to talk to him, Wesley and his telegrapher buddy George Grant went down to the recruiting centre and signed up. They tried to get into the air force but the air force wasn't taking anyone right then so they went with the army. When it was discovered they were competent telegraphers, they were assigned to the signal corps, and incidentally issued spurs and a whip.

I was mad at him. I thought he should have at least talked it over with me. I couldn't believe my kid brother was in any way ready to become a soldier and possibly go overseas to take part in a shooting war. He wasn't fully grown yet, he was only five foot seven and 135 pounds, but he was nineteen so there was no stopping him. I would have liked him to hold off until I figured out if I would also have to join up, then we could go together and I could look out for him. He liked the idea of us going overseas together but it was very unclear in the early stages of the war when and if married men would be called up and I wasn't about to force the issue. Meanwhile he was all excited to be getting out of Abbotsford and going off to see the world, and I couldn't really blame him. But I worried. Our family had already lost enough.

Part 3

INTO THE WOODS

14

Hauling Logs

The trouble with the Buckerfield's job was that it was seasonal and during the slack season when the farmers weren't buying seed or feed, I wasn't getting enough hours. I still kept in touch with the truck-driving crowd and dropped in on old Bill Schnare's garage where they hung out. One day I became aware of something new going on, something even newer than milk trucking: log trucking.

There's a lot of jaws been broken over the question of where and when trucks first got into the woods—hell, they can't even settle on where the first logging railroad was, and trucks are a lot harder to keep track of than trains.

There were trucks in the woods before 1939, lots of them, but they weren't getting all that far. Trucks were taking over every other hauling job there was by the mid-twenties so it didn't take any brains to try them on logs. Tretheweys had an old White around their mill, must have been 1922, and you'd see it struggling by once in awhile with some old stump rancher's logs chained on, but that was kind of a joke.

Trucks couldn't be used the way they were operating in the woods those days, they were too rough. Those old bush apes were used to clubbing ox teams on the skid road and crashing around in the woods with heavy steam equipment. They just didn't have the touch, their touch was too heavy—they'd wreck a truck just loading it. Everything in the woods those days was made to be thumped around. If they hit a flat car with a log, the worst that would happen would be it would jump off the track, and if that happened they'd just hook on a tong and yank it back.

I remember seeing them flip a truck loading with a duplex at Haney once. They set it back up real quick and kept on loading just like it didn't happen. The truck drove away under its own power, but as she took the turn out of the landing you could see the old wooden cab slouch off to one side like it was going to slide right off.

To those old-time loggers trucks were just too frail and fussy. It threw them off to have one on the claim. Gas engines made their heads spin. They could get along without them. It was the age of steam. They were still logging the valleys, rolling out big trainloads of first-growth fir all day. When the going got scratchy, they just pulled stakes for the next valley. Lay track down the middle, set up the skidder and the skyline, and haul wood for all they're worth.

In '58 I was driving for Blondie Swanson above Theodosia Inlet and you could look down and see where Merrill, Ring and Moore logged in the thirties. There were big spoked wheels, a mile across, side by side the length of the valley. It was all back in second-growth by this time and you didn't notice it at first but once you did you couldn't miss it, the old yarding patterns in the shading of the new growth. We were up 3,200 feet in the last bit of timber on the mountain, which is the real change in logging from their time to ours. While they had the big valleys full of first-growth fir to log, it's no wonder they laughed at trucks.

They say the first truck show on the coast, the first one designed to have all the hauling done by trucks, was Forbes Bay, just by the mouth of Toba Inlet, in 1926, and that may have been the first big one. I never saw it myself, but I heard tell of some outfit where they used a truck to drag logs over a skid road well before that.

There was another outfit that tried to use trucks on pole rails with concave wheels. You can see how they were thinking—they were thinking here's a horse that doesn't get tired, here's a locomotive that only costs $800. They treated it like a locie too, they built a raised track out of timbers, a fore-and-aft road it was called because the timbers were laid fore and aft instead of crossways like a puncheon road. It was two tracks, with squared saplings for guardrails, and open in the centre. At first they used sixteen-inch tracks, then the compensation board made them come up to thirty-two. Built on a gentle slope just like a railroad because of the no brakes, and no sharp turns because they couldn't figure how to make a truck so it would turn with a load of logs on it.

Come to any gully not real easy to fill and they built a timber trestle. Now let me tell you, coming down a plank road in one of those old hard-tired bastards, sitting out in the open on a board seat, a couple three-thousand-board-foot logs jiggling around up behind your head, no bulkhead for protection, that steering wheel kicking like a bull in your hands and mechanical brakes—you were earning your two dollars and eighty cents a day. Trestles rattling and jumping around, mud squeezing up between the planks? With mud or a touch of frost holding that thing on the track was like holding a greased pig. You sure tried, because to go off meant you went over, and not too many guys survived that. They nailed down everything they could find for rip-rap, to give the timbers some grip: branches, canvas, wrinkled tin. The standard was old strawline—light-gauge cable. It got better as it got whiskerier. But still they killed men like flies.

I can remember one of the old-time drivers talking about driving up at Brown Bay—that was what Brown and Kirkland called one of their early truck camps. He said you'd be looking through the gaps in your floorboards going over a trestle and seeing straight down through seventy feet of clear open space. Boards broke and jillpoked all the time—god! When he started out they asked him if he thought he could handle it and he'd said, oh yeah. One trip and that was it. He told the push, "I can see how you get a man to do that once, but I don't know how you get 'em to do it twice." In the Depression, with families starving, it wasn't so hard.

It was a ridiculous thing to do with a loaded truck if you think about it, try and support it for miles on a wooden platform, but coming to it after years of skid roads and railroads, it must have looked like the logical thing to do. It took a fortune's worth of timber, and you couldn't use it again like rails, so it was something only the big camps could afford. On top of that they couldn't keep the trucks running. I remember hearing that truck logging had failed, something in the same way you hear balloon logging failed.

But some outfits kept trying and got it working pretty slick. Jeremiason

Before WWII most logging operations were large-scale affairs that built railroads down the big coastal valleys to move the logs to tidewater. But as the valley bottoms got logged out and loggers moved up the steep sidehills, railroads weren't as practical anymore. CITY OF VANCOUVER ARCHIVES LOG P28

had a pretty good show up Vancouver Bay, and there was a bunch of Whites working at Holberg. The most famous I guess was Pioneer Timber at Port McNeill. The set-up at Pioneer was the work of the head mechanic, Archie McKone. There was a real gyppo Edison, Archie McKone. Every camp he was at was full of gadgets and cute ways of doing things he invented. There were a lot of Gyro Gearloose types in the woods at that time, I guess the problem attracted them: get those logs in the water without working so hard. The main improvement at Pioneer was the McKone pre-loader, which eliminated the delay and banging around of loading. The trucks had detachable bunks, the racks used to hold the logs on the truck, and they'd build the load on a spare set of bunks while the trucks were away, then when one came back he'd just drop the bunks he had and back under the loaded ones. It was used for a long time. Everyone copied it.

McKone had a pretty slick way of turning trucks around at the dump too. At Port McNeill it was a special problem because the bay is shallow and the road went a way out on piles. They could have backed up or built a long loop using miles of piles, but instead McKone built this turntable at the end so that when you drove onto it you hooked a cable, and the cable pulled on a drum that turned the whole thing around as the truck moved ahead, and by the time you got to the end you were back where you started, pointing the other way.

They made the fore-and-aft system work, but look at the trouble and expense to build something like that. They still couldn't go up really steep hills, and the timbered road was very inflexible. You left it where it was and brought logs to it same as a railroad. So it didn't cause any real major change. You still stuck to the valleys and used huge yarders with elaborate cable systems to reach way far out for logs.

McKone was a master craftsman and famous in the woods. He built trucks himself, from scratch. I ended up owning one of his creations at a later stage. It's funny, thinking about it, because Schnare wasn't anywhere near the man McKone was, he was just a little wizened-up old deaf mechanic from Abbotsford, and he never invented a damn thing, he didn't even bring anything into the woods, anything that other guys here and there hadn't tried already.

Schnare wasn't even a logger, he'd never been near the woods. But he was the guy, from his dirty little garage in Abbotsford, who saw where

Early hard-wheeled trucks hauling logs on a plank road. With a bit of frost or mud on the planks it was very hard to keep those hard rubber tires from sliding over the edge, and when that happened the driver's life expectancy was not very good. HARBOUR PUBLISHING

logging was heading before anybody else. He had some of the same ability to see ahead that McGarva had.

It really starts with the three-ton truck. Detroit started making three-tons I guess in 1932. They'd made some bigger trucks before that, and they'd made lots in the one-ton range, but these were the first what you'd call modern trucks. These were the same trucks Les adapted for milk hauling but it took awhile to get them into the woods. Schnare did a lot of our repairs when I was driving for McGarva and he used to make Les mad as hell.

"You guys don't know how to use trucks," Schnare would say. "I could put twenty tons on those trucks." We'd go as high as eight tons on them sometimes, and they'd just be dragging their belly pans down the road. Schnare figured he knew everything because he'd run steam thrashing machines on the Prairies, and we thought the old coot was just talking silly. I know what he was thinking now. He was thinking he'd make them into six-wheelers—put tandem axles on the back—like he did on all his trucks. It wouldn't have worked for us though, we had to zip into town and back, and hauling that much weight would have slowed us down.

Schnare was a pretty snarly old bugger, but there was always something going on at his place. Things were always happening to him and he was always telling about it, like the time he was in the York Hotel and the window stuck. Somehow the damn thing fell down on his arms and he had to shout down onto the street for someone to go in and tell the desk. He was close to sixty, I guess.

I was there when he got his first truck. He had a Ford dealership and he sold these two guys a 1934 three-ton truck for hauling into a tie mill. They didn't make any payments and finally Schnare went out looking for them.

"Cakzickers took off on me but I got the gaddam truck," he says. It was all battered and rigged up in some haywire way for hauling poles and he didn't know quite what to do with it.

"Mack, you tek that goddam truck," he says to Rendall McKinnon. "You could mek money hauling logs."

We all figured he was trying to suck somebody in, and he was I guess, but what happened was his son Stan, I guess Stan was seventeen or eighteen

Primitive White truck on a fore-and-aft timber road. At first they treated trucks like railroads and tried to run them on a track made of wood. It was awkward and expensive and dangerous.
HARBOUR PUBLISHING

then, he was listening to it all and afterwards he persuaded the old man to let him quit school and go hauling logs with this truck.

Well, by god if Stan didn't do alright, and the old man started to get interested. The next thing you know old Schnare was going around saying, "They don't know how to use trucks in the woods. I can haul four times what they're hauling with the same trucks." Still, nobody took him very seriously because all he ever had to do with trucks was working on them in the garage, he had never run them.

Schnare, he had quite a few other trucks he'd sold to other guys, and everybody was behind on them, it was the Depression and there was no money anywhere, so whenever he wanted one he just had to go out and get it.

So he took back two more trucks and sent them out hauling logs. Somewhere he found bogeys and made them into six-wheelers. They were the first six-wheelers in the woods that I know of and it was true it made them a far better machine, especially on the rough dirt roads.

Then he got the contract up on Vedder Mountain and he rigged up three more old Fords. That's when Schnare said to me one day, "Why don't you come driving with me and make some real money?" Things were slow at Buckerfield's and I'd been pining to get behind the wheel again so I said, "You bet."

They were logging up behind Cultus Lake in a patch of timber right up on the mountain. B & K had logged out the whole valley all up around the mountain, but this patch had been left because it was too steep to get the railroad in to it.

You couldn't see the fir in that forest. It as all cedar and maple, thick—you couldn't see the sky anywhere, and every once in awhile there'd be a big black pillar going up into the maple leaves. That's all you saw of these big firs from the ground. You honestly couldn't see any more than that, it was so thick in there. They smashed it all down, it was a different world. But God it was lovely wood. I've never seen fir like that again. The logs were so big the tongs wouldn't open wide enough to grip them, they had to chop notches. For a month I averaged just over three logs to the load, and there were lots of one-log loads. The biggest I think was 8,700 board feet. And it was a buckskin (an old windfall that had lost its bark)—and only thirty-two feet long. Nine feet I think, nine feet at the butt, and straight. It sat in the landing for a long time and we kept wondering which one of us was going to get it. Finally they gave it to

The Pioneer Timber camp at old Port McNeill. You can see the problem: once you get your truck and trailer out to the end of that long pier to dump its logs, how do you turn it around? Archie McKone's solution was a turntable the truck activated as it moved forward. HARBOUR PUBLISHING

Les Bates on Number Three with the reason that he was the oldest. Also didn't have a family.

Top heavy! If that log rolled six inches to one side the truck would go down the bank like a dog wrestling with a bear. Those one-log loads were cinched to the frame, that's what I hated—they would take you with them.

Schnare put me on a 1936 Ford truck and took me up the hill on a road the likes of which I had never seen before—tracks two planks wide and crooked and steep. Cats were dragging in huge logs five, six, eight feet through. Roy Wells was loading trucks with a crotch-line and haulback rig and Curly Chittenden was punching the Clyde yarder. When I saw them banging those huge logs around on those little old trucks I thought they were all crazy. Thankfully Roy would let you spot the truck, then hop out before they picked up the log. You couldn't stay in, the way they'd knock the truck around, it would buck you out, or else spear you on the gearshift. The goddamn old cab would crash and flap, I thought it would fly right off. Not that it would have been much loss—it didn't have any windows or doors as it was.

The goddamn things were so overloaded you could pop the rear end just starting out in the landing. You could twist off an axle anytime you wanted. Hitting a pothole you didn't even see, the truck would heave like a schooner in a gale and creak and squawk. It was bloody frightening with all that hill in front of you. And there was a lot I didn't know about driving with a trailer. If you hit the truck brakes before the trailer brakes and the cinches had worked a little loose, the logs would slip ahead and jam against the bulkhead, the wall of timbers that kept logs from sliding forward and squashing the cab. Then the truck would be load-bound, meaning the truck couldn't bend in the middle to steer. The front wheels would just skid across the corner into the bank. There was no way to move the logs and no power saws, so you got out the axe and chopped the ends of the logs back a foot or so so they would stop binding on the bulkhead. After I chopped twice through one six-foot butt I started catching on pretty fast. Coming up for my first load a plank flipped up and jillpoked the trailer off into the ditch. Then coming down the second time I got too close to the edge to let some French fallers pass and the goddamn old single-axle trailer pushed the shoulder out. I lost the load and they had to bring the Cat three miles to pull me out.

I was thinking, good God, how do these guys do it, because I'd driven half a million miles on the highway and I figured I knew how to handle a truck. But here I was, for the first two days I never got a load down to the dump. Schnare showed up the second day, and instead of firing me as I expected he would, he put his hand on my shoulder and said, "You're going to be all right. I've got a new Columbia trailer for you."

He could be good, but he was so miserable most of the time you don't remember. Your time was always short, and any bill he ever paid he'd scribble "S&S Trucking, 5% off" and shave a couple bucks off. That was just the price of dealing with Bill Schnare. But men paid it, that was the thing about logging. Men would do things for a guy like Schnare they would never do for MacMillan or the companies because he was a character, a person. You could talk to him. You might be making the tight old bastard rich, but that gave you a feeling of satisfaction in itself.

Well, after I got the new trailer I was away. That's another thing. I didn't know the reason I couldn't stay on the road was because of the goddamn haywire single-axle trailer I had. I thought it was something wrong with me, and so did the other guys. Schnare could see it was the trailer, but that was so obvious as soon as I made one trip, it was hard to even give him much credit for knowing it.

15

The Farmer Who
Changed Logging

Those trucks of Schnare's looked so goddamn awful you were afraid to get in them, in case they would fall down and you'd be trapped in the wreckage. They had mechanical brakes, which were of even less use in the woods than on the highway. One day I tightened my truck brakes up and on the first application the truck stopped dead. The back bogey slid back and pulled the brake rods so tight I had to back up to release them. After awhile you had all the soft spots picked out on the road where you could make an emergency stop if you had to. We shuttled back and forth, watching our turnouts to pass the other trucks. Late one Friday, I was dashing back for the last load and around a corner I met Ivan Blair hurrying down to get home early. We set our brakes and sat looking at each other, waiting for the crash, and knocked each other's radiators off. When we could see each other again through the smoke and steam, we were both laughing.

The reason Schnare could get by was that on the trailers he had real good brakes—five-inch drums with vacuum assist, which was new then. The first trailer I used, believe it or not, had no reserve vacuum tank, just a line from the manifold to the hand valve and direct to the boosters. Simple and foolproof, it worked well. Later trailers had some new features: a reserve vacuum tank and a relay valve, which was supposed to dynamite the brakes on a vacuum loss but that didn't always happen. I soon learned that on a frosty morning ice would form in the relay valve and when the brakes started to fade I had to stop the truck any way I could, and fast. Then I had to get out and make a torch with a gasoline rag on a stick and warm the trailer valve.

To stop the brakes from burning up coming down Vedder Mountain Schnare rigged up little water tanks on each trailer, and you'd just stop at the top of the hill and open the taps so the water trickled onto the brake drums to keep them cool. That was a hell of an improvement. With that, Schnare's trucks could handle the hills, and with the extra axles and big tires he could handle heavy loads on dirt roads.

Like I say, none of this was new or even new to the woods, except maybe the tandem axle idea. All these things were sitting around waiting for someone to put them all together on one truck. It was like coming up to a chess game, and suddenly realizing one side has his pieces set up so he can clear the board in three moves, but they don't see it because they're thinking some other plan. That was the way Bill saw logging in 1934. It had to be, or how else could some deaf old farmer with a dirty little garage out in Abbotsford walk in and take over like he did?

After I got the new trailer I had no more trouble staying on the road, but I still wasn't getting the loads. I couldn't get the goddamn old truck into high gear down on the flat. "I'll fix that," Bill says, "I got sumpnin will get thet truck moving." So one day he flags me down and he's got a supercharger. Well it was a little better, but I still couldn't get up there, she wouldn't hold on in high. So Bill says, "Here, I'm going to come with you. I know that goddamn truck'll go faster'n thet." It frosted you a little, because old Bill had never driven a load of logs himself.

So I get rolling and get into second and just about ready to go into third, and he shouts, "No, no, no!" He's signalling faster. So I keep my foot down on the gas and the poor little V8 is hammering and screaming, I wouldn't have thought it could stand it. "Okay!" he says, and I drop it into third. Going into fourth I wait 'til my foot won't stay down anymore, it's just shaking, but when I reach for the knob I can see him waving—it's so loud you can't hear—"No, no!" and I keep pressing until there's waves of heat pouring back over us and I'm watching for the pistons to fly up through the hood—"Now!" he says. Taking that extra bit all the way up, you could just get her to stick it in high if you kept her pinned right wide open, and that's how you'd go from Sardis right to the river, clear across the Fraser Valley.

I went through a motor every three months but that's what Schnare liked. Bill bought those Ford flathead blocks for seventy dollars each, and in the six trucks he had we were changing a motor almost every Sunday. He spent half his time scrounging old parts, and whenever anything bust, he'd be right there and shove in a new one. Breakdowns didn't scare him— he was a mechanic. That's where he had it over the loggers, they were afraid of things going wrong with trucks because they didn't know what they'd do if they did.

One day we were working on the rear end of one of the trucks, and got it fixed but when we went to button it up it turned out we had the wrong gasket. We were sitting there cursing when Bill came along and said, "What the hell! Put a piece of string around it!" So we got some butcher's string, wound it from bolt to bolt, tightened 'er up and away the truck went. After that whenever something went wrong, somebody would say, "Put a piece of string around it."

Tires were a number-one headache. They had to keep Cats off the road because tires were so poor that sharp rocks cracked by Cat tracks would pierce the low-grade wartime rubber. Jimmy Robson picked up a bucketful of sharp rocks off the road, took them into the B & K office and dumped them on a desk to show why he couldn't haul at their price.

One day a truck showed up at Schnare's with a load of tires. A couple of days later, Bill came around and asked, "Where did you put those tires?" Well, they were already on the truck and trailer wheels where they would do the most good. "My God, that was $2,000 worth of tires," he shouted. "I didn't mean for you to use them all up at once!"

We were getting paid five dollars a day and two dollars if we got over four loads, and one week in August I was top driver with sixty-five dollars. I had the pleasure of making $165 that first month, big money then. I figured there was nothing but money working in the woods.

Goddammit, I liked it. It was a big job and I was good at it. We had those haywire old trucks working so you couldn't imagine how it could be done better. You got so you could hear the truck, you got so tuned to its noises and the feel of it you could tell how it was working, you'd had the whole thing together and apart so many times you were conscious of every goddamn bearing and how it was turning. You'd see a new grease spot on the ground in the morning and think that goddamn seal's getting loose again, and if you didn't fix it at least you'd make sure the thing didn't run short of oil. If anything started to go on the brakes you'd catch the slight change in the pedal or notice a wet spot on the wheel. When you get that sharp you get to the point nothing's an accident, it's always you missed something or ignored something, nothing really serious happens so long as you're on the bit.

And if you did get into something, you knew how to get out of it. Say you lost your brakes—the water got plugged and the brakes started to burn up. A green driver wouldn't know what was happening until suddenly he was freewheeling down the hill, and there's nothing to do but jump and let the truck go and probably get run over doing it. A guy who was on the bit would have seen the steam getting thin in the mirror five, ten minutes before. Even if the green guy did catch that he would have probably dynamited right there and pushed the drums all out of shape or he would have headed straight for the ditch and put the logs through the cab. The

When Detroit began mass-producing 3-ton trucks around 1932 they probably didn't have this end result in mind. Abbotsford mechanic Bill Schnare modified highway trucks for log hauling by adding extra axles, which allowed them to haul heavier loads on dirt roads. This was far cheaper than fore-and-aft timber roads and a lot handier. HARBOUR PUBLISHING

guy who knew what he was doing would pick a good spot to go off, an in-curve where he could get the trailer hung up first, before the truck.

You got so slick at everything you'd start taking shortcuts, like using the brakes to help get around a corner—if you touch the truck brakes you turn sharper, if you touch the trailer brakes you straighten out. Even a little thing like a mud puddle. A driver who knows his brakes are hot would go half off the road to get around a little puddle, but a careless guy will plough right through it and the cold splash would crack the drums. Then the truck would run away and they'd tell his widow, "The brakes failed."

There's a million things, but you get so goddamn smart after awhile you get thinking nothing can happen to you.

I'm sure if a historian were to write a book about truck logging he would start with some old farmer with a Model T and never mention Bill Schnare, except maybe in a list. But I remember people talking after that show on Vedder Mountain. There were claims like that all over the country, that the big railway camps had left because they were considered inaccessible. Now Schnare and this little gyppo had gone in with an old 75 Cat and a haywire little donkey, punched in a dirt road, laid planks in the soft spots, kept moving the road close to the timber so the yarding was short, and they made real money.

There were sidehill stands all up and down the coast, every logger knew of a few, and all of a sudden here was a way they could be logged. Old trucks were suddenly at a premium, and anybody who could get together a haywire little Skagit donkey and a truck was going logging on their own. This was the real beginning of independent truck logging, small operators with a dozen or so men working small claims, who soon formed the Truck Loggers Association and challenged the big companies in the 1940s and 1950s, before the big boys used politics to put an end to it. While it lasted it produced what I think of as the golden age of the independent logger. Here was a way the ordinary guy could start up on his own and create work for a few of his friends and pretty soon you had thousands of gyppo camps operating all up and down the BC coast and through the Interior.

Schnare was picking up more old trucks wherever he could get them and taking jobs all over. He'd hear about some operator starting up or thinking of starting up. Then he'd go talk to them and first thing he'd have

Bill Schnare talking to one of his drivers, probably telling him he should be getting more loads and using less fuel at the same time. Bill was a tight old cuss but he played straight with his men and got the best from them. WHITE FAMILY

them sign one of his "contracts." They were the damndest things—he'd write them in pencil in a battered old notebook he had, with all his own wording, and they probably weren't worth a damn in a court of law but to him they were like the Ark of the Covenant. When we were finishing up at Vedder I remember he got all excited about measuring the distance we'd been hauling because he had it in the contract that if the haul got over twenty miles the price would go up. "I know it's over twenty miles goddammit, we gotta figger some way of measuring that road." What he finally did was, he painted a white spot on one of my back tires at the dump, then followed me all the way up in his car, counting the turns of the wheel. "Drive slow," he says. The way he figured it all out it came to just over twenty miles, and he made the logger pay a couple hundred bucks extra.

One day when I had some time off I got word old Tom Elliott had come up to Abbotsford and was visiting with the McGarvas. I hadn't seen him in a good while so I threw a dozen of beer in the back of my old panel van and headed over there. Nobody was home, just Tom, so I said, well come on for a ride. There was a little patch of timber up at Hope I wanted to look at up there, up on the hill. Anyhow, he said, "No, I don't want to go." I said, "Ah, come on." Then he looked in the back and saw the beer and said, "Well, when will you be back?"

"Oh we'll be back by four, five o'clock."

"Oh well, okay, sure." There was just a wooden butter box on the passenger side to sit on.

So we were drinking this beer and I looked at the timber and it really looked nice. You see, I was thinking like everybody else—get a truck, get a little Skagit donkey and go logging on my own. This was a few miles this side of Hope, so Tom said, "Well, we're this close, let's go on up to Hope. It's a long time since I was there." So we stopped in Hope, had a few drinks, then he said, "You know, now that we've come this far, I'd like to see that new highway they're building over to Princeton, let's have a look at that. We got time, don't we? But we better get a bottle of gin. We gotta have something to drink." We went out to the end of where they were working on the Hope–Princeton Highway and had a look. Oh, god, Tom is excited all to beat hell over this big construction project that is going to be a new route to the Interior.

"I wish it was open right now," he says, "I could use a little visit to the dry belt, get outta this goddamn rain... Say, how long would it take us to get up to Boston Bar? We got time to go to Boston Bar and still get back, don't we?" We went up to Boston Bar and had some beer but the sky still wasn't quite clear. Boston Bar isn't quite sagebrush country, it's got one foot in the coast and one in the Interior.

"Well let's go up to Lytton and spend the night," he says. "We'll get sunshine up there for sure."

I phoned Kay to say we wouldn't be back 'til morning and went on up to Lytton. I showed Tom the little pullout by the creek where my father and I had camped on our way up to Oliver in 1929.

"Si White was a prince of a man," he said.

We had a good time that night in the beer parlour at Lytton. People gather round when they hear guys like Tom start talking and he was in fine form. It turned out a lot of the oldtimers there knew people Tom knew and before long it was just like old home week. So next morning he says, "You know, we're this close, let's go over to Spences Bridge and see my cousin Agnes—it won't take us all that time."

We couldn't find Agnes, she was somewhere else, so I said, "We're not going to make it back today anyhow, we might as well go down through Oliver. I got some friends in Oliver who'll put us up, let's go see them." Oh sure. So we went over to Merritt and down through Princeton, and oh, he wanted to go through all the Similkameen and everything. He knew about Jackass John and the Similkameen gold rush of 1860 and wanted to locate Blackfoot Flat, the gold rush boom town. We frigged around there without finding much of anything then we went over to Oliver, stayed the night with the Whites. Gee, they were glad to see me. Tom said, "I didn't know you knew all these people... these are great people!" And they liked old Tom. Old Minnie, Bill's wife, she really went for him and he talked half the day in the beer parlour with Bill. Finally he said, "I wanna go down through Washington, whatta you say?"

I was counting my money by now but I had sixty bucks and that went quite a ways then, so ok, we went all along the Great Northern tracks while he showed me different places he'd worked when he was young. We went all through the Cascades and he pointed out the different division points and runaways they used to have before they made their tunnel. At one place we came to a big rock cut, so I had to hear about that. He said he'd worked for two brothers as a timekeeper when they came to this big cut. They worked and worked and drilling by hand, it was a huge blast. On the day it was set to go at eleven o'clock these brothers said, "Now Tom, you get your time books and you meet us over on the other side of the blast. We want you over there." The camp was on one side and the end of the rails was on the other side. When he got there, here was the speeder, the two brothers and the superintendent. The superintendent walked back to see the blast off. Tom was wondering about this. The superintendent comes back and says it was a dandy, it was a beautiful blast. They're all smiles and say to Tom, okay, coast is clear, you take those books back to camp where you got them. So Tom says, "What the hell is going on here?"

"Well, Tom" says one of the brothers, "You know, we didn't have a nickel left." They had borrowed all the money they could get and it was all tied up in this enormous blast. And if it had hung fire and failed to go off right, they were all going to pile on the speeder with all the financial records and get the hell out of there, leaving all the unpaid workers stuck on the other side.

We worked our way down the Columbia, got down to this Chinook Indian village near Astoria where he'd lived as a young man newly arrived out west. We were bumping along this dirt track and he said, "Hold on a minute, I think I recognize that stump." He pointed out a big cedar stump with a hollow in it and said, "I think that's the same stump I left my fishing net in when I was a kid!" I reached up inside the hollow, and sure enough, here was bunch of rotten old fishnet he'd left there fifty years earlier. That was the thing about Tom's stories, they were all true. You could tell they were true. He had no time for bullshitters.

Finally Tom said, "Holy Christ, what day is this? We better get home. I only told my wife I was going to be away for a few hours!"

It was the best accidental holiday I ever took.

Kay had been worried when I first went back to driving, knowing the long hours I'd worked on the milk haul and the rough crowd I got in with, but once she saw the hours weren't too bad and the money was good, she relaxed a little. Still, she never did completely adjust to living in Abbotsford. I had done too much drinking there and still spent a lot of nights at the

That's me with a one-log load on one of Bill Schnare's haywire Fords, giving the Compensation Board a heart attack. Schnare's first trucks didn't look like much but they changed the way we did logging in BC. WHITE FAMILY

Atangard with the old bunch, which was enough to keep her uneasy. So when Schnare asked me to take six trucks to Nanoose Bay on Vancouver Island where B & K was cleaning off a mountain patch much like the one on Vedder, she was all for it.

There was nothing to hold us, Beryl's store was booming along and Mother was doing fine with her little hat business, so we loaded up our belongings and moved to Nanoose Bay, just north of Nanaimo. Schnare had built a little camp for his crew out near Chilliwack and we had been living in one of his cabins since I went to work for him. We had no place to stay on the Island so I bought the cabin off Schnare and put it on one of the trucks. We got on the barge with it and when we got to Nanoose Bay I bought a small lot down by the head of the bay and set it up on blocks. Our own house at last!

When Wesley came home on Christmas leave in 1940, I told him I was still expecting to be joining him one of these days and got a surprising response.

"Don't do it!" he said. Then he went on to describe with some vehemence what a farce he's found army life to be. He told stories of waste and official incompetence and gun emplacements firing on each other across First Narrows and of bored gunnery crews taking potshots at innocent fishboats going past the big battery on Yorke Island in Johnstone Straits. He told of the bad food and the boredom and the demoralization of having to follow idiotic orders and urged me to do everything I could to stay out. "No use letting these idiots mess up both of our lives," he said bitterly. He had been bounced around all the coastal defence stations from Point Atkinson to Point Grey to Yorke Island to Little Mountain and back to Yorke Island and fed BS and made to participate in nonsensical exercises and he was thoroughly disgusted. "You keep out of this and look after Kay and Mother," he said.

I was really surprised by his change of heart and it certainly dampened any enthusiasm I might have been building up for signing up. But nobody knew what was going to happen. It looked like there was going to be some heavy slogging before it was over and I expected I'd be dragged into it sooner or later. It wasn't like the First World War when nobody knew quite why we were there and the experts were always predicting it would be over by spring. This time we knew Nazi Germany had to be stopped and it wasn't going to be easy. It didn't look like the Americans were going to help at this point and poor old Britain and its allies had all they could handle. But in the meantime there wasn't much we could do but get on with our lives.

Now here's something I've never quite got over. All through the Depression it was no money, no money. Families were broken up because relief wouldn't pay enough to feed two parents, kids were getting crippled up with rickets due to malnutrition and we were just told to keep tightening our belts. Calvin Coolidge was president during the twenties and he was just like these conservatives today—government couldn't afford to do anything, because that would create debt and debt would be bad for the economy. That thinking led to the 1929 crash, then in 1930 Hoover came in and it was the same story—tighten your belt down to the last notch, then make some new notches and tighten some more. In Canada we had R.B. Bennett spouting the same line. No money for starving families, no money for sick kids, no help for anybody—if you're suffering, well suffer some more. Suffering is good for the economy. Then comes the war in 1939 and suddenly money is no object. Money is everywhere. They are throwing up huge shipyards all over Vancouver and putting everybody who can walk to work at cost plus, and there's stories of crews sitting around in ship's hold playing cards all day just so the company can pad the bill. They are persuading all the women to leave their homes and go to work in munitions plants. Kay even went down to work in the Boeing aircraft plant on Sea Island for a time, building PBY flying boats. That was a great big lesson in economics for me. The very same guys who were saying we have no money to feed starving kids a few months earlier are now saying cost plus, sky's the limit for bombs and bullets, work around the clock, pile on, boys! You have to have lived through it and seen it with your own eyes to realize just what bullshit that is. It opened my eyes and it opened my whole generation's eyes. It created a whole generation of sceptics who wouldn't swallow the old line that the government can't do anything, it can't spend any money because government spending is bad for business and the interests of business have to come first every time. We came out of the war with a vast army of people wised up about that old lie and they started right in setting up strong unions and demanding a bigger share of the pie for ordinary people, which they got, and which now our governments are once again tearing down using exactly the same lines I first heard from Calvin Coolidge. The very same words! They call it neo-conservatism, but there's nothing neo about it. I've heard it all before. But people forget. Even a lesson as brutal as the Great Depression and the war only seems to last one generation.

As far as I can see economics is whatever the establishment can make you believe it is. What I have never been able to understand is—why does it take a war? Why couldn't you have propaganda campaigns and bond drives and deficit spending to end homelessness or fight global warming? My great hero was and still is Franklin Roosevelt, because he tried this in the Depression with his New Deal projects and oh, the bankers and Wall Street types denounced him like the devil incarnate and blocked his stimulation programs at every turn, and maybe that's why they only blunted the Depression, they never cured it like the war did. I somehow think there is more to it; I am not sure they ever gave the war on poverty their best shot.

16

Nanoose

The new show at Nanoose Bay was naturally up a mountain and the road wound back and forth on the way up, but coming down Schnare had them put a run straight down the face of the ridge. When you were coming up to the edge all you could see was the blue sky and the fishboats out on the gulf. Then you dove. One time I ran out of water near the bottom and the brake drums melted and welded right onto the linings. Had to cut it all up with an acetylene torch. Guys' tires were catching on fire all the time. You had your hand on the door handle a lot on that hill.

There was always a big argument about whether your brakes got hotter coming down slow or fast. Some guys claimed it was better to go fast because it meant the brakes were on for a shorter period of time. Other guys said the wheel still went around the same number of turns but it was going around faster so that made it get hotter. The fast guys argued back that it got hotter going around slow because you were pressing harder and there was more friction. They way I figured it, you have to think of your brakes as a heat pump. Their job is to drain off the potential energy of the truck at the top of the hill by converting it into heat energy on the way down. The longer you give them to pump off that energy, the cooler they end up, but I could never make guys see that.

Air brakes solved a lot of problems when they came in but it took awhile to get used to them. One time a local truck with air brakes coming

During the war the military grabbed a bunch of the bigger fishboats and turned them into makeshift patrol vessels we called "The Gumboot Navy." This is one of them photographed by my bother Wesley when he was stationed at the gun battery at Yorke Island in Johnstone Strait.
WHITE FAMILY

down with a load of logs had to stop. The driver left the truck running with the brakes set and went down to see what the trouble was. When he got back, his truck was sitting six feet below the road in the brush, with the motor running and its load of logs intact. The water had run out, air had leaked through the water tank and the pressure had dropped; the truck slid ahead a few feet, and then pressure came on and stopped it. This happened repeatedly, so that in a series of small jumps it eventually crept completely off the road. He couldn't have done it again for a million dollars.

It was at Nanoose there was this little guy head loading, Corky his name was. Bouncy kind of a guy, quick. Natural clown. Whatever he was doing, it looked funny. A head loader is in charge of loading the trucks and he signals the man running the loading machine which log to pull from the cold-deck pile and where to put it on the truck so you build a balanced load. Usually you see him standing out of the way on a stump where the loader can see him but Corky would be up on the load running around like a squirrel, dancing and waving his arms and carrying on as he helped the loader build the perfect load. It looked dangerous but he was so agile you got thinking nothing could happen to him. This day he was up on the load as usual, pushing on a log as it came down to get it to drop into the right place. I think what happened was, there was a Cat working there, and they snagged the line or something. Anyway, the log he was pushing on took an unexpected bounce and he jumped backward to get out of the way. He meant to land on the brow skid, the big log that was lying on the ground beside the truck, which should have been easy for him, he was wearing caulk boots with sharp new caulks, or spikes, in the soles and he never slipped, but the trouble with new caulks is that they tend to get clogged up with bark and stop gripping. This is what happened to him.

I was standing about fifty feet away watching. When his caulks failed to bite in like he expected he slipped right down on his ass onto the ground, his head went "crack" on the log. I remember somebody saying jeez, you can hear the echo. He just sat there against the log, and we thought he was clowning. Then somebody says, "Hey, you alright?"

He was dead. Of all the goddamned luck, right where his head hit the log there was one of these hard little knots sticking out, no bigger than a three-inch nail but sharp, and it went right through his skull. Damnedest thing you ever saw. We couldn't believe it. There were quite a few men killed around me in the woods but I think that was the only time I saw a guy catch it right before my eyes.

There was a wartime communications centre working at Bamfield where the underwater telegraph cable went across the Pacific, and our road ran under the telegraph wires where it crossed the E & N tracks. One day I was taking my trailer back to the shop and had it chained on the truck upside down to work on it. The reach stuck up in the air quite a bit higher than normal and on the way it caught the telegraph wires connecting Bamfield to the military in Nanaimo and pulled everything down including a pole. My god, I thought I was going to be placed in front of a firing squad. From all the fuss you would have thought I had personally caused the Allies to lose the war.

There was a lot of bullshit going on during the war. Every self-important local busybody got himself appointed some kind of marshal or watchman and got a special armband so he could strut around giving people orders, especially after Pearl Harbor. You'd see them marching around with buckets of sand ready to put out fires in case the Japs started bringing their subs into Georgia Strait and shelling Nanaimo, which the papers had people convinced was going to happen any day although I didn't believe it for a minute. Everybody was supposed to black out their windows at night and drive with shades around their car lights and everywhere you went here would be some of these hobby soldiers stopping you and putting you through a rigamarole. It gave me a big pain.

Quite a few other hauling contractors got going right after Schnare and by the late thirties there was a real boom in small-time operations going on all up the coast. Places like Texada Island and Jervis Inlet or up Johnstone Straits where the timber hadn't been extensive enough to interest the steam loggers or else had gotten too steep for railroads, men were swarming in with gas yarders and trucks. They'd yard a load into the tree, then to load they'd take a line rigged up with tongs, lead it through a block up the tree and pinch the end of it in the windings of the mainline drum. The tree was rigged with a lean so the tongs hung out over the truck. They called it a pinchline and it was just one of the ways of getting by with one machine. Stuff like that really got going in 1940 when Archie McKone and Jimmy Lawrence brought out a cheap, light gas yarder called the 10-10 Lawrence. You could get them for $1,200 minus the sleigh. It was the golden age of the independent logger. Up to that time most logging jobs were wage work for big companies, but now ordinary guys could start an operation of their own by saving up a few months' pay. Every time two chokermen went into a beer parlour togeth-

er, by the time they came out BC had a new logging outfit. It looked like the boom could go forever. There got to be a whole new profession called log brokers who did nothing but grubstake small loggers to go out and start up camps. They were mostly a sleazy bunch only a notch or two above the level of pimps or pawnbrokers and they made money but damn few of their clients ever did. Saul Seidler was a famous one, he had his own mill, but there were many at one time.

Just about the time everyone was

That's the head loader on top of the truck supervising the loading process. It could be a bit dangerous. CITY OF VANCOUVER ARCHIVES 586-3656

starting to talk about what a wizard Schnare was with cheap old trucks he turned around and bought four brand new fifteen-ton Macks. They were the first trucks of that size Mack sold in the BC woods, and a sharp car salesman named Charlie Philp got himself set up with the BC Mack dealership in order to deliver them. They had twelve-foot bunks and three-foot stakes and they cost $20,000 each. It was the most anyone had ever thought of spending on logging trucks and a lot of people thought the old man had made an awful mistake. People said they were too big for logging, too heavy for the roads and the small operations would never pay for them.

They went hauling at Port Douglas up Harrison Lake and nobody had ever seen anything like it. They had 502-cubic-inch motors and air brakes and they would go up twice the hill and haul three times the logs of anything else around. You couldn't stop them. That was 1938. After they had been hauling two years truck logging wasn't a small-time method anymore. It was the modern way to move logs. People had been saying trucks would never touch railroads in railroad country, but after 1941 nobody was putting any new money into railroads, they were punching in truck road. Northwest Bay was one of the first big camps to go all trucks, and in 1946 Schnare took sixteen new Macks into Franklin River for MacMillan. That was the real dawn of the new age of truck logging.

They had mobile loaders to scoot from setting to setting and the trucks were radio dispatched and they never stopped. They had Swedish steel for drilling rock to ballast the roads, they had power shovels to load it, trucks to haul it and Cats to spread it, and they were building road at the rate of thirty miles a year for the next two decades. Must have ended up with over 500 miles before they were done. The main spur was like the Trans-Canada Highway. Franklin River was designed around a new concept of logging, where you have small, mobile yarding equipment and you keep adding onto your road so you're always close to the timber. After that locies started disappearing fast.

Schnare sold out in the fifties. I don't know how much he was worth but when Matsqui District put out a bond issue for their sewers Schnare bought the whole goddamn thing. I remember the first time I ever saw Schnare, I was a kid selling raffle tickets and he grumbled and gave me a hard time, then bought the whole book of tickets. He had the first radio in

Part of Bill and Stan Schnare's S&S log hauling fleet lined up at Iron River, one of the big Vancouver Island camps in 1945. By the time the Schnares sold out in 1950, they had overseen a complete transition from rail to roads in the BC woods. WHITE FAMILY

Abbotsford. My dad and I went over to his place to listen to the Dempsey–Firpo fight in 1923. He died in 1956 at the age of sixty-six. His son Stan died five years later when a plane he was on crashed near Chicago, killing all thirty-seven people aboard. They had worked as partners from the start, calling their company S & S Trucking, although Bill was always the brains of the outfit. They were an unlikely pair to change the history of BC coast logging, but that's what they did.

Kay and I always looked back on those first years on Vancouver Island from 1940 to 1943 as the best time of our lives. We had gotten into the swing of married life and were loving it. We were away from all the evil influences of Abbotsford and the McGarva clan and making new friends like Tom and Lou Haines and Chick and Muriel Johnson, a young couple who ran a garage in Nanaimo and who introduced us to boating. The Island people were different from the valley people we'd grown up among. They were looser and freer and more attuned to the outdoors. Looking back from our new vantage point, we could see for the first time what people meant when they called the valley the Bible Belt. In the valley, even when you were cutting loose and kicking over the traces, you felt the pressure of rigid small-town morality bearing down on you. Here on the Island, nobody was religious and WASP morality was a complete non-issue. It felt a lot healthier, and it suited us fine. It was like we had finally arrived at the West Coast. It was a real novelty for me to actually have evenings and weekends off and we explored the Island in our car and went out in a terrible old inboard boat I bought. We explored the beautiful little islands out in front of Nanoose—Maude, Winchelsea, Southey, Yeo. The Winchelseas were like little wonderlands and we loved going swimming in their little bays and picnicking on their mossy knolls. Kay and I made a pact that when we got old and died, we would ask that our ashes be spread on South Winchelsea.

Chick Johnson's favourite water sport was shark hunting. We'd get a homemade harpoon and a bunch of rope and a box of beer and tear around the gulf in his speedboat until we found a basking shark dozing on the surface. Basking sharks are virtually extinct on the BC coast now but then they were considered such a nuisance the fisheries patrol boat would take a bunch of local citizens out and blaze away at them with hunting rifles. Another patrol boat ran around ramming them with a big knife. They were great huge dopey things that liked to lie on the surface basking in the summer sun and I never figured out why the government was so down on them, but it was enough for us to know it was open season on them and we did in quite a few. They would liven up pretty fast when you stuck a harpoon into them and would tow the twenty-foot boat around for hours before they ran out of gas and we got close enough to finish them off with the thirty-ought-six. They're supposed to be harmless filter feeders but once one grabbed hold of the transom in its big jaw and shook us until splinters were flying out. We'd tow them home and string them up from a tripod for photos but we didn't have the nerve to try the meat. Once some Chinese came down from Nanaimo's big Chinatown and carted one away but it must not have been too good because they never came back for more.

It was a wonderful time. We were young and in love. There is nothing like it. We were just alive. We were enchanted by the Island landscape. It seemed a bit magical. There was a place over in Cowichan where some guy

A popular Nanaimo sport in those days was shark hunting—for some reason the government was trying to exterminate basking sharks and we would spend weekends chasing them around in Chick Johnson's speedboat. That's me with the hair, Kay at my feet and Chick on the left. WHITE FAMILY

had carved all the tree stumps into the shape of heads. People over there did things like that, I don't know why, but there was a whimsical quality to it. The east coast of the Island had a lot English exiles all around Duncan and Shawnigan Lake and the Cowichan and maybe it was them who lent a make-believe quality with their mini-castles and oddball antics. There was one remittance man who had converted a big cedar stump into the cutest little house like something out of a fairy tale. We spent a lot of time admiring dream homes, tending toward the cute smaller places like old Filberg's cedar shake lodge in Comox, which is a museum now. It seemed a charmed landscape somehow and Kay was enchanted by all of it. I've gone back many times since hoping to recapture that magic spell but of course it's not to be done. It was mostly inside us.

It pains me to look back and remember how happy Kay could be, and realize what little chance she got in her sad, hard life, mostly because of my blindness. It was the last time in our lives together when she would be totally free to enjoy herself and let her imagination go, without babies to keep her up all night and bunkhouses to clean and crews to cook for and debts to worry about and all the things we fell into soon after. She had a great interest in art and literature and was always buying books and practising drawing whenever she had the chance, and she did a lot of that during this period. She had been good at drawing in school and had a fair talent for painting. We bought an easel and paints and she spent many happy afternoons sketching the little creek that ran through the property and other scenery, although her favourite subject was horses. She had a book of best-loved poems she'd work away at, though I think a lot of it mystified her.

I was never one for art and poetry much, except Omar Khayyam, but around that time I acquired a great interest in geology. I had discovered fossils in the rocks up on the mountain and wondered what they were doing there. You could tell they were sea creatures of some kind, and I couldn't figure how they got up there so far from the water. I got some good geology books and they opened up a whole new way of looking at the world. I was fascinated by the idea of the earth's crust churning and changing from one era to the next, and the clues geologists used to put the whole picture together, although much of what I learned about the formation of coast mountains at that time has since been overturned by plate tectonics. They knew that the mountaintops had once been a seabed but thought it had been heaved up by volcanic activity. Now we know that the whole east coast of Vancouver Island was part of an old continental shelf that was uplifted by continental drift during the Cretaceous era, 65–140 million years ago. We spent many contented afternoons just sitting round reading without a care in the world. I began to resent the disruption caused by going to work and even got up nerve enough to cashier my good job with Bill Schnare and get by doing odd jobs like shovelling gravel. We lived off the beach, and ate so many oysters Kay broke out in hives.

Here with a Loaf of Bread beneath the Bough,
A Flask of Wine, a Book of Verse—and Thou
Beside me singing in the Wilderness—
And Wilderness is Paradise enow.

We had a glimpse of what happiness could truly be but didn't take it seriously. We thought it was something that would always be there when we wanted it, like water to drink. But we were wrong. Happiness like that has to be cultivated and nourished if you are going to keep a good measure of it in your life. You have to give it space to grow. And all you young folks out there, don't put it off until you're retired. Every year that passes leaves you with less ability to really experience and enjoy life. I did eventually get around to having twenty or so years to do whatever I wanted when I was old, and I did do quite a lot of what I'd spent my life putting off—but you know, right now I can't even remember most of what I did. I guess I saw the pyramids, but it didn't make near the impression on me that those carved stumps in the Cowichan made when I was in my twenties and still had the capacity to be enchanted. If you get in the habit of always putting enjoyment last it withers and goes to weed and when you try to find it again, it's not there. Later in life I would see these nature lovers taking whole summers off to hike on Forbidden Plateau or cruise the Gulf Islands with their kids, and I scoffed at them as drifters and lightweights taking a free ride on real solid people like me. This was the great mistake of my life and I don't really know how to account for it. My father was a life-loving man who had the sense to devote his first forty years to adventuring and living to the fullest. When I think of him now, the first thing I think of is his great laugh. He was a man who could laugh and make others laugh. I hate to say it, but he may have been right when he said I had too much Carmichael in me, with their grim Presbyterian work ethic and mistrust of a good time. I tried to escape through drinking, and it worked for me but it left Kay out of the picture and entered a note of discord even in our good years.

In the fall of 1941 Kay suddenly got sick. She was nauseous and couldn't keep any food down. It tells you how naïve we were that it took us weeks to figure out she was pregnant. But our joy was tempered by Kay's condition. She was losing weight, losing sleep and felt like death warmed over. We went to the doctor and they gave her some medicine that made no difference. Her condition dragged on. She wasn't eating. She was losing the will to live. I went back to the doctor and said, look, she's not going to make it. This isn't normal, it can't be. You've got to do something. So very reluctantly he decided to end the pregnancy and booked her into the hospital. But the day before she was to go in, she felt a little better. We told the doctor and he said, "Well then, let's give it a day or two." Each day she was better and holding down more food. So they put the abortion on indefinite hold. Kay turned right around then. Within weeks she was not just better, she was positively blooming. She became a little plump and just kind of glowed with health. She also became very energetic, and started repainting the house and fitting out the nursery. On June 6, 1942, she went into Nanaimo General Hospital and gave birth to a healthy girl.

She was the perfect baby and we took more delight in watching her blink and burp than anything we'd ever experienced, but like all new parents we were blindsided by the way this tiny addition turned our lives upside down. Gone were the quiet afternoons spent boating or reading. Gone were the peaceful nights of deep sleep and the late mornings on weekends. Gone were the free-living friends and the spur-of-the-moment dinners and outings. And of course the biggest change of all is that you couldn't care less about that. All of a sudden there is something much more important in your life. Like most men I had never been interested in babies before I got one of my own and I was surprised by how fascinating they could be. She was a truly bright and beautiful baby and it was hard not to feel we had somehow been chosen to receive the new future Amelia Earhart or

First child—1942. This changed everything. WHITE FAMILY

Marie Curie every time she gurgled in such an expressive, intelligent way, so advanced over the way she had been gurgling the day before.

In those days you weren't visited by a public health nurse and they didn't send you home with a Gerber baby-raising kit or even a copy of Dr. Spock, which hadn't been written yet, so we were pretty well on our own. I was jumpy as hell and kept wanting to call doctors at the first sign of a cough or diaper rash and couldn't figure out how Kay could be so casual, but I slowly began to realize what we had here was one of the world's great mothers. Not just that she had been raising kids for most of her life already, she was built for it—calm, caring, endlessly patient—she had an easy, loving manner that was a blessing to all our kids and made up for a lot of what I lacked. On the other hand, I couldn't help but notice whenever there was a baby around I pretty much ceased to exist. Even that I didn't mind, though. With her cherubic little face and flaxen curls and sweet temper, our baby seemed to me beyond perfection. It was like a little angel had come to live with us. I would have suffered anything for her.

Your outlook changes when you have a child. Before, it is your own success that is important. Now it becomes your child's success. You want her to be healthy and happy and go to university and marry a good man who has the ability to keep her well. This becomes your number one goal now. I always tried to prepare my kids for the world so nothing could knock them down. I tried to let them see everything, do everything.

About this time Les McGarva surprised us by coming over for a visit. It was a long way from home for him, and I could see he was at loose ends. John was running his trucks again and he knew he was getting screwed over but he was too sick and tired to do much about it. His doctors had read the riot act to him and told him if he didn't stop drinking he would be dead within a year and he didn't know what to do. He tried to slow down on the booze but he'd been on it so long he just didn't know how to live without it. He was a mess.

I had gone back driving for a logger named Jim Robson, who had a fair-sized outfit in the Nanaimo area. I took Les up in the truck to show him the logging operation and he was really impressed. This was the first active logging he'd ever seen. "Jesus, this is real trucking," he said. He could see immediately that truck logging was going to take over from the railroads and it got him thinking.

"You and me should buy a truck and get in on this," he said. Well, I was ready to hear this. Since we started our family I was worrying about being a truck jockey all my life and felt pressure to get into something more substantial. I had watched Les make a fortune in the milk business and now I was watching Schnare make a fortune in log hauling and I didn't want to waste any more time just standing around on the outside collecting wages. I wanted to make my own fortune and I figured if an illiterate drunk like Les and a broke-down old farmer like Schnare could do it, a smart, hard-working young guy like me ought to be able to do it twice as good. And it felt good to finally be getting in partners with Les, it took away some of the bad taste about the way the milk business ended up.

Les wasn't stringing me along this time. He came over to visit a few more times and we scouted around and found we could get contract log hauling work without any trouble in the Nanaimo area. Then we went over to Vancouver and found a truck that looked good, a heavy-duty 1936 Dodge D 800 that was going for $5,000. We put it right to work and it hauled logs to beat hell. I was at the wheel of my own truck at last and it felt good. The D 800 was a big heavy truck for the time and a wonderful machine, the best truck I ever owned.

17

Palmer Bay

In October 1941 Wesley came home on leave from Yorke Island with the news that he was going overseas. He and his partner George had been frustrated by the long wait at do-nothing coastal defence postings and had been riding their officers to get to the front and see some action. One day the captain had come to him saying, "You and George are going to get your wish. You are going overseas, you have bugged me long enough." Wesley didn't know where they were going but they were issued tropical gear and were leaving in the next few days. He was excited, but I was dismayed. I had secretly been cheering his being stranded on the BC coast where he was safe and hoping it would last the whole war. Or if he did have to go overseas, I hoped it wouldn't be until I was able to go with him, but now I had to face the fact that chance was lost. I was worried. He still had the physique of a boy, and he wasn't strong. He was susceptible to pneumonia and had been in hospital for two weeks in March.

We didn't find out what had happened until much later, but if we had we would have been even more alarmed than we were. The Winnipeg Grenadiers had come through Vancouver on their way to help defend Hong Kong, which was in the path of the advancing Japanese army. There was no thought of actually stopping the Japanese, just of making a bit of a show. The Imperial Army had swept across China and was approaching Hong Kong with some 30,000 battle-hardened soldiers organized into eleven regiments and four battalions, backed with heavy artillery and forty-two

Kawasaki bombers. (I'm copying this straight off the internet.) Against this the Allies had 3,447 British and Indian soldiers, to which they added 1,975 Canadians from the Royal Rifles and the Winnipeg Grenadiers. The Winnipeg Grenadiers were under strength, under trained and under equipped. Instead of twenty-one troop carriers they had six. Instead of twenty-two anti-tank guns, they were given one. They had mortars but no ammunition for them. They were also short of signalmen, so when the call went out for reinforcements, Wesley and George were seconded and shipped out with them.

The Japanese attacked Hong Kong on December 8, 1941, the day after Pearl Harbor, and the British command under General Maltby surrendered on Christmas Day. Wesley survived seventeen days of brutal and completely futile fighting but was taken prisoner and placed in the brutal Japanese prison camp system. In all, the Canadians lost 557 men out of their contingent of 1,975. The *Canada at War* website states the Hong Kong "campaign" was "all for nought" and was a "military disaster." Worse, it was a planned disaster, knowingly entered into by Canadian and British officials who didn't want to throw away good army equipment on it but were fully prepared to throw away young men's lives. Wesley died of diphtheria on October 6, 1942, not quite a year after he'd set sail from Vancouver. To say my brother was betrayed by his country is an understatement.

Of course we didn't know anything about this at the time. I'm not sure we even knew for certain he was in Hong Kong until my mother received a telegram notifying her of his death in July of 1943, ten months after the fact. It took another two years of wrangling and untangling red tape before Mother finally received Wesley's service pay, which came to just under $400. I thought my anger and sorrow would eventually fade away but it never has. I still can't look at his picture. It's too painful. I cannot be rational about his life and death, we were so devoted to each other. I have put off thinking about him for so long, it is harder than ever to start. I couldn't appreciate his love or his loyalty or how much we meant to each other—I hadn't the experience to appreciate our relationship. If I did I would have spent a lot more time with him when I had the chance.

Wesley James White 1920–1942. WHITE FAMILY

After I got into contract hauling I found myself moving around a lot to chase the work. At Northwest Bay I hauled for Doug Dollar, a scion of the famous Dollar sawmilling and shipping family after whom the community of Dollarton on Burrard Inlet is named, then did a stint hauling down off Mount Sicker near Duncan for Blondie Swanson, the brother of the writer and inventor Robert Swanson. Robert, for what it's worth, is the man responsible for designing the horns that sound the first bar of "O Canada" at noon every day from the top of the BC Hydro Building in Vancouver. He earned himself a footnote in history by designing air horns that sound like steam whistles so diesel trains and ships could sound like they used to in the old days. In my day he was better known for inventing a type of fail-safe truck brake that dynamited if you lost air.

While logging Mount Sicker, we moved down to Duncan for a spell, where I put Kay into a pretty little cabin overlooking Maple Bay. I did a lot of running around. I even put the truck on the little *Cy Peck* ferry and took it over to Saltspring Island, although I ended up wishing I hadn't. I went to work for a haywire show hauling down the sheer side of Mount Maxwell over a road so steep I could never get up without running at it several times. The road surface was very loose, causing the truck to spin out, but there was a creek crossing near the top and I found if I turned the creek water down the road, it packed the gravel enough to get me up. That haul beat hell out of the truck, then they went broke and couldn't pay. I was finding being a trucking boss wasn't quite as straightforward as it had looked from the sidelines.

In 1943 I contracted to haul logs for Clare Smith, who operated a logging camp called Smith and Osberg Ltd. at Palmer Bay in Johnstone Strait, twenty-five miles north of Campbell River. There was no road into Palmer Bay so arrangements were made to meet a tug and barge going up to camp. I was told I would find the crew at the Willows Hotel in Campbell River. The Willows Hotel was about all there was to Campbell River in those days. It stuck up like a sore thumb right on the beach and sure enough the tug crew was there, and looked like they'd been there for longer than made for safe navigation. I joined in a few beers but couldn't relax because I was so nervous about loading my truck on the barge and worried that it was getting well on in the afternoon. They were in no hurry though, and eventually I figured out this was because they were waiting for the right tide to take the tow through Seymour Narrows past the deadly whirlpools of Ripple Rock. Fifteen years later this navigational hazard would be eliminated by the largest non-nuclear blast in peacetime history, but at that time it was still intact and still adding to its total of over a hundred shipwrecks. After hearing this, I decided to have a few more beers myself.

Eventually the skipper decided the time was right and I spotted the truck at a place the crew had indicated on the beach while they manoeuvred the barge into place. It was already loaded with a good-sized bulldozer, a couple of pickup trucks and what looked like a dump winch and had a decided list, which I realized was intended to even out once the weight of my truck was added. Then they set out a couple of timbers made from squared logs and signalled me to drive aboard. I couldn't believe it. The timbers didn't look strong enough to hold the truck, and even if they did, I wasn't a bit sure I could keep my wheels centred on them. I was climbing up at quite a steep angle, and the hood of the truck blocked my view of the timbers for quite a ways ahead. If I slipped off, it would be a ten-foot drop straight into the saltchuck. I yelled to ask if they had anything sturdier and they yelled back not to worry, they had loaded bigger trucks than mine. I doubted that, since there weren't many bigger trucks than mine in that part of the country, but there was nothing for it but to plunge ahead. I was doing fine until the barge took the truck's weight and heeled over like it was going to roll me off, but I kept creeping ahead and made it into the space they'd left for me. As soon as they had my wheels blocked, everybody scrambled aboard the tug and we were underway. As we approached "The Old Rip" as they called it, I went out on the stern to watch and noticed that the more skookum of the two deckhands was standing over the towline with an axe.

"What the hell are you up to?" I asked, alarmed.

"If the barge gets sucked into the hole beside Ripple Rock I have to chop the line fast or it will pull us down with it," he said. It turned out the skipper had spent a bit more time in the beer parlour than he strictly had to because we were now late for the tide and the ebb tide was moving extremely fast. We zipped past Ol' Rip without a hitch, although the tide rips on the downstream side tossed tug and barge around in a manner that looked quite alarming to my landlubber's eye and made me wish I'd paid more attention to blocking the truck wheels, but we made it through and reached camp without incident. Unloading was much less nerve-wracking now that I knew the timbers wouldn't buckle and drop me into the water.

It was a medium-sized camp for those days, about fifty men with one trackside and a cold decker, that is, a smaller yarding outfit that would pull logs in from the farthest reaches and pile them in a "cold deck" where they could be reached by the main yarder and pulled the rest of the way in to trackside. They called it trackside because that was where the end of the tracks would be if it was a railroad show, and they didn't see any need to come up with a new term just because we happened to be using trucks instead of railcars. The system used two spar trees and some fancier yarding methods like a skyline, where a heavy line between two trees was used as a kind of trolley wire along which a carriage travelled with bunches, or "turns," of logs suspended from it. It wasn't as complicated as some of the big skidder shows to the south, but still there were enough lines running this way and that it looked like some giant spider web. It is hard to see how we used so many men to put out the same wood six guys would move now, but the cookhouse had a crew of first and second cooks, one or two flunkies and a bull cook, then the foreman and a timekeeper, three on the boom crew, three or four road builders, a mechanic, a saw filer, three or four truck drivers, eight or nine in the yarding crew, four for loader crew, eight or nine fallers as well as one or two cold deck crews at five each and the high rigger.

As the war progressed it became very hard to keep the various operations working efficiently with short crews and many inexperienced men. It was becoming evident that Smith was having his trouble keeping the operation profitable. Douglas fir was in record demand but Palmer Bay is just on the northern border of the climatic zone where Douglas fir grows naturally. Hemlock and cedar predominate on the North Island but in those days hemlock and cedar fetched very low prices.

The yarder used wood for fuel to fire the boiler—oil was not to be had in wartime—and I can still see the joy on the face of the fireman when a big fir log was yarded in. The bucker immediately had the chaser spot the log in the wood yard and soon had it reduced to firebox-sized chunks. I can still hear Clare lamenting that if he could only sell the fir instead having to burn it for donkey fuel he might actually make some money.

Of course they could use hemlock to fire the boilers, but hemlock produces a lot less heat than fir and the result was unsatisfactory. The fireman could not keep up enough steam to keep the yarder working full bore and on a long pull they would often have to stop and wait for the steam pressure to build up. The exhaust steam was vented up the stack and when the engineer opened the throttle on a hard pull the firewood just seemed to evaporate up the stack. Pity the fireman and the wood buckers, as well as Clare Smith. The days of power saws had not arrived yet and every piece of wood was sawn and split by hand, then stacked if the machine happened to be yarding close in but likely as not was passed to the fireman and straight into the firebox to keep up steam when on a long pull. Firing steam donkeys was not for the faint of heart.

Palmer Bay was a very old camp site. It was an early camp of the old Hastings Lumber Co., BC's first big forest company, and it was claimed that the first steam donkey on the coast worked there. This would be ground lead, that is, they'd pull the logs flat on the ground. As they reached further back from the beach, they had to build a clear roadway for the logs

I was nervous enough placing my truck on an overloaded barge towed by a skipper who was none too sober, but having to navigate past Ripple Rock where over 100 ships had gone down was more than I bargained on. HARBOUR PUBLISHING

to skid down, so they wouldn't hang up on stumps and rough ground. To keep the logs from digging in, they laid logs crossways in the mud, forming what was called a skid road. They had to use very long lines to reach to the back of the claim and the steam donkey that wound the line in had to have a very large drum to hold it all. This was called a "roader" donkey and a lot of the old gear used on those skid roads was still laying around. They used things like big rollers mounted on stumps so the line could pull logs around corners. When the road got too long for the roader engines to reach all the way back, that's when railroads would usually be brought in. Here for some reason instead of using railroads they had decided to use trucks, the early kind with hard rubber tires that had to run on a timber-stringer road, with squared timbers placed lengthwise, or "fore and aft," to provide a solid surface for the hard truck tires, which were no good on soft ground. This old timbered system was still in place down on the main line and still mostly in good enough shape for our modern trucks to work on, although they put in branches surfaced with gravel for the final steep climb up to the high country where we were logging.

Palmer Bay was a fascinating place. There was an old schoolroom in one of the older buildings and everywhere you could find the debris of sixty or seventy years of logging. The bay is named after a well-known old-time family and I encountered one of them, a man over seventy who met the Union Steamship boat at his place and was seen to walk ashore across floating boom logs carrying a 150-pound oxy-acetylene tank on his shoulder.

The job was turning out well for me. By volunteering to take the firemen and donkey punchers up to the tree an hour early to get steam up, I always got the first load, which meant I also got the last load most times and the money was piling up, but I hated being away from Kay and the baby. All the men in the camp could think of was drinking, drinking and more drinking, which didn't have the appeal for me it once would have had, especially the stuff they were drinking. It didn't take long for the store-bought booze to run out, so the only way to survive was to become your own brewmaster, and every bunkhouse had some kind of homebrew bubbling and fuming away. Normally this was forbidden in coastal camps but

A roader show similar to the system originally used at Palmer Bay. The donkey engine pulled the logs in along the ground instead of using a spar tree to gain lift as in later years. HARBOUR PUBLISHING

with men so scarce you could get away with pretty much anything short of murdering the push. Homebrew was considered ready as soon as it had any alcohol content, never mind what it tasted like, and most of it looked and tasted like something that collects in the bottom of the compost bucket.

A few of us got the idea that it would be a big improvement to our lifestyle to run some of this sludge through a still, which might lessen some of the barf-inducing effect while improving some of the intoxicating power. It turned out nobody had any idea of how to make a still, and neither had I, but it seemed simple enough—you'd get a bunch of brew, throw it in some kind of a sealed vessel that you could heat and collect the vapour from, then lead the vapour off into some kind of a condenser that would cause the pure alcohol to revert to liquid form. Among my junk I had a battered old ten-gallon milk can we'd stolen off the FVMPA years earlier and it seemed like the perfect still. It had a tight-fitting lid and all it needed was to drill a hole and solder in a piece of copper tubing, of which there was lots around camp. We wound about twelve feet of tubing into a coil to enhance condensing and stuck the free end into a jar to collect the moonshine.

It didn't work worth a damn. First we were in too much of a hurry and put too much heat under the can, which caused it to just boil off very polluted water. When we got the fire slowed down enough not to do that, nothing came out of the end of the tubing at all, and we discovered it was all escaping around the lid, which wasn't as tight as it looked. If we'd had the patience to keep fine-tuning, it might have worked, but we were all too thirsty and decided the taste of rotten potatoes wasn't so bad after all. Clare wasn't happy about the amount of drinking going on in camp and once when I was discussing it with him and his superintendent, Gunnar Johnson, I pointed out the camp boat had a big alcohol compass with about a quart of pure alcohol in it and said how it was funny nobody had got that yet. After Gunnar left Clare said, "You shouldn't have said that in front of Gunnar, he's the worst one of the bunch." Sure enough, next day I checked and the compass was bone dry. Gunnar was a good old guy and a fine logger but he was just helpless in the presence of booze. He knew it as well as anybody and later jumped off the Lions Gate Bridge in Vancouver but they fished him out and patched him up and he went on to live for many more years.

In order to get out to see Kay once in awhile I managed to bring the panel truck I was driving in those days over the logging roads to Rock Bay, the old Merrill, Ring and Wilson camp that was only a few minutes by boat down Johnstone Strait from Palmer Bay, so I was able to get out when I had a couple days off. Of course it was a long run through the bush to Campbell River and there was no gas station at the Rock Bay end, so I had to bring a can of gas with me from our camp to fuel up the van. I looked around for a can big enough to fill the tank, and the best thing I could find was the milk can we'd been using to make moonshine in. It still had copper tubing soldered into the lid and was all smoked up on the sides but it was clean on the inside, so I filled it from the camp's bulk tank and put it in the boat. Well now, of course gas was rationed during the war and the gas we had in camp was special permit gas, meaning it was meant for use in a war industry and not in private vehicles. The way they kept track of gas that was for war work was they placed red dye in it, so this gas was bright red. It was illegal to drive a private car with red gas, but every vehicle coming down from our area had it because it was all you could get. So as soon as the road crosses the border into the Campbell River municipal district, here's a cop sitting there checking every vehicle for red gas. He draws a little gas out of my tank, checks it, and writes me a ticket. The fine is pretty steep, about a week's pay.

"What's the use of giving us gas to do war work if you won't give us gas to get to the work?" I say.

"You'll have to ask the magistrate that," the cop says. The provincial police were a pretty low-life bunch, most of them. Then he spots the sooty milk can.

"What's in that?" he says.

"Nothing, it's empty," I say.

He pulls the lid off and there's about a cupful of red gas in the bottom. I never like to pour out the last bit in case it's dirty. So he seizes the can. Well, I'm pissed off. This is real bullshit. What are we supposed to do, ride bicycles through fifty miles of bush to get back and forth to our war work? I decide I'll go to court and fight it. I show up at the police station on the appointed day feeling pretty nervous and the clerk says, "Take a seat, the corporal wants to talk to you." I wonder what this is all about, and the door opens and who should walk in but Corporal Wesley, my old friend from my Abbotsford days who used to bum rides into Vancouver in my milk truck. He's got a big grin on his face.

"When I saw that milk can come in, I said, 'Don't tell me. You took that off a guy named Frank White.' I knew you could be the only guy around here who'd have an FVMPA milk can," he said. I had no idea he'd been transferred to the wilds of Vancouver Island, but apparently he had been keeping better tabs on me than I had on him.

It was good to see a friendly face, but I still didn't know what kind of trouble I was in.

"You know, you're damn lucky I was here or they might have charged you with being in possession of a still. It's pretty obvious that can has been used as a still," he said.

"Yeah, but it didn't work worth a damn," I said. We both laughed.

The Willows Hotel was about all there was to Campbell River in 1943. HARBOUR PUBLISHING

Eventually I go up in front of this tweedy pipe-smoking Englishman. One of the provincial cops reads the charge and I get up and say we had to use the red gas or we would have been stuck up there, and I had just put enough in the car to get to the first gas station. This magistrate gets a pained look on his face, removes his pipe and starts talking to the cop who's acting as prosecutor just as if I wasn't in the room, "I am going to find the accused guilty. These people are just going to have to learn to obey the law!" So I have to pay this goddamn fine. It's the only time I was ever fined in my life, other than a traffic ticket. I couldn't get over the way he sneered "*these people…*" What did he mean by that? I didn't normally think of myself as a member of any group. Did he mean people from the mainland? Loggers? Local yokels? Rightly or wrongly I took it that he meant the lower classes, rubes from the colonies who hadn't read *Blackstone's Commentaries on the English Common Law*, although by chance I had. It rankled. I guess I was a bit sensitive. There was quite a collection of these displaced Englishmen around Abbotsford and they always managed to speak in a tone that made you feel like you were something that got stuck to the bottom of their shoe, even though most of them didn't have a pot to piss in themselves.

I got hold of one of the empty bunkhouses in Palmer Bay, scrounged a bit of basic furniture, and moved Kay and the baby up to camp, which was much better for me, although I got up so early and spent so much time monkeywrenching the truck in evenings and on weekends I hardly saw them. One of the men shot a deer and discovered that it had a newborn fawn, which he brought down to camp. It had to be fed with a bottle, and Kay had the only bottles in camp, so we undertook to look after it. It became as tame as a lap dog. It grew up in the house so it continued to live in the house even after it got too big for comfort, which didn't take it very long. We discovered an interesting thing about deer. Their brain is about on par with that of a chicken. No, that may be doing discredit to the chicken. It was the dumbest thing I ever ran into. Every time you turned around it would be up on the counter knocking down dishes. Once I smelled something funny and looked around and there it was standing on top of the red-hot cookstove. Its hooves were so hot they were smoking and the damn thing was picking up one foot after another and kind of shaking it, and I guess it would have stood there and burnt right up if I hadn't grabbed it. It couldn't have been housebroken in a million years but luckily deer poop is pretty rug-friendly. The main challenge was to get to it before the baby, who seemed to think Bambi's pellets were raisins. When a commercial fisherman who was overnighting at the camp wharf caught it out wandering and clobbered it over the head, we didn't know whether to be mad or glad.

Clare Smith had an office in Vancouver and would hold the contract money there a couple weeks at a time, then get it to Kay, who would pay the bills, make the truck payment, take our share and send Les his share. One day Kay noticed the bank account was empty when it shouldn't have been so I got hold of Clare and asked him what was going on.

Clare said, "Jesus, I don't know how to tell you this, but your partner was in and took all the money that was owing. I'm sorry but there was no way I could deny him."

This was Les all over again. Neither he nor John could ever leave any money lying around anywhere. If there was anything, they'd go and get it. I knew then I wouldn't be able to keep working with Les on the basis we had been. I would never know when he was going to swoop in and scoop the money, and I would never be able to get a square accounting of what he took or what he did with it. Clare was on my side, he had to be since I was the one doing his work, so he agreed to hold back all the money for the next period and put Les off if he came around. When the next payment was ready, I picked it up and went out to see Les in Abbotsford. I met him at his old table in the Atangard and I laid it on the line. I said okay, now this is how it's gong to be. I'm going to give you this money and you're going to sign the truck over to me. He didn't like it but I had him over a barrel because without me to run it, he'd lose the truck and get nothing. One of Les's old drinking buddies was with us and he never quit saying I'd screwed Les but it wasn't true. He came out money ahead and I came out with the truck.

I only saw Les a couple more times after that. He was in pretty bad shape. About the last time I saw him I found him out back behind his place sitting under a tree with his gun beside him. "I came out here to shoot myself, but I can't do it," he said. He had quit drinking but it was no good. He said he'd rather not live than live that way. I tried to think of what to say, but everything I could think of sounded stupid so I didn't say anything. Any other time we would have gone out and tied one on, and without that there was just nothing. He was only thirty-eight but his life was over more surely than mine is at ninety-nine. The next I heard he was dead. He'd gone back drinking and his heart gave out.

At Palmer Bay our daughter Marilyn shared her bottle with an orphaned fawn and they became fast friends. WHITE FAMILY

That was in 1945 and I knew it marked the end of something for me. It was a turning point just like it was when Father died in 1929. John McGarva died of a heart attack too, not long after. Rita died of cancer early on, too. The only one that survived was Florence, who remarried and lived to a decent age. They had a son Andy and a daughter Marlene who was just born when I was with them but I never got to know them. It was a bit strange having people who had been such a part of my life just walk off stage and never return but that's the difference between real life and a made-up story. It's something you get used to, at least here on the West Coast. The scene keeps changing and the new one doesn't always have much to do with the old one. I've often thought how different we are from the old country, where you walk to work past the graveyard where your father, grandfather and great-great-great-grandfathers and -mothers all lie, and you're walking on the same stones looking at the same trees they looked at. I can't even imagine what that would be like. But like I said before, the dead don't really leave you. They stick around.

I didn't really give Les much thought at the time he died, I'd had enough and I was ready to be done with him. I probably thought that was it as far as Les went. But looking back, I can see he influenced me more than any man except my own father and he probably had a more direct hand in shaping my adult life. He got me into driving trucks, he got me into owning trucks. But that was on the surface. It was through him I finally stopped being a lost kid and found my place as a man among men. Drinking was part of that but only a part. Les had a wonderful outlook on life really, one I tried to copy but never could pull off the way he did. He thought a man was a damn fool to go by the rules. He saw rules as something the guy ahead of you in line dreamed up to keep you down, and it was your job to get around him. All the laws and norms of behaviour and prevailing opinion that went to make up society was just so much bullshit to him, something to be turned on its head and got around.

Him and Bud Haddrell were a lot alike in that way but they had different ways of going about it. Bud would always try to figure out what you wanted and make a deal to get it for you, but Les had this thing, he'd try to charm you. Get you drunk if he could but if you were too smart for that he'd charm you and show you such a good time and get you thinking he was the greatest guy in the world and before you knew it he would have your farm, or whatever. He operated on a bigger scale than Bud. Bud sold drinks to people who were thirsty, one person at a time. Les sold a new way of doing things to a dairy industry struggling with outdated methods. Of course Schnare did that too, and that's another guy I took a lot from. I learned what a truck was from him. Les was afraid of a truck—he didn't know anything about them and as soon as one started to give him any trouble he'd trade it in on a new one so he never did have to learn what was under the hood. Schnare would pull some godawful old wreck in from the bushes, rebuild the motor, add a bogey, beef up the frame and send it out hauling twice the loads it had hauled when it was brand new. A machine was just a bunch of parts to be rearranged to him. But sometimes I think I learned the wrong things off those two guys. Les was a hard drinker who made money and Schnare was a haywire mechanic who made money so I became a hard-drinking haywire mechanic who didn't make any money. I've often thought I'd like to go back and ask them if maybe there was some little detail I missed.

18

Garibaldi

I n all the commotion surrounding the move up to Palmer Bay I hadn't been picking up my mail and when I finally got around to it here was an important-looking brown envelope from the Selective Service Branch. It was my army call-up. It said I had two weeks to put my affairs in order and report to the recruiting centre at Little Mountain in Vancouver. Well, because this letter had been sitting around, the two weeks were up the next day and if I didn't report, a warrant would be issued for my arrest. The army had started to run out of volunteers so the Mackenzie King government had held a conscription plebiscite in 1942 and now they were calling up some of the older married men they'd left alone in the early going. As luck would have it there was a steamer going through that evening so I jumped on it. I got to Vancouver and reported to the recruiting office on time. I was pretty upset and worried and hoped I would be able to talk to somebody in charge about getting my war-work exemption reinstated. At least I figured I would be able to explain that I needed a two-week deferment because I had a wife and baby to get situated and a business to wind up, but they weren't taking any questions. It was just stand here, stand there, take off your clothes, bend over, you're in the army now, chump. Every thing they could do or say to belittle and humiliate a guy, they did. So I go through the mill and I'm told to report for induction the next day.

This is an unmitigated disaster. I have no way of getting in touch with Kay. She doesn't know she's stuck with truck payments to make and nobody to run the truck. Clare Smith doesn't know he's just lost his contract hauler. How are my wife and baby going to survive? It's the end of the world. I couldn't believe such a thing could be happening.

Out on the street I spot a familiar figure striding along leaving the headquarters and heading out to the parking lot. It's my old nemesis, Judge A.M. Manson, the hanging judge, who I haven't seen since he declared me a hostile witness at the great milk-truck trial of 1936. The reason he is there is that he's gotten a wartime appointment overseeing the Selective Service but I didn't know that. To me he is just a man of power and influence I might appeal to in my blind desperation.

I came running up behind him and laid a hand on his arm and he jumped like he was being assaulted. I blurted out my problem. "I'm in a hell of a fix, and I just hoped you could maybe speak to somebody who could get me a couple days deferment so I could get my affairs in order and get my wife and baby taken care of," I said.

"Did you say you're working for Clare Smith?" he asked.

"Yes, he's a logger who owns a camp up in Palmer Bay and I'm his main hauling contractor," I said.

"That man has been on the phone to me three times a week bitching that he can't operate because we're taking all his men," he said.

"Well he'll really be stuck now because he won't have any way to get his logs down the hill," I said.

"I tell you what, young man," Manson said. "You catch the first boat up to Palmer Bay and you keep hauling logs until you hear from me. You can do more to win this war up there than getting your ass shot off in France."

I don't know how I ever had the nerve, but I said to him, "I'm a contractor and it would be no good if Smith figured he had me stuck there for the war, a guy has to be free to shop his services around."

"I understand that," he said. "You just get back up there hauling for Smith and if there's any trouble you just call me."

"What about this order telling me to report for induction in the morning?" I asked.

"You just leave that with me. I'll take care of it."

So I gave this piece of paper to him and caught a boat back up-island the next day. Old Manson was as good as his word. I never heard from

Selective Service again. It was a funny damn business. Some guys seemed to get their logging jobs classed as essential wartime services and others didn't. The authorities seemed to be playing it by ear a lot of the time. Anyway, Smith closed down in 1944 and I pulled the truck out and went on a contract on the mainland up at Garibaldi. I never bothered to tell Manson or anybody else and nobody ever said boo.

That was quite a show, Garibaldi. It was owned by a man named Les Kurz, who was completely unlike any other boss logger I'd ever met. He was one of these European Jews who'd been chased out by Hitler. I had it in mind that he was Hungarian but now I'm not sure why I think that, he might have been Czech or Austrian. Kurz is a German name but I don't think he was German. I believe he later changed the name to Kerr and him and his sons built up a major forest company called Lignum. Anyway, Kurz had scared up the most godawful ragtag bunch of alcoholics and old wrecks for a crew you ever saw. By this late stage of the war good men were impossible to get. The super, Zeke, was some toothless old coyote who'd been in the woods since they were using stone chisels, but he was so rummy half the time he didn't know where he was.

By 1943 they were starting to conscript married men and I got my call-up. I took the boat to Vancouver and was inducted into the army—for about an hour. HARBOUR PUBLISHING

The first thing I saw him do when I got there, Les had some nice hand-knitted wool socks drying in the office and Zeke stole them. Naturally Les saw him wearing them, they had fancy zig-zags you couldn't miss, and he just couldn't believe it, that his superintendent would steal his socks. He just shook his head in disbelief.

Another time we went in for breakfast in the morning and the cook was passed out on the floor with lemon extract all over his face. Zeke had it in for the cook anyway because he'd caught him sneaking a sandwich after hours and threatened to behead him with a cleaver, so Zeke was grumbling to Les and me how you couldn't dare leave anything with alcohol in it like shoe polish or shaving lotion sitting around or the cook would drink it on you. After he left Les said, "You know that's funny, because that is exactly what the cook said about Zeke."

One day old Zeke was standing on a stump out in front of the tree, so bleary and shaky he didn't see that he was in the bight of the haulback and all that was holding it was a little sapling. The sapling pulled over and the line picked old Zeke right up by the ass like a hundred-yard bowstring and flung him seventy feet. Joe Beef, who was another relic from the Vancouver skid road—I never did know his right name—he was pulling rigging and Zeke came down right beside him. His ribs were sticking out and he was bleeding and screaming, and Joe Beef says, "Ah, shuddup y'ol sonuvabitch, that's just the shoe polish coming out." They got him plugged up and shipped out to Squamish.

That night in camp Joe Beef was telling us, "You know, ol' Zeke looked just like a leaf floatin' down through them trees."

This Les Kurz, it all must have been quite a shock for him because he was from the upper crust in Europe, his wife was a concert pianist and all that, but the funny thing was he seemed to really enjoy these guys. Not just enjoy them, he admired them—he used to say there was no other men like them in the world. Everybody liked him, too, he was a real gentleman. He had no business to be running a camp, though; the only reason he ever got any logs in the water was we put them in for him. That camp just ran itself—these old bastards were pretty slow until the sun got up, but nobody ever had to tell them what to do. It was the only camp I ever saw where they didn't give signals. They'd just glance at each other and maybe give a nod. They knew all the moves by heart.

I was getting paid by the log, so every time I got over twelve logs in one load I would pass out packs of cigarettes for everybody on the loading crew. It didn't take them long to get saving all the small logs for me, and leaving all the big ones for the company truck. The only guy who didn't fit in was this pissant named George on the company truck, and it didn't make a damn bit of difference to him but he was always meowing. "Look at all the money you're making." Last I heard he was still up there, driving a school bus.

There was a kid there named Bob Hallgren who was smart as a whip. I said you put the kid on head loading and we'll take care of it for you. It was a big job for a green kid, but he handled it like a pro. Between him and me we kept the logs moving for them. I even kept their old truck going for them. That was Bob's start in the logging business, and he went on to become a vice-president of one of the big companies, Rayonier. They had the old Pioneer Timber camp at Port McNeill and Bob masterminded its transformation into a municipality. For awhile there he was known as the "Father of Port McNeill," although he's pretty much forgotten now.

I enjoyed working for Kurz. I told him I was having a hard time getting

As the war ended I traded in my trusty Dodge and bought three of these 1937 Mack BX's Bill Schnare had originally used at Harrison Lake. They had been great trucks in their day, but a lot of logs had gone down the hills since then. HARBOUR PUBLISHING

sleep with all the noise in the bunkhouse, so he invited me to move into the office with him. We had some great discussions. I was quite a reader in those days and I never ran into anybody I could really discuss any of these things with, geology, American history, economics, but he was very well educated and seemed to be right up on all of this stuff.

I was making money and it looked like it could go on for awhile so I decided to move the wife up. There was no place suitable so Kurz says, "Why don't you go ahead and build one? I'll see you get all the lumber you need." He had a little mill up the line closer to Alta Lake, where the Whistler ski resort is today. So I got busy and built a nice little cottage. I think I enjoyed that more than any building I ever did. I had only a vague idea how a house went together and yet it turned out I knew more than I thought. I had once helped one of my cousins, Bob Gledhill, rebuild his house in the valley after it burnt and there was one old guy, an English guy, who'd been a carpenter and showed me the basics. I had a sense of satisfaction building that little shack I never quite recaptured again with the dozen or so houses and shops I've built since. It was very cozy once Kay moved in. It's great country in there, surrounded by all those mountains, and they loved it. We hiked up into the Garibaldi meadows, which were just a vast ocean of wildflowers. A couple of us even climbed the Black Tusk, a crumbling volcanic plug that dominates the skyline up there. It's all loose and disintegrating and brick-sized rocks were falling around us, it's a wonder we weren't killed.

Our baby was growing up. She was about three feet high then; I'd send her under the trucks to grease the throwout bearings. She could do it standing up and she loved it, but she had snow-white hair and it would be black, jeez Kay would holler. One day she tripped on a cut-open barrel and put about a three-inch gash in her leg. It didn't bleed, but this white baby fat just bushed out like popcorn, like it was under pressure. I damn near fainted, but the first-aid man just shoved it back in and slapped on a bandage.

We were in Garibaldi when we got word the war was over. Les called me in and offered me a drink. "Here's to your brother," he said. He had tears in his eyes. He'd lost a lot too.

The war ended in May and our second child, Franklin Howard, was born in April. Kay went over to Abbotsford and stayed with Beryl for the birth because we had nobody to help around Garibaldi, there was no doctor or nurse close by. It was fun having a baby in the house again, though nothing like the dizzying thrill of the first time. At first I thought, okay, this time I'm going to pay more attention, take more pictures and do everything I didn't do the first time, but of course I ended up paying even less attention and taking fewer pictures. But also worrying a lot less. It seemed before I knew it he was walking and saying his first words and getting his first haircut—though that took awhile. He had beautiful snow-white hair and Kay let it grow out like a girl's; he didn't get it cut until we moved back to Nanaimo where there were other kids and they teased him. We called him Howard to avoid confusion, which soon became Howie, or as he said it, How-woo. He was a typical second child, quiet and resourceful. I found myself calling him Wesley by mistake and from an early stage found myself transferring a lot of the feelings I had for Wesley to him. He filled that empty place in my emotions to such an extent I had to think to tell them apart after awhile. But I was so busy those first few years I barely saw him.

A friend of mine got to be super for MacMillan over at Northwest Bay and offered to set me up with a contract for more than one truck. I didn't like to leave Garibaldi, but this looked like the kind of break I'd been hoping for so I sold my faithful old Dodge and got three used Macks from Charlie Philp, some of the same Macks Schnare had first introduced in 1938. I figured I was on my way to being a big-time contractor. It was a good haul and I was getting the wood but the big company situation was an altogether different world from what I'd been used to. You never knew what was going on. One day they would say, go to the west side, haul three loads. Then at noon they'd say, go to the east side and haul a load. The only people who had an idea what was happening were the bosses, and they just said, "We'll let you know in plenty of time what you're supposed to do." It was like being in school. Nobody was trusted to have any brains but the head office guys.

But at least my friend was in charge so I could feel safe. Then he got transferred. Turned out he'd been wrangling with the old guard group from Nanaimo, and they were too much for him.

As soon as he left they started putting the screws to me. There was a side that was so muddy my trucks were the only ones that could get into it and they told me if I would handle it they'd see I got looked after. I was losing an axle or rear end every day, and I would be up all night monkeywrenching. I'd have breakfast in camp and go back to work without seeing the wife for two or three days at a time. It was on this job I lost the ability to sleep at night, something that has cursed me ever since. One time the Cat had to push me and wrecked my trailer. "Use one of ours," they told me, "Go ahead, take it." Come the end of the summer my scale was so low I couldn't hardly cover my parts bill. Not only was there no compensation for the rough going, I got a bill for $1,200 for trailer rental. Anywhere there was bad going that's where I'd be sent. I didn't have radios on my trucks, and the dispatcher would talk to the company trucks, then they would stop my trucks and give them orders. George Robinson, the head loader, told me, "You can't stand this. You come back here and I'll have some good loads for you." He'd lay aside a few good loads, then one of my drivers would flag me down and say, "They want us over at the other side."

After awhile they brought in a young kid with a haywire old Ford. He was from Nanaimo, and around Nanaimo they'd hated contractors from the mainland ever since Schnare came over. Besides that they were all Masons together. This kid could do no wrong. He was getting as much wood as all three of my trucks.

I can see now, I was trying to tell myself it wasn't happening. I'd seen men screwing each other around like that when I was a kid working for Safeway, but the whole reason I liked the woods was nothing on the job was more important than how you treated the other guy. It just gave me a sick feeling to think that was changing.

I bitched to the dispatcher, but that was like bitching to a drill sergeant. "You're getting the same as everybody else. Just go do your job and don't worry about how we do ours." Other places you'd make a guy like that come clean quick enough, but there they've got you by the short ones, they make sure of that. With me it was my contract, with the men it's seniority and the blacklist. The whole thing with the old-style logger was, he was a journeyman, he was a pro for hire, and if he didn't like the way you looked at him in the morning he took out his time and caught the boat.

In the spring of 1945 Kay did the best thing she could to help me get over the loss of my younger brother by giving birth to a healthy, spunky little son. We named him Howard after Kay's father but it took me a long time to stop calling him Wesley. WHITE FAMILY

One day as I was driving up the road I saw a fourteen-year-old kid shuffling along looking like he had the weight of the world on his shoulders. I pulled over to offer him a lift and he got in. He was crying. His name was Gordie Cochrane and he lived with his father, Bill Cochrane, who had a gyppo camp on Texada Island. They had come over to Northwest Bay in their camp boat, the *Miss Victoria,* and they'd got in a row and the old man had pulled out and left him on the beach with only the clothes on his back. I figured I could use a kid to help grease the trucks, maybe it would free me up to get home a little more often, so I offered him a grease monkey job. Well, this was some kid. He'd grown up in his old man's camp and not only was he a crackerjack at fuelling and greasing the trucks, he could repair tires and change a broken axle. There seemed nothing he couldn't do, although when he told me he could also drive truck I took it with a grain of salt. He wasn't even driving age. But he kept bringing it up, so one day I let him take down a load with me watching, and by god, he could handle that load of logs like a pro. I let him spell me off now and then when I was in town getting parts, and then one of the regular drivers quit and I put him on steady. He had a tendency to drive too fast, but I was a fast driver myself and I didn't mind a guy booting it as long as he wasn't taking chances. I told him how to handle all the different situations and by god if he didn't come out as top driver one month.

When a chance came up to get one of the Macks out of Northwest Bay and put it on a contract on Texada Island, Gordie was my best driver so I sent him over with the truck. He did fine. The outfit liked him. Then one day I got called into the office and handed a message. Gordie's truck had run away. I rushed over—it was at Cook Bay on the south end of Texada so it wasn't far from Northwest Bay—and I found my best Mack down over a bank under a load of logs, totalled. He'd stopped at the top of the hill to drain the water out of the air tank but when he finished he didn't shut the valve off properly. He was careless that way. Halfway to the beach the air ran out and away went the truck. It was a hell of a hill and he had the sense to jump right away before the Mack really took off so he was just scratched up a little.

I just walked away and left the wreck to the insurance company. The way things worked out, I should have got Gordie to wreck all the trucks—I would have been money ahead. Back at Northwest Bay, things were going from bad to worse. In the end I was just so frazzled from the runaround they were giving me, I had no choice but to break the contract and pull out. They didn't squawk—that's just what they wanted me to do.

That's when I began to see it was all over. When Schnare started, trucks were new and risky and the companies were willing to pay someone else to work out the wrinkles. Now trucks were proven and the companies were all getting their own. They'd put in a new law so trucks could be depreciated thirty percent a year and it worked like a tax dodge. Instead of declaring income as dividends they were piling it into big diesel fleets with fourteen-foot bunks, radio control and all the rest.

Now I could see why old Schnare had been in such a rush. He saw the door open, and he'd been around long enough to know how long it would get left that way. I turned my two remaining trucks back to Charlie Philp along with all the equity my sleepless nights and thirty-hour days had built up and decided to get out of logging. I was pretty disgusted. Here I'd been working like a goddamn fool for five long years and had come out with nothing to show for it. What had I done wrong? I thought about how Les would have handled things differently. Laugh at his little squiggles on the backs of matchbooks if you want to, but Les always had the dollars figured out first, before he committed himself. I was too in love with the idea of getting a fleet of trucks without figuring out just where the money would come from.

Les got into some deals that didn't work out, but he bailed out of them quick. Me, I tried to hang in and make up the difference by working all night. That just got you in deeper. Les would have figured out there was no use trying to battle those bastards at Northwest Bay at the start. Or else maybe he would have got drunk with the right people and got on the inside track. It kinda hurts looking back at what a sucker I'd been, working my guts out like that while those bastards were sitting back laughing at me, knowing I wasn't going to get anywhere because they were going to see to it I didn't. I can see now what I was doing wrong—it's plain as day. You have to take care of the political stuff first. Les always fixed things up behind the scenes with the key people like Louie Powell and got them coming his way first, then he'd do his part. I had the naïve idea I could ignore the political stuff and just make my impression by working harder and hauling more

I was mad at Gordie Cochrane when he put one my prized Macks over the bank at Cook Bay but the way things worked out I should have paid him to wreck all my trucks. WHITE FAMILY

logs than the other guy. That didn't work in the corporate world. It was who you know and I was poor at the backroom stuff. I see my mistakes plain as day now, but of course hindsight isn't worth a plug nickel. It's being able to figure it out on the fly that counts in business.

It's hard to believe that I was still in my early thirties when I wrapped up my career as a trucker. I still had over sixty years to go. It doesn't seem that way. In many ways it seems that was the main part of my life, and the rest has been a matter of filling in time doing this, that and the other. I couldn't tell you in so many words just what the hell I did do with the rest of my days. I logged a little and excavated a little and operated a service station, but I have to think about it to draw up the list. Those later years seem to have only lasted half as long as the first thirty, instead of twice as long. It's one of life's cruel facts that you live a lot more intensely in your first thirty years than you ever will again, and no matter what great things you achieve in later life—and I did have my share of adventures later— nothing else will ever have quite the impact as those first three decades. I remember every day of it. I don't have to check any dates.

And I still think of myself as a truck driver. A truck driver who went on to build houses and run logging camps rather than a logger who started out driving trucks. I notice my kids, when pressed to describe their ancestry, also often say their father was a trucker. I guess it sums up a way of life and a kind of personality better than something like entrepreneur or independent businessman, which I tried to be but never became in the same way I became a trucker. It gets in the bones. Many years later, in the 1970s, I took a break from running my service station and went back on a logging truck haul after thirty years away. The trucks in the meantime had grown to triple the horsepower and load capacity as Schnare's old beaters. I couldn't even figure out how to start them at first. But once I got out on the road, I felt at home and was soon showing the young fellows how it was done. They got mad at me and accused me of being reckless, but the truth was I was driving more safely than they were, just doing it smarter. Those instincts you develop in those early years just burn into your brain and stay there all your life.

I've learned a lot of trades since—house building, landscaping, water management—but I've never mastered it to the degree I did driving truck. I would have gone up against anybody driving truck and been confident of coming out on top but I never felt that way about anything else in my long life. It's good to have one thing you can say that about. I'm not sure but one is all you need, even if it does only take place in your early years. It takes the pressure off if you've proved yourself once.

Of course I can only say this now, looking back after sixty years. At the time I got out of trucking I couldn't take any satisfaction from it because I hadn't made any money at it, and that's what I had set out to do. Now that doesn't seem as important as the fact I was there, in the bad old days when trucks were just coming on the scene and changing the way the world worked. It was the happening thing in those years and I was right there in the middle of it, helping history unfold. It was a full life and I wouldn't have missed it for anything.

Index

About the Author

Frank White (1914–2015) started writing the story of his life as a pioneer BC truck driver in 1974 when he was only sixty. His boisterous yarn in *Raincoast Chronicles 3* about wrangling tiny trucks overloaded with huge logs down steep mountains with no brakes won the Canadian Media Club award for Best Magazine Feature and was reprinted so many times everyone urged him to write more. He started in his spare time but kept having so many new adventures he didn't finish until his hundredth year under heaven (which he didn't believe in). In the end he had written enough for two books, this one and a sequel, *That Went By Fast: My First Hundred Years* (Harbour, 2014). The former truck driver, logger, gas station operator, excavationist, waterworks technician and homespun philosopher lived to see 101 years. He shared a home in Garden Bay, BC, with his wife, author Edith Iglauer.